'Donnelly ha   giants of
women's rugby past can be recognised for their enduring
commitment and sacrifice.'
– Sara Orchard, BBC

'A vitally important book, bringing to life the rich
history of women's rugby and highlighting some of the
game's true pioneers. Inspiring and thought-provoking,
it is a reminder of how far the game has come and of the
huge opportunities ahead – a must read.'
– Maggie Alphonsi, former England player

'A much-needed treasure trove of women's rugby history
– insightful, informative and inspiring'
– Sarah Mockford, Rugby World Editor

'The story of women's rugby has never been documented
in one place, by anyone before. This thorough summary
of the 130 years of history of the women's game is a
fantastic testament to the progress of the women's game,
and crucially it doesn't shy away from highlighting
that there is still much work to be done. A much-
needed book.'
– Melodie Robinson, former Black Fern

'This is a story of sisterhood that could only be told by
one of our own. Ali pulls the history out of the heads of
those who lived it and weaves this together with research
from around the world. In doing so, allows the next
generation of women's rugby to continue to carry the
game forward, over the advantage line.'
– Alice Soper, Women's Rugby Advocate

Ali Donnelly

SCRUM QUEENS

The story of
women's rugby

Foreword by
Stephen Jones

First published by Pitch Publishing, 2022
Updated 2025
2

Pitch Publishing
9 Donnington Park,
85 Birdham Road,
Chichester,
West Sussex,
PO20 7AJ
www.pitchpublishing.co.uk
info@pitchpublishing.co.uk

A CIP catalogue record is available for this book
from the British Library.

ISBN 978 1 80150 229 0

Printed and bound in the UK on FSC® certified paper in line
with our continuing commitment to ethical business practices,
sustainability and the environment.

Printed and bound by CPI Group (UK) Ltd, Croydon, CR0 4YY

Contents

Dedicated to the memory of my sister, Denise, who had absolutely no interest in rugby, but who would have bought this book (or at least demanded a free copy) and pretended it was fascinating anyway.

And to my Mom, Mary, who instilled in me an early love of books (frequently falling asleep with one on her chest) and who liked rugby just about enough to humour me.

You are both so dearly missed.

Foreword

Stephen Jones, the *Sunday Times*

THIS IS the book that had to be written. It begged the author to do it. In a way it's the book that seals the first revolution in women's rugby and sets it up for a radical, wonderful and even-moneyed future. Ali Donnelly has been a player, coach, media manager, campaigner and journalist of renown for women's rugby – and almost all of this in her spare time – after professional duties and motherhood. Astonishing. Maybe the Irish have found a way of having more than 24 hours in a day.

And at the heart of it all has been Scrumqueens.com. Ali's legendary website was probably the most heroic operation I have ever come across in rugby and maybe in any sport, and it bound together all the fledgling links in sport wherever they raised their heads.

It has been rightly lauded and awarded, improved every year of its existence, and is absolutely impossible to emulate. The ability to sniff out an international rugby match in the most remote countries, where you would least expect it, has become legendary. There is no question in my mind that she has been one of the true driving forces of the growth of the sport, equally as important as the great players.

She has had to be rugged, often had to swallow anger and pride, no doubt. She has been inexhaustible, needle-sharp; she has had the courage to speak out against those who felt that they had louder voices. And in doing so, she has proved her relevancy and campaigning brilliance. And she has given the sport worldwide a history, a reference and a sisterhood.

It was (frighteningly) over 30 years ago that we at the *Sunday Times* concluded that we could no longer ignore the growth of women's rugby. We heard about the staggering efforts of the four heroes of the first World Cup led by Deborah Griffin. In the build-up to the final, in my first interview with a player – Sam Robson, the England centre – I remember her technical grasp of what England needed to do in the final against the USA, and how inspirational she was for her sport.

Some years after in England's north-west we went to interview a teacher, and England's captain, Gill Burns. How can anyone so modest, so quietly spoken, be such a global hero? No idea, but she managed it and her lovely mum still sends me a gorgeous home-made Christmas card every year.

More recently, after featuring scores of the game's giants in our newspaper, and finding every one inspirational in its own way, I collaborated with Heather Fisher in telling her retirement story. You try telling a story as incredible as Fisher's in only 1,400 words.

Women's rugby is ever-growing as a story. Sometimes is it The Story.

So sorry, Ali, we know you are frantically busy, but we also know that you were always going to write this and that so many people have been eagerly awaiting it. We also know that the book will provide another set of rock-solid building blocks for the runaway growth of rugby for women and girls.

The author reflects herein that sometimes; you can still come across people who challenge the right of women to play rugby. Well, they can read this, and weep.

Introduction

I GOT involved in rugby by chance.

We moved to a new area when I was 15 and the nearby town of Midleton in East Cork had a women's team.

Up to then I'd largely been playing Gaelic football, but the travel to training was now a bit of a hassle and I thought I'd try something else nearer to home.

I bumped into someone who mentioned the rugby team in Midleton and though I knew nothing whatsoever about the game, I decided to try a session.

I grew up in a house full of sport. All five of my brothers were involved in something – football, athletics, boxing and karate mostly, but never rugby. We considered it a 'posh' sport, deathly dull with all its stoppages, and until I started to get involved myself, I don't think I'd ever even met someone who played it.

I couldn't give you any detail about my first training session, but I knew immediately this was *my* sport.

Unlike the other teams I played in, where everyone was around my age, this was a group of women from all walks of life; women in their 20s, women in their 30s, mums, teachers, students, professionals, all who knew far more about life and rugby than I did. I was in awe.

Walloping the tackle pads, getting caked in mud, thumping a ball that could land anywhere off my laces, learning something new every single minute of every session. I was hooked and have been ever since. I quickly learned two things.

One was that if you wanted to play women's rugby in Ireland then – this was the late 1990s – you had to be prepared to travel. There were only about 12 teams in the whole country at the time and so 12-hour round trips to Belfast to play Cooke and regular trips back and forth from Dublin and Limerick became the norm.

The second was that people had surprisingly strong views about women playing rugby and a large number of those views were negative.

This was something of a shock to me. I'd been playing sport for years and was oblivious to the idea that anyone would take issue with the involvement of women and girls. I'd grown up mostly playing Gaelic football for my club Carrigtwohill, where if you got to a final, half the village would turn out to cheer you on.

If you won, you'd thrillingly be driven in convoy up and down the main street hanging out the window, medals held high in the air and horns beeping madly before the lot of you clamoured into Frank's Chippers for chips and a potato pie. Yes, double potato. This was Ireland after all.

No one seemed to care that they were cheering on the U14 girls' team. You were playing for the village and that was that.

But people did care about women playing rugby and many were stridently opposed to it.

This opposition meant that those who did play had to battle to do so.

This was not, I learned, a battle for equality, but rather a battle to simply be included and taken seriously.

After a few seasons with Midleton I moved to Cork city for university where I began to play at University College Cork and with a new club Highfield.

As I moved from my teen years into adulthood, I began to understand that my experience in the Carrigtwohill U14 team had been unusual – something reserved almost uniquely for the nature in which Irish towns and villages get behind their beloved local Gaelic teams, no matter what the age of the players or their gender.

The reality for the vast majority of women playing sport I quickly realised was quite different and women were in fact fighting everywhere just to be treated fairly – and in the case of women's rugby, often to simply not be laughed at.

My own rather naïve take on this then was that it was desperately unfair, and if only people would come and watch our games, then their minds would be changed. I hadn't of course reckoned with the fact that at the time, the standard of the women's game was unsurprisingly poor.

Rugby had a rich history in Ireland. The first men's Test game was as far back as 1875, but women had been largely shut out from the sport till the 1990s.

The teams I joined and played against in those early years were playing catch-up on a level that is hard to even quantify.

All of us were brand new to the sport – of course the standards were not comparable to the men's game, but endlessly compared we were, and it was maddening to me, as my eyes began to open to wider gender inequalities in sport, that we were so often treated as a novelty and not, as I had expected, as something to get behind and support.

This was true all the way to the top of the game, where the Irish Rugby Football Union (IRFU) at that point were barely involved at all.

There were outliers though, and I began to get to know some brilliant people who were doing their best to progress the game and get more women involved.

In 2001 I got an email from a man called Mark Andrews inviting me to join the committee of the group who ran the Irish women's game.

Mark was an influential figure in women's rugby in Ireland who had arrived from Australia in the mid-1990s when the Irish women's game was starting to get up and running.

He'd become involved in every part of the game across the south-east of Ireland, as an administrator, as a coach and as a referee. He was also chair of the Irish Women's Rugby Football Union (IWRFU), the volunteer-led governing body running the Irish women's game.

Mark had heard I was writing match reports about the games I was involved in, and he was interested in me coming on board to help generate much-needed publicity.

By now I was in my second year at university, studying politics, and seriously thinking about a career as a journalist. I was writing anything and everything for local papers to build my portfolio and given I was a student with plenty of time on my hands, I hit reply and said I was up for it.

Having come to grips with the fact that there were massive disparities in how men and women were treated in rugby, this was my first real step on my journey towards becoming a more serious advocate and campaigner.

I discovered almost immediately that the fledgling game in Ireland, and the challenges facing the national team in particular, was beholden almost entirely to a small but fiercely dedicated group of volunteers led by Mark.

I became determined to do everything I could to help.

For the next few years, I shared car journeys with my Highfield team-mate and friend Deirdre Lynch, travelling the country to meet up with the committee to discuss how to grow the game, and how to get more people involved.

It's remarkable that just over 20 years ago, the IRFU still catered and ran a sport almost exclusively for men and boys. They offered minimal help as the women's game got off the ground, even when the national team became more established on the Test stage.

In Ireland, as in many other countries, the administration of the game would remain divided on gender grounds for many more years.

In the interim, this group of incredibly hard-working people kept the national team playing, ran the club game across the whole of the island of Ireland, and through my new role, attempted to generate media coverage.

I eventually figured out that the best way to start building any sort of profile for the game was to think local. I spent evening after evening compiling the names of all the local papers connected to every player in the national squad. Through a process of calling, emailing, persuading and writing as much as possible myself, slowly but surely Ireland's leading players started to become better known.

A first ever Six Nations win in 2003 galvanised the momentum, and star players like Fiona Steed, Sarahjane Belton and Patrique Kelly were at last generating some name recognition within Irish rugby circles.

With the support of Rohan West, a brilliant volunteer and long-time champion of women's sport, we set up an IWRFU website. Now players all over the country could follow what everyone else was doing and find out more about who was playing where and when.

Through my involvement with the IWRFU, and later through building Scrumqueens.com, I realised that what I had experienced in Ireland – where volunteers drove the women's game forward, often in the face of much opposition – was being replicated all over the world and indeed had been for decades.

The more I got into the sport, the more I began to discover stories of amazing people who had a determined vision to make rugby a sport that could be played by women and girls everywhere.

I moved to London in 2007, a year before women's rugby in Ireland was taken in-house by the IRFU but I haven't stopped writing about the game since. My passion for wanting to tell the stories of the players, the coaches, the administrators and the volunteers who have made women's rugby what it is today has not changed since that first email from Mark, who has since sadly passed away. And through this book I want to play my part in preserving its history.

I set up Scrumqueens.com in 2009, initially to help generate profiles for the teams travelling to London the following year for the World Cup. I happily wound it up in 2025, feeling our work was done, and I am enormously proud of the role it has played in the game, not just highlighting the sport's many brilliant people, teams and competitions, but also shining a light on the game's many inequalities and campaigning for better. It is one way in which I believe I have given back to a sport which has given me so much – introducing me to the best friends of my life, including my wife Sarah who I met through playing at Teddington, and leaving me with fabulous playing and touring memories.

Women's rugby is the story of a sport persevering through tough and often seemingly insurmountable obstacles; through a lack of investment that is still a problem today, through subtle and overt sexism, through opposition and disinterest from those in powerful positions in the sport, and from societal misgivings about women and girls getting involved in such a physical activity.

I am thankful that, even though there is still some way to go, the women's game now is unrecognisable from the one I first got to know. I know that those who have worked so hard to push it forward have done it through making enormous sacrifices, often at significant personal cost and without any real recognition.

This is an effort to tell the story of the women's rugby pioneers who thankfully refused to take no for an answer and the story of the game's progression through the evolution of major international events.

Those of us still involved now owe all these brilliant people a debt of gratitude. I hope this book at least starts to recognise what they have done for the women's game.

Chapter One

Kick-off

ON 30 December 2020, Becky Hammon, the assistant coach of men's NBA team the San Antonio Spurs, took over running the game when the team's male head coach was thrown off court after arguing with officials. It was a historic moment – no woman had ever been the lead coach in an NBA league game before.

Or no one could be sure if they had.

Afterwards, ESPN tweeted its 36 million followers: 'Spurs assistant Becky Hammon filled in for an ejected Gregg Popovich. She's believed to be the first woman to act as head coach during an NBA regular-season game.'

The tweet attracted some ridicule. Surely with all their resources and knowledge ESPN could do better than that. Either she was the first woman to act as head coach, or she wasn't.

ESPN, who can tell you absolutely everything about what the men of the NBA are achieving on the court – how many assists, how many points, how many blocks – faced the same challenge everyone else does when it comes to reporting on historical moments involving women in sport. It's incredibly difficult, almost impossible, to know accurately what, when and where anything happened for the first time.

The modern stories of women in sport are increasingly well documented, with TV coverage, great volumes of online and print media exposure and growing social media content, but the decades of history and the women who came before are not.

Most women's sports, including rugby, took root independently of the national governing bodies running their sports, who catered in the early years almost exclusively for men and boys. Yet today they largely rely on those same organisations, still dominated by men, who once shunned, silenced, banned and excluded them, to keep the story of their true origins and history alive.

Unsurprisingly many of the game's national governing bodies don't accurately publicly document the story of how women's rugby actually began in their countries. Some simply don't know and haven't done the research. Others, however, know well that the history doesn't suit the narrative of inclusivity they now promote and, in most cases, they would frankly rather not highlight their past treatment of the women's game.

It should be acknowledged though that in the three years between the first print run of this book and its second, things have improved considerably on this front with increased visibility and exposure meaning we know more about our game's past now than ever before.

Writing in the *Guardian* about women's cricket in 2019, journalist Kirby Fenwick, wrote about the fact that sporting organisations too often airbrush the history of their women's game. She noted that Cricket Australia's website neglected to even mention the Women's Cricket Council who ran the women's game across the country for 70 years for women. Rugby has been guilty of this neglect too

Even as I first wrote this in late 2021, there was little to nothing on the official websites of leading rugby nations that told anyone the true history of how the women's game got up and running initially in their countries.

The 'history' page on the Scottish website didn't mention women at all, ditto Ireland which had a convenient list of all its international captains but only the male ones. If you wanted to read about the Black Ferns, the brilliant New Zealand women's team, you must navigate through AllBlacks.com, a website named after the country's men's team. There you would find nothing either about the amazing work of many pioneering New Zealand women who tried to get women's rugby up and running long before the New Zealand Rugby Union ever got involved.

Although many unions are starting to lean into the history of their women's game with occasional pieces of content, most prefer to start the story of women's rugby in their countries only when the game was integrated into their organisation, often ignoring the decades of hard graft and activity beforehand.

Even with all we now know, patchy record-keeping means the accuracy of many 'firsts' in women's rugby is questionable. Where records do exist of specific markers or milestones, the sport often remains completely in the dark about them.

In 2007, the 25th anniversary of the first ever women's international Test game, for example, passed by almost unrecognised, even by the nations who took part. It was France v Netherlands by the way, and there's more on that to come later.

Limited retained written accounts of the earliest years of the sport have been unearthed and it is only now, or at least only in the past decade, that enough dedicated media coverage of women's rugby means that its more modern history will be secured for future generations.

What is particularly hard to swallow about this lost history is the narrative that rugby had once been for men only and that governing bodies were actually progressive for having allowed women to join in from the 1960s. That, as this book will highlight, is just untrue. Women's rugby had a rich history before being suppressed by authorities going as far back as the 1800s.

It's true that women fought for the right to re-enter rugby from the 1960s and from there it grew into the game we have now, but the erasure of the sport's earlier history means that only now is more information coming to light.

On that front, things are improving considerably. Detailed research by journalists, historians and academics is starting to build a picture of women's rugby in the very early years. Footage is emerging of the game from as far back as the 1920s and there is genuine interest in understanding more about how women first got involved.

The attempts to rectify the near invisibility of the people who helped get women's rugby where it is today, with a professional Olympic sevens game and a part-professional and burgeoning Test 15s game, are starting to shed light on the impact of some genuinely inspirational men and women.

Several projects and developments mean momentum is steadily building to ensure the history of the earliest years is understood.

New Zealand academic Professor Jennifer Curtin, for example, has traced the start of the women's game in her country back to the late 1800s. Women's rugby writer John Birch's research unearthed the memoirs of Emily Valentine, who describes playing rugby in 1887 in Ireland. More recently a partnership between De Montfort University Leicester and the World Rugby Museum at Twickenham has resulted in a comprehensive study of women's involvement in rugby by Lydia Furse, who has now successfully completed her PhD on the topic.

Though we may now take for granted the fact that thanks to regular television coverage, the game's biggest moments will be archived and recorded, there are years of work ahead to find out more about what happened in those early days, to celebrate the initial milestones and never forget where women's rugby came from.

That is why I wanted to write this book. The following pages tell us about what we now know, how the game took off in its early years, and looks at where women's rugby is heading.

It attempts to highlight some of the major moments on the field too through the narratives of the biggest and best games, and weaves in the stories of some of the players and officials who have done so much to get the game into the shape it is in today.

This will not be the only book written about the history of women's rugby, but it is one of the first. I hope it is a springboard for many more so that the stories from our brilliant game can be forever preserved.

Rugby's first lady

The story of Emily Valentine, so well told by John Birch who ran Scrumqueens.com alongside me, is one of the earliest documented records of any woman playing rugby at any level. While there are some records of attempts for social games to be played before this, there is nothing definitive, and his research produced a remarkable tale that has gained global interest.

The story began in the 1880s at the Portora Royal School in Enniskillen, Ireland. The school had a wealth of famous alumni with former students going on to have high-profile careers in football, cricket, athletics and the arts. Playwrights Oscar Wilde and Samuel Beckett both attended the school.

But it's the tale of a ten-year-old girl that entered women's rugby folklore.

The school was going through a particularly difficult period in the 1880s after the departure of a headteacher who took many pupils with him to a new school and a decision to stop taking on boarders.

The arrival of new assistant headteacher William Valentine in 1883 brought three new pupils who all loved the game of rugby – his children William, John and Emily. They played among themselves and with friends.

Although the school didn't have an official team, intra-school matches were played every Saturday and matches against Enniskillen RFC were recorded.

The discovery of Emily's journals revealed that one day in 1887, the boys were playing a match and they were short of players, summoning their sister to come and join them on the field. Her memoirs vividly recall the moment.

> At last, my chance came. I got the ball. I can still feel the damp leather and the smell of it and see the tag of lacing at the opening. I grasped it and ran dodging, darting, but I was so keen to score that try that I did not pass it, perhaps when I should.
>
> I still raced on, I could see the boy coming towards me; I dodged, yes I could and breathless, with my heart thumping, my knees shaking a bit, I ran. Yes, I had done it; one last spurt and I touched down, right on the line. I had scored my try.
>
> I lay flat on my face, for a moment everything went black. I scrambled up, gave a hasty rub down to my knees. A ragged cheer went up from the spectators. I grinned at my brothers. It was all I had hoped for.

Her story is remarkable, not just because its history has been preserved and was told so many years later for the first time, but also because it would be another 100 years before Ireland's first women's rugby club was formed.

It's unlikely that what Emily Valentine did at the time was unique. There were probably plenty of other girls who picked up the ball and ran with it or got involved informally. But hers remains the earliest recorded written story.

We know, thanks to archive newspaper reports, that a version of women's football was being played in England in the 1870s and 1880s, but it is not entirely clear whether it was football or rugby, with write-ups describing the scores invariably as goals or touchdowns. Furse's PhD also points to research from Dr Victoria Dawson indicating that in Hull, also in 1887, two women's teams played against each other but the crowds were not amused and invaded the pitch.

It's clear now that the women who did play rugby in the 1800s likely did so either sporadically, anonymously or in the face of misgivings from many around them. While Emily had the support of her brothers and loved her involvement, there will likely have been many more women and girls desperate to play but simply not allowed. Perhaps they played in secret.

Women were certainly playing sport at the time. Women competed at Wimbledon from 1884, the first women's cricket clubs date back to the late 1880s and the 1900 Summer Olympics in Paris introduced women's events for the first time.

But rugby itself was only 60 years old as a sport when Emily Valentine describes playing in her first match in 1887 and it is likely that the earliest attempts of women to get involved in such a physical sport would not have been encouraged.

Though the start of women's involvement in other sports, most notably football and cricket, faced similar challenges – although by now cricket was being played by women regularly and it was widely played in girls' public schools by the early 20th century – the contact and physical nature of rugby made the idea of women playing even less acceptable, and press clippings and coverage from the era show that attempts to get it up and running were fiercely resisted.

While a young Emily Valentine was reflecting on the joy of playing and scoring in her first rugby game in rural Ireland, serious efforts around the same time were being made on the other side of the world to get women's rugby up and running in a more formal way.

Though it would only be a couple of years before New Zealand would become the first country in the world to give women the right to vote in parliamentary elections in 1893, attempts to empower women to play rugby – which had only existed for 20 years in the country that would go on to dominate the sport – faced significant opposition.

Dr Jennifer Curtin's research, plus club histories from the brilliant New Zealand Rugby Museum, describes the efforts of another remarkable woman, Nita Webbe, to organise a women's team and an international tour in 1891.

There is evidence that women in New Zealand were attempting to play socially. A game had apparently been played in Wellington in 1888 between a team from Wellington Girls' High School and the Hallelujah Lasses Club, although it was considered a one-off.

Webbe, just 26 years old, came up with a plan that can only be described as radical given the era. She decided to get 30 women together, divide them into two teams of 15 each and, after several weeks of training, tour the Australian colonies before returning to play a series of matches around New Zealand.

Inspired perhaps by other changes afoot in New Zealand, where women's suffrage was a powerful political issue and women were seeking more rights across all aspects of life, Webbe was taken with how popular rugby had already become in just a few decades, particularly among women who made up vast chunks of the crowds attending games all over the country.

She placed advertisements in several major newspapers around the country to attract women to come and set up a team in Auckland. The deal was that women could apply, with parental consent, and if selected, Webbe would pay the players ten shillings a week. Her advert said that players were to wear gymnasium suits with a jersey, knickerbockers and short skirts, and their hair was to be cut short.

Though there was interest from women to take up the offer, her efforts were greeted with scorn in local media with the consensus being that the game was far too rough and dangerous for women.

The *Auckland Star* ran the following editorial after Webbe's advert appeared:

THE PROPOSED FEMALE FOOTBALL TEAM

We subscribe most heartily to the doctrine that every sphere in which women are fitted to take their part should be as freely open to them as to men, but there are some things for which women are constitutionally unfitted, and which are essentially unwomanly. A travelling football team composed of girls appears to us to be of this character. Moreover, making every allowance for vitiated tastes in the popular craving for amusement, we cannot conceive of either men or women who have sisters of their own being attracted by such a spectacle, or encouraging a number of girls to forsake womanly employment for the purpose of entering upon a life of an itinerant footballer. It would also be well for the parents of girls who think of engaging in this enterprise to consider what will be their position if the enterprise proves a financial failure, which we sincerely hope and believe it will be. Have they obtained substantial guarantees that they will be returned to their homes, or are they liable to be left stranded – homeless and penniless in some distant city? If any respectable girls are determined to persist in this foolish enterprise, we strongly advise them to make it an indispensable condition that return tickets shall be placed in their possession before leaving Auckland, so as to ensure them a safe passage back to their homes when the venture has been proved a financial failure, as it unquestionably will be if we rightly gauge the taste of the New Zealand public in the matter of amusement.

Webbe fired back immediately with a lengthy letter defending her plan:

It is only quite recently that your paper announced that an English team of lady cricketers were about to tour the Australian colonies, yet not one word had you to say against it. And now a team of lady footballers is projected here, you charitably hope it will end in a financial disaster. The football team are being taught by a regular trainer to play a clever game without any of the roughness characteristic of men's play. Strict observance to the rules will be enforced, and when they play in public, I am confident that the verdict will be not only that there has been not the slightest breach of propriety, but that a cleverer game has seldom been seen here. If it is permissible for ladies to participate in gymnastics, swimming matches, and cricket teams, is it not equally permissible for ladies to play football! To draw a line between them would be to make a distinction without a difference.

There is evidence that Webbe managed to get her players together – a newspaper in Poverty Bay wrote in June 1891 that 30 girls were training in Auckland – but the overall mission never got off the ground. About a month later, newspapers reported that the scheme had been abandoned with suggestions that Webbe and her husband Frederick did not have the money to carry out the plan.

But while that specific tour might not have gone ahead, women's rugby in New Zealand did start to put down real roots in the years that followed.

The transformational impact of war

The war years of 1914–18 brought with them an inevitable decline in men playing sport. As women became more active in the labour market, taking to the factory floor as men took to the trenches, opportunities emerged for them to step into the spotlight in sport.

In numerous countries and across a variety of sports, social and exhibition women's games began to emerge. These were almost exclusively to raise funds for the war effort and to offer some social entertainment at such a challenging time, and that made the involvement of women far more palatable to the public.

The women who wanted to play rugby in New Zealand seized their moment.

Many were already well connected to local rugby clubs. Curtin's research highlights that groups like the single and married ladies of the Combined Sports Bodies Committees played at Athletic Park, Wellington, in May 1915, and a match endorsed by the Wellington Rugby Union occurred the same month at half-time of a men's match in June to raise money for the Wounded Sailors and Soldiers Fund.

It was a novelty game, short and entertaining, but, as Ron Palenski points out in his book, *Rugby: A New Zealand History*, it was significant given where it was played. Even more remarkably, it was refereed by a woman too. The whistle was carried by May du Chateau, daughter of 1884 All-Black Harry Roberts and the sister of another, Teddy, who played for his country before and after the First World War. Du Chateau might well be the first ever recorded female referee, a role that only in the past decade has started to see women break through at the highest levels. Similar games were held elsewhere in Wellington, on the West Coast and in other parts of the country.

Meanwhile, there had been some fledgling efforts to get women's rugby started in France, Wales and England, though in the face of public opposition. The women who were trying to play rugby were doing it behind closed doors and, bar scant reporting here and there, there remains a dearth of evidence of what was unfolding in the 1890s in these countries.

Though it was sporadic, there was some interest in the game in England among women, as Col. Philip Trevor in his book *Rugby Football* from 1923 documented. His chapter 'The Game's Popularity – Rugger For Girls' told the story of his daughters asking him to help them with a game they wanted to play in 1913 with friends on the beach. It was a full 15-a-side game of rugby, with more players available if the need arose.

Col. Trevor, who acted as referee, marvelled at the skills of the girls in his book and described how they improvised with kit by wearing bathing hats to lessen the chance of being 'tackled' by their hair.

As it had in New Zealand and later Australia, the First World War also brought opportunities for women to play rugby in Europe. Perhaps the most well-documented game of the time took place at the Cardiff Arms Park on 16 December 1917, when Cardiff Ladies beat Newport Ladies 6-0.

Despite photographs existing of the game, many of the players involved remain anonymous, though academics are seeking to rectify that through continuing research. Records that do exist identify that the Newport players represented the local iron mill firm of John Lysaughts Ltd, while Cardiff Ladies turned out for Wm. Hancock Ltd, the local brewery.

As with almost all matches that took place during the war, the proceeds were donated to charity and this match was played in aid of the 'Comforts Fund' for the men of the Cardiff City Battalion. The choice of this charity made sense because the 16th Battalion Welsh Regiment had close links with Cardiff RFC, not least through many of its personnel, and it's likely that several of the Cardiff Ladies had spouses, partners or brothers serving in the battalion.

The best-known member of the Cardiff team is Maria Lillian Eley, or Maria Evans as she was in 1917. Born on 12 January 1900, she was only 17 when she turned out at full-back against Newport. She lived to the age of 106 and in March 2000, at 100 years old, she was the guest of honour of Cardiff

RFC at a match against Caerphilly at the Arms Park, where she was introduced to the crowd.

When asked in an interview with the *Penarth Times* how she accounted for her longevity, she simply replied 'rugby'. Reflecting on her time playing the game, she added:

> We loved it. It was such fun with us all playing together on the pitch, but we had to stop when the men came back from the war, which was a shame. Such great fun we had.

While this game is largely recalled as the most high profile of the era, records kept by the Cardiff Rugby Museum discovered it was not the first time that women had played rugby at the Arms Park. According to a report in the *Western Mail*, there had been an even earlier women's match at the ground, three months before on 29 September 1917. This time, though, there were no Cardiff-based participants. The two teams were 'girl munitions workers from Newport'. As these were termed the 'Wasps' and the 'Whites', it seems likely that the Wasps were wearing the traditional Newport strip of black and amber.

Thousands also reportedly attended the Arms Park to watch this earlier game, which ended in a 3-3 draw. Why this contest involving teams from Newport was held at the Arms Park remains unknown. The two sides are known to have met again in Barry in March 1918 in front of 4,000 spectators, so it is possible that the Arms Park game was one of a series they held around south Wales.

However, until details of any earlier fixture materialise, the Arms Park can still lay claim to being the venue of the first recorded women's rugby match in Europe.

Back in New Zealand, teams began to be established independently and unrelated to the fundraising efforts of the war.

Dr Curtin wrote about another team from the North Island who were photographed. It was formally posed with 17 players lined up in three rows, arms crossed, wearing uniforms of jerseys, shorts and boots. Three male officials from the Horowhenua Rugby Union are also seated in the picture. Assuming the team were dressed to play against an opposition, the picture indicates that competitive games were now being played more widely.

As the game of rugby became more and more popular in New Zealand, other pioneering women came to the fore. In Wellington, another marvellous woman was stepping up. Phyllis Dawson decided she had had enough of women playing second fiddle to the men's game.

Founding and captaining the Wellington Ladies Rugby Football Club in 1921, Dawson helped organise two 15-a-side matches in the team's first season, and she was hoping for support from the local men's rugby union clubs in 1922.

She attempted to secure a seven-a-side match as a curtain-raiser to a local men's match, but the lack of opposition and lack of support from the local men's clubs, including access to pitches on which to play and practise, curtailed her ambition. As seemed to be the way of the time, she vented her annoyance through local media asking readers:

Which is better for a band of young girls: to be out in the open air, playing games or sitting in a stuffy drawing room with no other aim in view but to look genteel?

Across the water in Australia a similar story was playing out, but it was rugby league and not rugby union gathering momentum.

In the summer of 1921, two pioneering young women from Sydney, Molly Cane and Nellie Doherty, penned a letter to the NSWRL, the governing body for the sport, asking for support in setting up a women's league.

By June a league was up and running. In September a remarkable crowd of 20,000 gathered to watch Sydney take on Metropolitan, with pictures appearing in the papers showing the huge crowds.

Despite the apparent appetite from the public for women's rugby league, the governing body got cold feet and pressure from authorities ensured that the women did not play again. Women's rugby of any form disappeared from the record books in Australia until the 1930s, when leagues were established once again in New South Wales.

France join the party

Back in France, an alternative version of rugby was fast becoming popular.

The game was called barette. It had emerged in the 19th century as a football code with varying rules in different parts of France. In some areas of the country the ball or barette was passed by hand, in others a kick, but by the end of the era a version that resembled rugby had become hugely popular.

Dr Furse suggests that after the war a new form of barette emerged. Whereas the original game of barette had been closer to a form of touch, the new barette was a full-contact sport directly adapted from rugby union, the only major difference being that tackles were limited to around the waist, teams were 12-a-side, playing time was shorter and pitch dimensions were slightly smaller.

Perhaps this new version, clearly an implicit form of rugby, was a clever ploy to try to avoid the problems that had befallen similar physical women's sport elsewhere but either way over a short period, it became very popular.

Coached and promoted by former French rugby international André Theuriet and Dr Marie Houdré, a fan and player of the sport, barette received its public debut on 2 April 1922 at the Stade Elisabeth in Paris.

Barette was strongly supported by the Fédération Feminine Sportives de France (FFSF) with leadership from the pioneering Alice Milliat, who was fast becoming one of the most influential figures in the world for championing the involvement of women in sport.

Milliat believed sport offered an opportunity for greater gender equality across society. She wanted the 1924 Olympics to include track and field events for women, but these were considered too physically strenuous by the organising body. In its place she launched the first Women's Olympic Games, held in Paris in 1922, where women competed in events like the 1,000-metre race and shot put.

Her lobbying and organising are widely credited with forcing the inclusion of more women in a broader range of sports in the Olympics and her work came full circle in 2024, where the third Olympic Games to be held in Paris included around the same number of male and female athletes for the first time in Olympic history.

Despite, or perhaps because of, the support from the FFSF, newspapers reporting on the demonstration of barette in 1922 were under no illusions that this was rugby rebranded and many were deeply unsupportive.

Within a few months, the Fédération Française de Rugby (FFR), the organisation set up to run rugby in France, introduced a ban on barette being played on any rugby grounds. It was not dissimilar to the FA ban on women playing football in England the year before, when it was claimed that 'the game of football is quite unsuitable for females and ought not to be encouraged'.

But the Stade Elisabeth was not a rugby ground and the new sport did not fall under the auspices of the FFR, so the game did not disappear despite the ban. If anything, it expanded.

By 1926 there was a national championship with at least nine clubs. When the FFR tried to enforce its ban in 1927, after a barette game was proposed as a curtain-raiser before a men's championship game at Stade Jean-Bouin, there were protests through the media in support of the game by people who had come to admire the perseverance of the players.

The following year the FFR caved. Barette was played before games at Stade Jean-Bouin from 1928, the ground which over 80 years later would host a World Cup Final between England and Canada.

Then, with the sport at its height, reports suddenly all but disappeared from the French press. The financial collapse in the mid-1930s of the FFSF shortly afterwards left the sport on its own.

Despite the media silence, it seems probable that the game did continue away from the media spotlight because, in 1941, it again appeared in record books. This time it was to announce its demise.

Alongside rugby league and women's football, Furse's research tells us that barette was banned by the Vichy French government, a right-wing collective who promoted the values of 'Travail, Famille, Patrie'. Women were encouraged to take a more traditionally feminine role in the home.

Whether barette had disappeared before 1941 anyway or whether this ban was the final blow is impossible to say, but barette did not reappear after the Second World War. It was another 20 years before the next generation, perhaps unaware of what had gone before, would form L'Association de Rugby Feminin (ARF) and women's rugby would be reborn in France.

What is the final significance of barette, apart from another tale of what might have been? Dr Furse picks up the story for us:

> Playing barette was more than the simple act of picking up the ball and running with it; Barette was also a symbol of female physical emancipation. The feminist

imperative behind barette may not have impacted upon each individual player, but the activity was discussed in the public sphere as an act of gender-boundary crossing.

The achievements of barette do live on though – Marie Houdré was symbolically the first name in the new French rugby hall of fame in 2019.

The efforts of women like Nita Webbe, Phyllis Dawson and Molly Cane counted for little as the world headed into the Great Depression in the 1930s and the traditional role of women in society was restored. In between the world wars, as men returned to the workplace, women returned to their roles in the home, as wives, daughters and caregivers.

Records and journals suggest that women's rugby, despite considerable early success, faded away before a resurgence in the 1960s when formal leagues and competitions sprang up and women-only unions began to establish themselves in the lead-up to the first Test games in the 1980s.

However, in some pockets, versions of women's rugby continued.

In Australia, women's rugby league continued throughout the 1930s. Pictures exist of teams playing in the New South Wales areas of Tamworth and Armidale; the games ran until halted by the Second World War. Photographs of women's teams also exist from New Zealand from the same period.

There were even some competitive games played in the 1940s. Ron Palenski's book documents a women's match at Carisbrook in Dunedin. The four-team competition appears to be the first documented women's rugby competition in New Zealand. A team called St Kilda won the event over Dunedin North. The *Otago Daily Times* provided a memorable report: 'Some of the players gave the appearance of knowing the general idea of Rugby football, but the majority were more willing than scientific, and the referees could do little about it.'

For all this, the progress that women's rugby had made in a few decades began to falter significantly. Little action, bar informal playing here and there, was recorded until well after the Second World War.

Chapter Two

A rebirth

THOUGH THERE are some reports of women playing socially and informally in England, New Zealand, France and Australia, and women's teams are mentioned in many official club history books in the 1940s and 1950s, it was not until the 1960s that it started to make real inroads again.

It was a pattern repeated in many other women's sports, where the 1960s and 1970s would prove to be vitally important periods after decades in the wilderness. Women's football had been banned in countries including England, Germany and Brazil for varying periods of time from the 1920s to the 1970s. The bans were justified by a narrative that playing sport would impact on a woman's ability to have children or that it simply wasn't her place.

After its initial faltering start, this time when women's rugby re-emerged, it would be for good.

Much of the action took place on university and college campuses. Student teams were starting to crop up all over Europe, but particularly in France. In the mid-1960s, two groups of students in Lyon and Toulouse decided to run an exhibition game to raise money for charity.

The players had limited experience playing the game but had brothers and friends who did. The match took place at Bourg-en-Bresse, where newspapers and images of the game highlighted that thousands of people packed the grounds to watch it. So successful was the outing that a regular series of games began between women's teams with clubs being formed as students graduated, initially mainly in the south of the country. All over Europe, as pioneering rugby-playing students left university, an adult women's game began to emerge.

Arguably Bourg-en-Bresse ought to be recognised as the birthplace of modern women's rugby in Europe. The club still exists today and was the base from which French and European women's rugby grew.

Initially women's rugby tended to be confined to charity matches between male and female teams – though coverage in the UK's *Daily Herald* included pictures of girls' teams training in Thornhill near Dewsbury in Yorkshire in 1965 and Tadley in Hampshire in 1966. There are no records of whether these teams arranged any formal games, and so it is not until May 1968 that the first fully documented and recorded official women's club match of the decade took place.

It was of course in France, in Toulouse, at the home of a local team – the Toulouse Fémina Sports – who took on Villemur-sur-Tarn. Again, the match was reported to have attracted thousands of spectators. The players and coaches involved in the game reached out to France's governing body, the FFR, to ask them to take on the women's game.

The answer, for now, was no.

The players decided to form their own association. In 1970, Annie Bannier from Pau and Isabelle Navarro and Odette Militon, both from Tarbes, founded the French Association of Women's Rugby (AFRF).

Slowly but surely, women's teams were being established all over France and the first French championship took place in 1971. Twelve teams took part and ASVEL Villeurbanne were crowned the inaugural winners.

With email still years away and media coverage rare, nobody in the game knew for certain what was happening in other countries, but across the Atlantic in the USA, universities were also building a head of steam.

Beginning with teams at the University of Colorado, Colorado State University, the University of Illinois and the University of Missouri, the American game began to grow rapidly. The governing body – the United States Rugby Football Union – was formed officially in 1975.

A women's committee, effectively the first governing body of US women's rugby, was founded a few years later in 1980 made up of representatives from the four territories – East, Pacific, Midwest and West. The group was led by Elissa Augello with a handful of other dedicated young women including Mary Larkin, Marcy Borge and Jennie Redner.

While the US was already producing some exceptional players, these administrative pioneers were critical to the growth of the US women's game in those early years. Their voluntary efforts in the 1970s and early 1980s to move the women's game forward, as well as the work of others including Jami Jordan, Lee Chichester and Kathi Morrison, were vital. It was through their leadership that the USA had its first club championships, its first collegiate championships, the first overseas tour by the nation's best players, the first women's national team and, later, the first World Cup-winning team.

Club sides were now also starting to appear in Canada, who enjoyed better support from their union than their US counterparts. Back in Europe, university students in the Netherlands were also starting to take up the game.

That teams were popping up mostly at university campuses was not surprising. It was much easier for women to access playing fields, students had time on their hands to get to grips with a relatively new sport and there was less opposition to physical sports like rugby than there was likely to have been at standalone rugby clubs, which remained largely a domain for males.

In the USA, many of the university towns with flourishing women's rugby teams like Madison, Tallahassee and Chapel Hill also had strong feminist communities with notable artists and writers living in the area. Women playing physical sports was much more acceptable in these communities.

By 1980, competitive championships were up and running in the USA and provincial games had started to be established in New Zealand. In Sweden, women's rugby had also taken off. A first National Cup was fought between Malmö, RC and Karlstad. The first teams were also being formed in Wales.

The women's game in Asia was starting to take flight with women's rugby in Japan getting off the ground. Rugby was already popular as a sport for men in Japan and was widely shown on television. Though there had been limited chances for women to get involved, there was strong interest, especially from mothers who saw their sons playing the game and loving it.

The now legendary Noriko Kishida was a mother who picked up a ball for the first time when she was 37. She became an integral part of the establishment of the Japanese women's game, where she is still heavily involved to this day. Kishida told me:

In the late 1980s, one of the wards in Tokyo was planning to run a rugby clinic and this was going to be for men and women which hadn't really been done before. A lot of women turned up to it and that event was really the start of women's rugby in Japan.

Around the same time, in Nagoya, there was also a women's handball team which was owned by a company, and those handball players were talking about playing rugby too. Once those women's players experienced what rugby was like, they started to establish their own teams and from there the women's game grew.

Kishida helped found the Japanese Women's Rugby Football Union in 1988 and would go on to play at the 1991 World Cup, making her debut at 45 years of age. The club team she played for, the Liberty Fields, would later be made famous by a documentary funded by Guinness charting their desire to play rugby despite deep societal opposition.

On this topic, Kishida told the filmmakers:

> It was back in the day, when getting harassed, sexually and otherwise was a given. Men expected women to be young, pretty and willing to quit their jobs for marriage. We lose if women can't play rugby. The reason why we've kept on going is because we don't want to lose. I wanted society to accept that women can love this kind of sport too, not just men.

The amateur Japanese Women's Union were smart enough to look to New Zealand to develop their game and sent club teams there to tour as they built their expertise and experience.

Given the reputation the All Blacks had already started to forge in the men's game, it was no surprise that many others too looked to New Zealand to try to improve. American teams were the first to venture there for tour games, when a group of players from San Diego, the superbly named Rio Grande Surfers, headed to New Zealand for a tour in 1980.

This was amateur rugby at its best. Players were housed with the opposing teams and the tour was only four matches long, all in the North Island. The visiting team was undefeated. They played a Wellington XV that was selected after trial matches, but also against sides which seem to be scratch teams never having played before.

Women's rugby got coverage in newspapers and was firmly back on the map, 90 years after Nita Webbe's efforts to establish the sport in New Zealand.

US teams began to descend thick and fast on New Zealand's shores. The California Kiwis RFC arrived in August 1980, a tour that was also four matches long, the first a warm-up with an U17 boys' side. The new set of tourists also went undefeated.

The following year, the San Diego State University Aztecs made the long journey south, again playing four club sides in North Island. The Aztecs also went undefeated, perhaps highlighting just how far ahead the US were in their development of the game at the time.

Finally, a New Zealand team returned the favour. In 1982, Linwood RFC became the first Kiwi side to tour overseas, heading to California for a series of matches.

The game was also establishing itself elsewhere.

In England, the home of rugby, steps were being taken to run the game more seriously. In early 1982, the University College London's women's team went on a tour to France and played, among other teams, Pontoise. It was the first recorded overseas tour by a UK team.

In Canada, the Ottawa Banshees were founded in the late 1970s, the first women's rugby club team to be officially formed. More clubs popped up locally through the 1980s. Women's provincial championships were up and running soon after and the first Canadian Championship for women was held in 1987 in Calgary.

After decades in the wilderness, the game was finally gathering momentum and the groundwork was laid for the first ever Test match in 1982.

The road to the first Test

Women's rugby in France was now well established with leagues already ten years old. Several Dutch universities also had teams up and running. At the university in Utrecht, the game was so popular that a women's team had been formed at the town's main rugby club.

The seeds of the first ever Test games were sown as a result of a meeting about women's rugby held in France between Henri Fléchon and a delegation led by Leo van Herwijnen from the Dutch rugby union, the NRB.

Fléchon had already become a hugely important figure in the development of women's rugby in France. In the early 1970s he had been a rugby referee with no connection with the women's game, but he was incensed at the FFR's efforts to kill it off by banning referees from officiating in it.

Fléchon refused to take part and the ban fell apart. Within three years he found himself president of AFRF. Later he would lead the negotiations to get women's rugby accepted by and eventually integrated into the FFR.

His meeting with the Dutch delegation was originally arranged so the Dutch could find out how women's rugby was organised in France, but Fléchon himself was particularly impressed by the way the Dutch governing body, the NRB, had recently officially recognised women's rugby. Returning to the Netherlands, the Dutch enthusiastically put into effect everything they had learned in France and decided to form a national team.

The year 1982 was already going to be a major year for Dutch rugby since the NRB was 50 years old. As part of the celebrations they invited France to play a women's game. It would be the first Test match in women's rugby.

Unsurprisingly the amateur French women's union accepted the invitation immediately and set about organising a team and coaching staff.

Claude Izoard, who coached with the Violettes Bressanes in Bourg-en-Bresse and was vice-president of the AFRF, was named coach. Judith Benassayag was appointed captain. Twenty-two players from five French clubs were selected and a weekend training camp was organised for the players and staff to get to know each other and learn to play together. The players selected had to pay for everything; their own transport to the game, their own hotel bills, even the shirts they would play in.

The Dutch organised trials and selected a team by the end of April before arranging several training games. The home side would be coached by Jopie Nessels and captained by Lisa Groenedijk. Many of their players had little or no experience of full 15-a-side rugby.

On Sunday, 13 June 1982, the two teams arrived at Utrecht Rugby Club to play the historic game. The French players had arrived the night before after a 500km bus journey.

France wore white. They were not allowed to wear the symbolic rooster on their shirt as they were not affiliated to the FFR, so they wore a tricolour badge instead.

In a recent interview reflecting on the game, French player Monique Fraysse, whose twin sister Nicole was also in the team and only distinguishable because of her hair colour, recalled both how special lining up for the anthems was, and what it was like sizing up the opposition in a Test game for the first time.

Representing France meant that women's rugby would be able to move forward. It was also a personal reward. We were there, we were not going to back down. I recall the shape of the Dutch players, all dressed in orange. They were young, tall, strong and they passed the ball very well.

There was no score in the first half, despite early French dominance, but France upped their game in the second half with star turns by fly-half Odette Desprats, leading to a try for winger Isabelle Decamps, only worth four points at the time.

Despite other opportunities on both sides, the score remained 4-0 to France and the visitors would record a famous first win. A return fixture was quickly organised, and the teams continued to meet annually throughout the rest of the decade.

If the pace of the growth of women's rugby in the 80 years after Emily Valentine picked up a ball had been glacial, the progress in the years after the first Test was nothing short of meteoric.

USA point the way

Test rugby was up and running in Europe. Meanwhile the USA were making serious strides domestically, laying the foundations in building a team that would go on to become the world's best in 1991.

The first ever National Championship in Chicago in 1984 was run magnificently. Had they known about it, Europe's leading sides would have been amazed at how professional and organised the competition already was on the other side of the Atlantic.

In Chicago, where the National Championship would be held, a raft of high-quality players was emerging. There was already an annual championship held in substandard county park facilities in Oakbrook and Schaumburg, both northern suburbs of Chicago.

Another locally held competition, the men's Inter-Territorial Tournament, had access to much better pitches at the nearby Polo Grounds.

Envious of the better grounds the men had, organiser Mary Larkin called the Polo Grounds to inquire about renting their facility instead for the first US Women's National Championship. She was told that the men had not yet put down a deposit for the 1984 event.

Larkin and her team quietly got to work, organising fundraisers including car washes and raffles to raise the money to get the insurance policy she needed to secure the venue before the men could get their act together.

Within a few days of putting the booking application in, she received an angry call from the president of Chicago Lions

RFC, the powerhouse in Chicago and Midwest men's rugby at the time.

She recalls in a recent post for the brilliant US Women's Rugby History Project website:

> He was furious. He was screaming into the phone, claiming we had no right to take the Polo Grounds as they had had them for all those years. I told him that Oakbrook still had not received their deposit nor their insurance from the previous year and that we had signed a contract. Our relationship with the Chicago Lions soured.
>
> Not that we ever had a close one. They made it clear from the very beginning that they did not approve of women playing rugby and they convinced the Midwest Referees' Society not to support the Women's Nationals that year. Thankfully we were rescued by the East and West Referees' Societies.

The 1984 Women's National Championship set a high bar for the tournament going forward. The grounds and the games were superb given the standard of the time. The Polo Grounds were so large that, in addition to the National Championship, the organisers were able to host a second competition, the Invitational Classic. They invited eight teams including Pittsburgh, Southern Illinois University, Illinois State University, St. Louis, Richmond Iris and Michigan State University. Richmond Iris dominated the pool and won the title.

The National Championship entries included Beantown, UC Berkeley, Chicago, Florida State, Iowa City, Minnesota, New Orleans and Texas A&M. Florida State defeated Beantown 11-6 to win the championship with Candi Orsini, later a star player for the US, named the tournament MVP.

Orsini was a remarkable woman and player who had begun her rugby career with Florida State in 1975. She led them to 13 finals appearances and four National Championships during a 23-year span which included helping the USA to win the World Cup in 1991.

Orsini had something rare for women's players at the time – a media profile, thanks largely to her day job as a stunt woman. She described it in an interview with *Sports Illustrated* in 1996:

> When I got to college, I intended to play softball and volleyball, but I also joined the rugby club. By the time I graduated, I knew that if I wanted to continue playing rugby, I would have to support myself somehow. A lot of people, even my team-mates, say I'm crazy, and they ask me when I'm going to get a real job. But stunt work is a great way to make a living. I like constant excitement.

Orsini's brilliance included, it was an empowering weekend. It highlighted, although hardly anyone else knew it at the time, that the US were much further ahead in their development than the rest of the world.

As they left US shores to get more experience, people would soon find out.

Chapter Three

A decade of firsts

COMMUNICATION BETWEEN the countries who were trying to develop the game was challenging, but the first international Test match was the catalyst for the acceleration of the game beyond recognition through the 1980s.

Having kicked Test rugby off, France and the Netherlands continued their annual fixture throughout the decade. Elsewhere across Europe and North America, the game began to put down sustainable roots.

The historic match in Utrecht provided a jolt to others involved in the embryonic administration of women's rugby. Just a year later, the Women's Rugby Football Union (WRFU) was formed to look after the game across England, Scotland and Wales. By then, several teams were already well established, especially across England. Word of mouth brought teams together and action revolved around an annual tournament in Loughborough.

A game in the early 1980s between Leeds University and University College London (UCL) subsequently proved important. Carol Isherwood, a player from Leeds, was introduced to London players Sheila Walsh and Deborah Griffin. Together they would all go on to become pivotal figures in the establishment of the game across the UK and the development of the first World Cup.

UCL organised the first overseas club trip by an English side to France to play Pontoise and, as the Dutch had found on their fact-finding mission to France a few years earlier, the French were well organised with a burgeoning club scene and established leagues. The touring team and organisers were impressed and returned to England determined to get the game off the ground properly in the UK.

The emergence of gifted players like Wasps' Karen Almond on the club scene highlighted that serious talent existed if it could be pushed in the right direction and the idea for the WRFU was born.

There were 12 founding teams as members of the new organisation including Leicester Polytechnic, Sheffield University, UCL, the University of Keele, Warwick University, Imperial College, Leeds University, York University, Loughborough University and Magor Maidens from Wales. Isherwood, who had begun playing with friends before lobbying Leeds University to set up a women's team, was named the chair.

The group wrote to the home nations' rugby unions to tell them what they were planning and the first meeting of the new organisation took place at the Bloomsbury Theatre in Euston in 1983.

Media coverage at the time shows the plans did not meet universal support. A *Times of London* diary entry read:

I bear Christmas tidings that should have every Twickenham diehard spluttering into his preprandials; a group of determined ladies has just established a national association for women rugby union players. The women's game has existed, mostly at universities, for many years now, but the ladies are extending their range. Tricia Moore, spokesperson for the organisation is not sure if it can get away with calling itself the Women's Rugby Union (the acronym might be confused with the Welsh). She says: 'Our games tend to be more tactical than the men's game, with a good deal less gratuitous violence. But it is still a very aggressive game; we play to exactly the same rules as the men. It is played in good spirit though, about as ladylike as it could be, in the circumstances.'

The early years of the WRFU focused on growing numbers and establishing clubs outside the university system. It involved heading back to France too, whose blueprint was now firmly on the radar of many European nations, including Italy, who had started to play regular games against them.

Unbeknown to those organising activity on one side of the Atlantic, on the other, women's rugby in the USA was about to make a major leap forward. There were plans for the best players in the country to tour Great Britain and France.

While women's rugby was still in its relative infancy on British shores, the game in the US, buoyed by the experiences of touring in New Zealand and the success of the National Championship, had accelerated rapidly. The 1985 tour, by a team calling itself the Wiverns, would arguably change the game forever.

The Wiverns come to town

While nine of the founder members of the WRFU were student teams, the exception being Magor Maidens, by 1985 a few non-university clubs were being formed by graduates who wanted to keep playing after their studies. But, apart from one-day festivals, there was still no competitive rugby in the UK on the eve of the arrival of the Wiverns.

They were not the first US team to visit the UK – Magor had hosted a team from North Carolina the previous year – but the standard and quality was at a level no one had seen before.

Leading the squad was coach Pat Foley, who had the idea of getting together the best players across the US for a tour.

The idea spread enthusiastically through the American rugby community. Huge numbers put their hands up to be involved, despite the personal cost and time involved. Foley had more than enough for a very competitive 36-player squad.

The team needed a name. It didn't have the support of the US Rugby Union, whose only contribution was to withhold both the names 'Eagles' and 'United States', so they needed something creative. Foley came up with Women's International Vagabonds, Emissaries and Rugby Nomads, which resulted in a convenient acronym, and the Wiverns were born.

Thanks particularly to Title IX, a law that prohibited discrimination based on sex in schools and colleges and ensured more equitable funding for women's sports, women's rugby in the United States was years ahead of where the British game was in 1985. Inter-university rugby had been expanding since the Universities of Colorado, Colorado State, Illinois and Missouri launched rugby programmes in the early 1970s. They were benefiting from quality coaching and funding.

By 1985, the USA had over ten times as many teams and players as Britain or France and a national club championship had been in place for over five years. As a result, the Americans arrived to find that they were older and significantly more experienced than almost all of the teams they would meet.

Foley arranged three matches in England, against Yorkshire Select, Midlands Select and the South of England, before the team moved on to France for two more games, against club teams Chilly Mazarin and Soisy. All of this was to take place in just two weeks in November.

The tour rules and policies issued to each player ahead of the trip, dug out for me kindly by Kerri Heffernan, made clear that management had high expectations of the players.

Our primary goal is to provide the greatest display of running and handling rugby ever seen in the British Isles and France by either women or men. We want to score as many tries as possible to show the rugby 'purists' that women can play rugby as well as men, if not better. Do not be conservative – take chances – you have 14 of the best rugby players in the world supporting you. Every one of you is getting a chance to shine, use it.

The talent and skill of the Wiverns created a stir among the women's rugby community who saw them play and train. In an interview to remember the tour with John Birch on Scrumqueens.com, England's Emma Mitchell recalled how the Americans made an impact in the Loughborough gym with their ability to lift heavier weights than most of the men's rugby team and their more proactive approach to fitness.

> The Wivern side had been lifting weights in the Loughborough gym and some of the men's first 15 had been surprised at how much the Americans were lifting – some were even embarrassed to see the women lifting far more than them!
>
> My Loughborough team-mates Liza Burgess and Amanda Bennett took in three or four billets, and I remember them being shocked when one of the players asked for a ten-mile training run route around Loughborough for a recovery run the day after the game. They were also a little aghast to come home from lectures and realise that the Americans had had the gas heating on all day – we used to limit heating to an hour in the evening in those student days!

The *New York Times* wrote a report of the tour and remarked on the difference between the visitors and their hosts.

Many of the British women talked to their friends between matches, while others sipped a beer or two in the nearby cafeteria. An unidentified young player was also quoted as saying, '[The Wiverns] are marvellous athletes ... but they take the game a bit seriously for my tastes.'

The tour kicked off in York on 17 November with the visitors cruising to an 11-try 44-0 win over Yorkshire Select. Eight players made it to the scoresheet, with Cynthia Bystrak, Jan Rutkowski and Carolyn 'BB' Alley getting two each.

Three days later the team arrived in Loughborough and, although there was only a three-day gap between games, the size of the squad allowed a totally different XV to be fielded. A big crowd turned out to watch the game on the Towers pitch, partly due to the Wiverns' prowess in the Loughborough gym.

The host team was the Midlands Select, with players from Loughborough, Keele, Warwick and Leicester Polytechnic, as well as Swansea. They lost 44-0.

These games were vital in accelerating what would happen next in England and Wales. Players like Bennett, Liza Burgess, Kiki Lee and Sam Robson all appeared in the first Great Britain game against France a few years later, while Emma and Jane Mitchell would go on to become key players for England.

For the Americans, players like Candi Orsini, Kathy Flores, Morgan Whitehead and Chris Harju were standouts. Six years down the road they would be the cornerstone of the USA team who would go on to win the first World Cup, with England their opponents in the final.

The tour was beginning to gain traction in the local media. *The Observer* sent reporter Geoffrey Nicolson to the next game, just two days later against the South of England, at Wasps.

It was to be a significantly closer match than those that had gone before – the closest of the tour – though for 11 of the party it was their second game in a week, and for six the second in just two days. The final score was 20-0 with Kerri Heffernan, Kathy Flores, Ruth Bernick, Karen Keith and Chris Harju getting the tries.

It was a sign of the times that Nicolson's half-page article largely ignored the game and concentrated rather more on the fact that women were playing at all. The headline 'Rugger dolls no pushovers' gives a flavour of the text that followed.

The Wiverns headed to Shenley for an annual festival organised by the WRFU and went through the tournament unbeaten before heading to France. There they met Chilly Mazarin in Paris. Their opponents were one of the leading French teams but the result was much the same as in England: eight tries and 38-0. A 'third half' – a shortened match of two ten-minute halves for the other half of the squad – was also arranged. This time the Americans won 21-0.

The final game came the day after, with a match against Soisy, a game that would live long in the memory of US player Kerri Heffernan:

> I was in the forwards and recall that the front row was getting the hell beat out of them – punched and kicked. I was at six and the opposite prop just kept punching me in the head – they were for real. We won handily – we still had superior skill, fitness and speed – our backs were tremendous and once out the ball was usually on its way to the line.

The tour came to an end having left an indelible mark on the game in both England and France. The Wiverns inspired significant improvements. Both countries were now clear what standards were required and had a better idea what the game could become.

Everyone involved vowed to become fitter, stronger and more organised.

It was also seminal for the US players, planting the seed for the idea for the first women's national team. That would become a reality in 1987.

Great Britain get up and running

Overseas tours were now becoming more regular with club sides from the US, the UK and France travelling more often. Plans were afoot in New Zealand for a club team to travel to Britain towards the end of the decade.

With the Wiverns' ability and impact fresh in their minds, the WRFU turned their attention to the inevitable next step, the creation of a Test side. Communication between the WRFU, French and Dutch organisers of the women's game was becoming more regular. With France and the Netherlands now playing annually, the time had come for the Brits to take the plunge.

But there was a challenge. The WRFU represented not just England but Wales and Scotland too. The decision was taken therefore to invite France to London to come and play a game against a Great Britain side.

Since the union had been established, the number of club sides had grown from 12 to over 70 across the three nations. The player base was there and when well-regarded coach Stefan Czerpak from Newbury came on board to coach the team, the plans were formalised.

Carol Isherwood told me about the discussions that took place.

At this stage we knew the Dutch and French were playing games and we had been on tour to France and had some talks with them about what they were doing. We'd found out too that Italy were also playing Test games and we knew we really had to get on this.

We had a meeting where we were arguing the toss about it. Was it too soon and should we focus on the grassroots first or should we do it before we were left behind? Ultimately, we agreed that Test rugby would create an important shop window where people would realise we were a serious sport. We decided to invite France and go for it and we agreed that we'd play as Great Britain.

Having done that we spent the rest of the meeting designing the shirts we were going to wear! By the time I had finished with it, it looked suspiciously like a rugby league shirt with a great big cross down the front!

The organising of the game itself, to be played on 19 April 1986 in Richmond in west London, was left largely to the host players who would be playing in the match. The French players would self-fund their trip.

Such were the financial constraints of the time that Great Britain trained the night before at Rosslyn Park before heading their separate ways to stay at friends' and relatives' houses scattered across London.

The administration around the game was a challenge for the volunteers involved. One of the organisers for the home side arrived at Heathrow to collect the French team with a coach, only to realise that they had in fact landed at Gatwick. The French players made their way to west London on the tube, none the wiser to the mix-up as an empty bus headed back down the motorway.

Back in Richmond, the Great Britain match shirts had yet to arrive hours before kick-off. When they did turn up, they were far too big and players resorted to taping up their sleeves before running onto the field.

The game attracted both media and public interest. The stand was packed as the players took to the field.

France, more experienced, applied serious pressure up front and though they scored early after pushing Great Britain off their own ball, the hosts soon settled into it. Karen Almond was the home side's standout player. Her two tries were written up in local media reports as being high-quality and she helped the hosts to an unexpected 8-4 lead.

Eventually the French showed their experience with a second-half try and, though Great Britain lost, there was elation at the final whistle that the match had taken place at all and that it had generated such interest, much of it positive.

The *Sunday Times* reported positively on the game:

Karen Almond of Wasps was Britain's most powerful and effective player. She came scything through on to a break by scrum-half Hill (another outstanding player who always made the ball available) and from five yards out had too much momentum to be halted. Then, on the outside of a blind-side move, she swept around the French flank for a second try and an 8-4 lead.

If the first half was splendid, with Britain apparently forging ahead, the second was somewhat anti-climactic. Eventually the French ended the stalemate when their left winger rounded the defence and, with all the players tired, there was no coming back for the British. Increasingly there were errors, and the referee picked up all of them.

Indeed, if anything came badly out of the game it was the laws, now seen in all their overkill glory, as innocent mistakes produced a stream of penalties.

The British women were able to react to the final whistle with elation, however, as they hugged each other. They had done well, and so had women's rugby.

The game was the first of eight that Great Britain would play over the next few years, even though Wales and Scotland started to break away to form their own unions and play their own standalone Test matches. A year later, both Wales and England felt ready in fact to play their own Test games but agreed that at a European Cup that was to be played in France in 1988, they would continue to play as Great Britain.

Further strides were being made in the club game, with Wasps playing Richmond at Twickenham Stadium in the first appearance of women's rugby at the country's national stadium. Karen Almond starred again as she led Wasps to a 19-0 win.

Historic rivalries begin

They didn't know it at the time, but many of the players involved in the first Test game between Wales and England at Pontypool Park in 1987 would go on to become highly influential figures in the development of women's rugby across Britain in the decades to follow.

Wales were captained by Liza Burgess, who had already starred for Great Britain and who would go on to lead her country 61 times during a 93-cap career. She helped to found Saracens and later moved into coaching in the Welsh women's set-up.

The Welsh also had players like Amanda Bennett, who went on to coach Wales women and England A before becoming a senior administrator in sport. Fran Margerison, a true pioneer of Welsh women's rugby who has sadly since passed away, was also in the team. Margerison was already playing a pivotal role in the establishment of the Welsh Women's Rugby Union and she became its first chair.

On the England side, Nicola Ponsford was at hooker, later going on to become one of the most influential women in the development of the game in England, while Isherwood, a future World Rugby Hall of Famer, was flanking.

The first game between the two teams was the start of a historic rivalry. Wales were coached by John Grice from Swansea University and had selected a team made up mostly of players from universities and prominent clubs such as Magor

Maidens, Pontypool, Swansea Uplands and Blaenau Gwent, along with some English clubs.

England won 22-4 in a match played at a high standard. It was clear that both sides were generating enough talent and depth to help field a strong Great Britain team in France the following year to contest for the European Championship.

That 1988 event was the first ever such European event and the first multi-national women's rugby competition of any sort. France and Great Britain were joined by the Netherlands and Italy.

Little is known about the Italians and their early progress, though they had established a women's union some years earlier and clubs had begun to emerge in the north of the country. The Italians were organised enough that they had already played three Test games against France and had run the more experienced French side close enough in Rome the year before, losing 4-16. Early international Federica Bortolato remembered the early days of the Italian team in an interview with Scrumqueens.com:

> I have many memories of playing with the Azzurri: from training camps where we stayed together to cut down costs, to the evenings spent rehearsing the national anthem, the remarkable performances which involved in cutting and sewing badges on blue jackets which had been designed for men and having to shorten all the trousers that we had been given. But we didn't mind that if we could play.

Great Britain were coached by Jim Greenwood, whose influence on the early years of women's rugby was significant. The players later recalled that Greenwood had the team doing cool-downs after the games – a tactic considered cutting edge at the time!

France and Great Britain made it to the final, with the hosts winning 8-6. By now it was clear that there was enough competition in Europe for the game to start to organise more formal windows of competition.

After the tournament, a meeting was held and attended by delegates from Britain, France, Italy, the Netherlands, Belgium and Spain. They decided to form an international women's confederation, similar to the International Rugby Board, to coordinate and promote the women's game worldwide. It would be called the Women's International Rugby Board (WIRB) and it was expected that the USA, Canada and New Zealand would also come on board.

By now, France were well ahead of their European counterparts in their pace of growth. They had around 30 clubs playing in a league system and a women's federation affiliated to the FFR and recognised by the French sports ministry, therefore receiving a subsidy from the government.

In Britain, a five-year development plan was devised to increase the number of players, raise playing standards and encourage more women and former players to become involved in administration, refereeing and coaching. The plan was a precursor to funding that would be received from the English Sports Council to help grow the game.

With the European game gathering momentum, several other countries were getting their act together, including from some unlikely sources. Sweden had beaten Great Britain to the punch to become the third country to play Test rugby as they played the Netherlands in 1984 and again for the next two years running.

The USA had not rested on their laurels after the success of the Wiverns tour and their first Test game with Canada was planned in 1987. In Canada, where activity had begun in universities in the 1970s, provincial games were springing up through the 1980s. With support from the Canadian Rugby Union, a national side was established to take on the USA.

The USA was still not permitted to wear the Eagles logo on their shirts for the match, with the governing body resistant to fully supporting the women's game, though it was sanctioned as an official Test even though they called themselves a President's XV.

The USA won the match 3-22 in Victoria, British Columbia, and also won the rematch of what became an annual series for the next ten years.

Kathy Flores, who had made such an impression for the Wiverns on their European tour, captained the US team from number 8. Though the scoreline looked comfortable, she recalled the incredibly physical nature of the Canadians when I sat down with her in San Francisco to talk to her for this book.

> I'd played with a Florida team that was pretty good and strong and so we often dominated teams, but this was different. The thing about Canada is that they were much tougher than we were. They have always been incredibly physical and tough. We tackle hard but at the breakdown we are not as physical on a constant basis like they are. We won the game alright, but it was an awakening to say 'oh this is international rugby', because nobody had ever done it and we were the first.

She also remembered the lack of respect the team faced from its own rugby family in the US.

> We were all just generally very excited because not only was it our first international, but we were playing alongside our men. We won our game, but the guys didn't as it turned out. At our banquet, some of the US men had tied their ties around their heads, were banging their utensils on the table and being generally pretty rowdy. We were fairly aghast at the time and since it was our first time we

didn't know if this was standard behaviour so we stayed quiet. Then the US men's captain got up and spoke and said he was upset because 'these women are sitting here while my wife is not allowed to come to the banquet' and gave his view that rugby really was a man's sport.

Clearly that didn't exactly make us feel very welcome! What's funny about that story now is that these days it's told as if the women were the ones with the ties and banging their utensils but there you go, that's what it was like and we had to face that at the time.

Flores passed away in 2021. She is remembered as one of the true pioneers of women's rugby, not just a World Cup winner but also the head coach of the national team becoming the first woman in the role.

New Zealand reawakens

Meanwhile, in New Zealand, progress was also being made with the influence of a coach who was playing a huge part in driving the game forward. Laurie O'Reilly was a Christchurch lawyer who coached the Canterbury University men's team. He was approached by some aspiring women's players for some coaching advice.

His involvement increased when his daughter said she wanted to play rugby and he became the Canterbury women's coach in 1985 and the first New Zealand coach a few years later. He had a clear understanding with all the teams he was involved with. 'You are rugby players who happen to be women,' he once wrote, 'not women who happen to be rugby players.'

The game started to thrive, in part thanks to O'Reilly's enthusiasm and connections, and he helped gain the backing of national figures such as Russ Thomas, the New Zealand Rugby's chairman, the body who ran the game there. In 1988, O'Reilly wanted to establish a touring squad from Canterbury to travel to the US and Europe in what would be the first matches by a New Zealand side against non-American opposition.

The team was to be called the Crusadettes. The players and coaches spent a year raising funds. O'Reilly wrote to teams all over the world, waiting for letters to return to confirm whether the team could play and if they had somewhere to stay.

A group of over 40 players saved enough to make the trip which took in the USA, England, Wales, Italy, Spain and France over an eight-week tour – a trip that modern-day amateur players would likely consider impossible.

The team played every second day, sometimes twice a day. The tour generated press interest back home with an article in *The Press* challenging forward thinking on the women's game.

Rugby is no longer a man's sport exclusively, but a worthwhile game for both sexes. The challenge has been issued for the promotion of, and participation in women's rugby in New Zealand.

The 1988 touring team won 17 matches from 21 abroad and racked up a staggering 520 points with only 67 conceded. Losses were rare. London side Richmond got one over on the talented visitors, while Italian team Treviso also notched a win.

Like the Wiverns before them, the Crusadettes left a mark on Europe. It was clear that New Zealand, when they got their act together, were going to be a standout team. The tour was also a turning point for both Canterbury and New Zealand Rugby. Ten members of the squad played for the 'Gal Blacks' at the 1991 World Cup in Wales with Anna Richards, who would go on to become a three-time World Cup winner and is still considered one of the best women's players ever.

When they got back to New Zealand, the Crusadettes' success became a catalyst for those running the game there to start taking women's rugby seriously.

New Zealand had already become the go-to place for touring sides looking to develop their game. A year later, a New Zealand Select was put together to play US representative side the Pacific Coast Grizzlies.

O'Reilly coached the team to a 13-7 win and the Grizzlies have the record of playing against the first New Zealand representative side on 22 July at Lancaster Park, where the match was a curtain-raiser to Canterbury against Argentina. The Grizzlies played six other matches, two against provincial men's sides Wellington and Auckland.

Next a team from England made the trip. Richmond toured with a strong squad, playing nine games against club and provincial sides and winning them all. Keio University from Japan also toured New Zealand in 1989, with the Japanese Women's Rugby Football Union having been established the year before.

In Taranaki, a group of players were also using their influence to further the game.

In 1988, Vicky Dombroski, who would become the only female coach of the Black Ferns (the name now used by the New Zealand women's team), wrote a letter to the New Zealand Rugby (NZR) asking for more support. She had a reply from John Joseph 'JJ' Stewart, a former All Blacks coach and member of the union's council. Stewart replied and said that the NZR was 'most favourably disposed towards women taking an active role in the game'.

He went on to say the first step was to encourage clubs to include women's teams. Then the clubs needed to approach their provincial unions to organise a club competition and to 'seek representative opportunities for selected players'. Later Dombroski would reflect that this letter was the catalyst for women's rugby in New Zealand and things really did start to change in 1989.

O'Reilly had become more convinced than ever that New Zealand were ready to play as a Test team. He was the driving force behind a tournament that became known as RugbyFest in 1990, a two-week festival of women's rugby held in Christchurch.

Week one was dedicated to club rugby. Those involved played every day against teams including Japanese club sides from Tokyo and Nagoya. The second week was dedicated to international games where the US, the Soviet Union and the Netherlands played. It ended with New Zealand taking on a Rest of the World team.

Though run close by the US, the New Zealand side was too strong. In the final game against a combination of the other teams, New Zealand won 12-4 to round off the tournament.

Richards later told me more about O'Reilly's influence and the tournament itself.

Laurie was very passionate with decent coaching experience behind him. He was a lawyer with huge contacts in rugby around the world which really helped us, and he was held in high regard all over New Zealand. He was brilliant at identifying girls who were good at other sports who might do well in rugby, and he did a great job in persuading people to come across. Helen Littleworth, who ended up as a captain, was an ex-NZ hockey player. I was a netballer as was Helen Mahon; Leslie Brett was a touch player, so he was recruiting talent from all over. The festival in Christchurch was a whirlwind. We played pretty much every day and it was exciting to beat America, who had more experience than us. We played in Lancaster Park too which was huge back then and though the games aren't counted as capped games – we did play in the Black jersey.

O'Reilly's impact had been massive in those formative years, not just in organising and coaching the game, but also in advocating for it.

In a piece for the *Journal of Physical Education New Zealand* in 1994 he set out his views that women are physically and psychologically suited to rugby and that they find a spirit and freedom in rugby that is absent in other sports. He bemoaned the existence of sexist attitudes towards women's players. Until his death he was a massive champion for the women's game in New Zealand. New Zealand and Australia now play regularly for the Laurie O'Reilly Trophy.

As the players in New Zealand celebrated a historic tournament, back in London, plans were accelerating for another huge first.

A women's rugby World Cup.

Chapter Four

World Cup pioneers

AS THE 1990s were ushered in, the women's game looked vastly different than it had ten years before.

New Zealand's RugbyFest was a model for what could be done, highlighting that teams were willing to travel to play international rugby, whether officially sanctioned or not, and that standards had increased enough that a more global tournament could be considered.

In London, Richmond had been invited to take part in RugbyFest. As they had only travelled to New Zealand the year before for their unbeaten nine-match tour, there was no way they could afford to go again so soon. But the invite and the success of the event in Christchurch got the members of the WRFU committee thinking. With committee member Deborah Griffin agreeing to do some scoping for what a bigger international event might look like, she returned to her club to ask for some help.

Griffin had started playing rugby at UCL in one-off fixtures against King's College in the late 1970s and had quickly become a vital figure in the development of the game across the UK as a member of the WRFU committee. She recruited three more Richmond players – Alice Cooper, who worked in advertising and PR; Mary Forsyth, an accountant; and Sue Dorrington, who had commercial experience – to form a core team to look at what was possible. Working with the help of Carol Isherwood and other volunteers, they soon found it to be a project which would drive them to exhaustion and to tears of despair and delight. But it would eventually earn a place in the history books.

The group sent letters all over the world inviting teams to take part in the first World Cup. They received enthusiastic and positive responses from New Zealand, Canada, Wales, Japan, Sweden, the Netherlands, the USA, Italy, Spain, the Soviet Union and, at the very last minute, France. With England also involved, 12 teams were confirmed to take part in the event.

The team now needed venues and financial backing. The first would prove much easier than the second.

Having spoken to both Leicester and Bristol, they picked Cardiff to host the event with the Arms Park made available for the final. South Glamorgan County Council agreed to host the gala dinner for free at the end of the event after the final on 14 April. Vernon Pugh, a lawyer and highly regarded Welsh rugby administrator, then helped find venues for the pool matches.

The group secured support from the Welsh Sports Council, but money was extremely tight. As the event grew closer, the quartet on the organising committee realised they were going to fall well short of the investment they had hoped to secure via sponsorship and glumly set about writing to all the teams taking part to tell them they couldn't help to pay for anything – certainly not flights and now not likely accommodation either.

Every team wrote back with the same message. We're still coming. It was early evidence of what became clear later. Teams were thrilled to be taking part at all and grasped the magnitude of what Griffin and her team were trying to do, to host a global event on a shoestring budget with little to no support from the International Rugby Board (IRB) nor many official governing bodies.

What Griffin and her team managed to pull off was remarkable, not least because they were juggling it alongside their day jobs and, in Isherwood's and Dorrington's cases, alongside their own efforts to make the England squad to play in the tournament.

Isherwood also organised a coaching conference in Cardiff alongside the event and Griffin had had a baby just months before it kicked off. Forsyth too gave birth a week out from the opening matches.

The entire tournament was packed into a schedule lasting just over a week, with some players playing four games in eight days.

Although Griffin admitted afterwards that the experience was a huge challenge, she looks back fondly at its impact:

> Everyone was so pleased to be there. I don't remember the teams, apart from the Soviet Union, causing any real trouble so they just went along with everything and helped out. We had a dinner which was put on at the end and the Japanese arrived in full kimonos looking absolutely fantastic and it just meant so much to them all to be there. The letters we got afterwards were just amazing. They all felt it was something that put the game on a new footing.

The tournament had very little input or support from the IRB. Their main contribution was to argue with the organisers about the competition logo. Alice Cooper, who acted as a press officer throughout, explained that the issue delayed a huge amount of planning.

> We'd asked James Young of January Design to do the logo for us as a favour but it proved to be a bone of contention. The original brief had been to avoid any confusion with the men's event. However, no sooner had we launched the logo

than word reached us that the design was unacceptable to some IRB rugby chiefs, and we must change it – the angle of the ball, the 'speed stripes' and the fact that it was enclosed by a box being considered too similar to the men's Rugby World Cup logo. In spite of considerable inconvenience, cost and wastage, we reluctantly changed the logo and sought approval from all parties.

The USA become the world's best

With Griffin and her team marshalling things so well off the field, a genuinely competitive tournament was about to play out.

England were captained by Karen Almond, who had proved such an outstanding talent for well over a decade. Gill Burns at number 8 was fast becoming one of the world's best too, despite being a relative newcomer to the game.

New Zealand had Anna Richards, who would play such an impressive role with her side through to the 2010 World Cup, and they had the most recent international experience behind them from their tournament in Christchurch.

Wales had been at the forefront of the development of the game with Magor of course one of the founding members of the WRFU. They were led by Liza Burgess, who already had plenty of international games under her belt for her country and for Great Britain.

The USA were expected to be dangerous, especially by anyone who remembered the Wiverns tour. The outstanding Kathy Flores and Patty Jervey were involved again.

The Netherlands had been playing for years at this stage so had experience, including in the European Cup, and they brought a young side with lots of students who were still gaining knowledge of the sport. They, like the Soviet Union, had also played in RugbyFest the year before in Christchurch. Japan hadn't played in that competition but they had been to New Zealand and tasted some form of international rugby.

The Swedes were selected from a small number of clubs who had to pack in a very short programme of games in late summer before they became snowbound. Squad member Jennie Öhman recalled her selection in an interview with Scrumqueens.com:

> I started to play rugby in 1986 thanks to a relative of mine who had a friend who was playing. I also played handball, another physical game, and I thought it would be fun to try another sport. Then in 1991 different club coaches in Sweden were asked to select the players they thought had the skills to represent Sweden in the World Cup. The preparations were in several training camps during weekends and from these camps the World Cup squad to Wales was selected.

France were expected to be strong and reach the semi-finals at least. The Italians had been building their experience and had played Great Britain twice coming into the competition.

Finally there were Canada, who had three losses to the USA under their belts and travelled with high hopes, and Spain, where the women's game had been growing in and around the Madrid area since the late 1970s and where a Catalonia representative side had already played against France, Italy and Wales.

The weather for much of the tournament was atrocious. It was so bad that on the day of the opening fixtures that hardly any other rugby games were played anywhere else in Wales or England. As the opening match loomed between New Zealand and Canada, it lashed with rain. There was no chance games could be moved given the tight schedule. Even all these years later if you ask players about it, they can still vividly recall the conditions of the opening matches.

There were four pools of three teams. New Zealand were matched with Canada and Wales. France faced Sweden and

Japan. The USA were pitted against the Dutch and the Soviet Union. England, Spain and Italy were also matched up.

New Zealand kicked the competition off memorably at the Glamorgan Wanderers ground with a traditional Maori tribal dance in front of a crowd of over 1,000. Debbie Chase led the haka before her side impressed to see off Canada 24-8. Chase scored two tries herself while Helen Mahon, a pacey wing, ran in a hat-trick. The New Zealand backline was brilliantly organised by Richards, then playing scrum-half.

Canada were captained by Ruth Hellerud-Brown, who was questioned by the amazed media afterwards about how full-on the game had been physically. 'I wouldn't say it was a dirty game,' she replied. 'I've played in much worse. The most important thing was that there was no hair-pulling and stuff like that going on; we can take the boots.'

England kicked off against Spain and played well enough to win 12-0 with tries from Cheryl Stennett and Burns. France hammered Japan 62-0 and the United States snuck past the Netherlands 7-0 with a less-than-convincing performance, albeit in atrocious weather, winning thanks to a four-point Patty Jervcy try and an Andrea Morrell penalty.

Interviewed recently on World Rugby channels, Jervey remembered well the weather being a rude awakening against the Dutch:

It was a cold, miserable outing – torrential rain and wind. I recall being elated that we pulled out the win as we celebrated with hot tea in the shower. The only problem was that we were shaking so hard from the cold that the cups were empty by the time they got to our mouths!

The opening matches generated some media interest, with Paul Nelson in the *Sunday Times* providing a memorable report from the first round:

The lack of kicking ability, both from ground and the hand, is one of the glaring differences from the men's game. But, as many long-suffering supporters would suspect, it improves the game as a spectacle. Once the purist has stopped tut-tutting over the kicks to touch that fall short, he is impressed by the amount of running this produces once hoofing the ball into touch is no longer an option.

Even if the opening day's play had not been so compelling, the World Cup is already a significant triumph for its organisers and for the women's game. Despite a desperate lack of funds, the tournament having no sponsor and the regrettable sniping of men who see the game's development as an intrusion into their territory, the tournament has brought together 12 teams from around the globe on a shoestring.

For some, the sacrifices have been enormous. The team from the Soviet Union were still arriving in dribs and drabs yesterday, with no money, little food and supplies of champagne, caviar and vodka with which to barter for the basic necessities.

The Soviet Union team would prove to become infamous as the days wore on. The national team had been established just a few years earlier in Barnaul under coach Sergey Chechenkov and they had travelled to New Zealand to play the year before at RugbyFest.

They did well in New Zealand despite a daunting start against the hosts, only going down 8-0. Two days later they played and lost to the Netherlands 12-4, before ending their first experience of international rugby with a 32-0 loss to the United States. Nonetheless it was an encouraging start, so they would have approached the World Cup with some confidence that they could make an impact.

The USSR Women's Rugby Union had been set up subsequently with 12 club teams actively competing from Moscow, Tashkent, Barnaul, Tver, Nalchik, Alma-Ata, Kazan and Chernovtsy. The team came to Wales on the back of the first ever Festival of Women's Rugby in USSR in Tashkent earlier that year.

But they had arrived at Heathrow for the World Cup with hardly any money at all and had hoped to raise funds to pay their keep by selling cut-price vodka and caviar when they reached Wales. Customs officials were called to deal with the problem but found it almost impossible to break the language barrier and they eventually left the team alone.

News of their financial plight spread quickly throughout Wales and offers of help came in thick and fast. Companies and individuals contacted the organisers to support the team with money, meals and transport. A pie manufacturer and a restaurant owner came forward to donate food and an anonymous donor offered £1,200 towards their expenses. The mother of Bess Evans, the Welsh women's hooker, gave £100.

The Soviets would go on to lose all their games, but they had left their mark, as *The Guardian* reported at the time:

Customs officers called on the headquarters of the Soviet women's rugby team in Cardiff yesterday after reports that the tourists were penniless and had been selling cut-price vodka and caviar in an attempt to pay their expenses during the inaugural women's World Cup.

The women were said to have travelled through Heathrow airport's green channel with five 5ft cases of liquor, but at South Glamorgan Institute yesterday customs investigators found it almost impossible to break the language barrier and eventually left.

It is understood that no charges will be brought against the team, who had only enough money for their air fares and hoped to barter their goods for food during the week-long tournament in South Wales. But half of their goods went missing at Moscow airport and since arriving they had resorted to rationing their breakfast meal and sold some jerseys and sportswear to raise cash.

Yet even while customs officers were questioning them, offers of help were coming in. Companies and individuals contacted the party with offers of cash, meals and transport.

Such acts of kindness came too late to build up the Soviet women's stamina for yesterday's match: they lost 28-0 to the Netherlands – but showed a profit on touchline sales of souvenirs.

Russian player Larisa Masalova recalled in an interview in 2009 how happy the team was, just to be there.

For most of us it was the first time we travelled abroad or even the first time we ever got passports. There was no target: it was just to get some experience vs great international teams. When the team arrived at the hotel, we Soviet girls were so surprised: we never had had twin rooms! That was amazing!

The competition would be the last time the Soviet Union took the field. Political upheaval meant that by the time the next World Cup came around in 1994 the USSR's place was taken by two teams – Kazakhstan and Russia – who would come up against each other in that tournament.

The USSR was not the only team whose traditions and peculiarities would become an integral part of the legacy of the 1991 World Cup. Japan, despite also losing all their games, were hugely popular. Competitive women's rugby in Japan was still very new, having gained a foothold thanks to the interest of many mothers across Tokyo who had seen their sons get involved and love the sport. Although rugby for women was largely frowned upon in Japanese society due to its physicality, women's sports were relatively well respected there, with the Olympic gold-medal-winning women's volleyball team hugely popular.

The Japanese team were noticeably much smaller than all the other teams with tall scrum-half Ayako Horikita, who weighed a mere seven stone, and stood just 4ft 9in tall. Horikita saw only ten minutes of play in Japan's first match against France before breaking her collar bone.

The team went on to lose 0-62 that day, performing a sporting bow every time a try was scored against them, an endearing tradition they carried on for the rest of the competition. Their sportsmanship was also on show at the end of every game when they presented small gifts such as origami to their opponents, while every member of the team played in a scrum cap, regardless of their position.

New Zealand's haka also impressed crowds and opposition. They had been granted special permission to perform it from Maori elders who said yes on the basis that it was afforded proper respect, although Nino Sio and Elsie Paiti were not granted permission from their respective South Sea leaders and had to watch from the sidelines as their team-mates performed pre-match.

Despite not funding the Gal Blacks, as they were then known, NZR did allow the team to wear the silver fern, synonymous with New Zealand rugby, on their jerseys for this tournament.

Having paid mostly their own way to get there, teams had to make do with budget accommodation in the local area. The England team were even kicked out of their own beds for a night when the hotel they were staying at realised they'd double-booked a major event. The team had to spend a night together in sleeping bags in a conference room.

On the field, England, France, New Zealand and USA looked like closely matched teams.

The USA were standout athletes and could play at a pace and energy that was hard for teams to match, but the weather continued to catch them by surprise. Kathy Flores recalled to me how much of an impact it had:

> We had the Netherlands and Russia in our pool stages and the weather was just awful. The worst. In the very first game we played, the score was 4-0 and at one point the rain was coming down sideways. One of our girls was so cold she was hyperventilating. At one point there was a scrum and she looked like she couldn't move, and someone had to grab her and pull her off the field. We were running around trying to stay warm, jumping up and down like crazy people. It wasn't something we were really used to!

The games came thick and fast. While those four sides would emerge from the pool stage to meet in the semi-finals at Cardiff Arms Park, there were other early-round highlights.

Sweden beat Japan 20-0, the much closer result driving the Japanese on for the next few years, laying the groundwork for them to beat the same opposition at the next World Cup in 1994. Jennie Öhman recalled:

> The first World Cup was very exciting with a lot of new opponents. The Swedish national team had played mostly against Germany until that time. Our win against Japan was a nice memory, and I also remember that the French women were a little rougher than I had experienced at that time!

New Zealand made their way to the semi-finals by beating Wales 24-6 at the Llanharan grounds with several hundred of the old mining village's locals turning out in full voice to support the national team. New Zealand were expected to continue on to the final but faced a stubbornly tough USA team who beat them in the semis 7-0. Chris Harju slotted a penalty and Barbara Bond dotted down a pack try for the Americans.

Anna Richards remembers the disappointment of being knocked out vividly to this day:

> It was a tough game and there were no huge scoring chances or anything like that. They got a try and a penalty, but we got battered. They were more structured and knew the game a bit better than us at that point. It was hugely disappointing for all of us to lose. We had gone with high hopes and in some ways, it was the thing that drove me to keep on playing rugby because I hate losing.

It was to be an England v USA final as the English saw off the French 13-0 in the semi-finals in perhaps their best performance as a team yet.

The USA were slight favourites going into the final. They had been playing well enough and their backline was particularly feared, with an ability to score from anywhere. England had hardly rotated their squad, going into the final with a group of players who had played practically non-stop for just over a week.

The final itself generated a decent crowd with around 3,000 on the sidelines. The organisers had made a real occasion of it, with a full regimental brass band, mini-rugby curtain-raiser games, national press and *Rugby Special* coverage on the BBC.

England raced into an early lead thanks to a penalty try converted by Gill Burns. However, a second-half brace from Claire Godwin and a late score from scrum-half Patty Connell wrapped up a 19-6 victory for the USA team whose spine remained from the famous Wiverns tour of the UK and France in 1985.

A match report in *The Times* reflected on an exciting game:

> The United States became the first world champions in women's rugby union after biding their time before pulling England apart by 19-6 in the second half of the World Cup Final in Cardiff.
>
> In the first half, England had kept the Americans penned back in a tight and turgid show of muscle. The 'locks from hell' and the 'turbo props' could do little to counter a disciplined display from the England forwards. Facing the heavier American line-up, the English pack finally proved that organisation can counter brawn, scoring a penalty try from a well-worked five-metre scrum. Converted by Gill Burns, the English drew first blood to go 6-0 up. But the United States, tackling with power and skill, were always going to come back. The turning point came after half an hour when a Francis fumble allowed the United States to press forward, winning a penalty. Harju converted, there were points on the board and the Americans were given a new lease of life.
>
> Within two minutes of the second half Godwin forced the ball over after England had failed to counter the American pressure. Now the States were on a roll and the English could do nothing to stop them.

England would rue their tactical naivety in the game. They were up against a streetwise pack and backs that were extremely dangerous though they would learn the lessons for the next World Cup. Burns told me recently:

> We were naïve. America had a squad with much experience and our team was relatively new and not so streetwise. We

knew we had a strong enough team to win but let the Americans in with two easy tries – we had a pack that was easily good enough to dominate but our game plan wasn't enough against the accomplished USA squad.

The win ought to have become a watershed moment for the USA team. They had beaten a powerhouse rugby nation and became the first World Cup winners. The team was even invited to the White House and was hosted by First Lady Barbara Bush, but it was England who would go on to develop most in the years that followed.

That the 1991 World Cup happened at all, given the numbers and the finances involved in women's rugby at the time, is something of a miracle. Most of it was down to the sheer determination of Griffin, Dorrington, Cooper and Forsyth, with Isherwood too playing a vital role.

They had no sponsor and had to beg and borrow equipment. They lost track of how much of their own personal money they put into the competition. They took time off work, worked through maternity leave and had limited to no experience organising major events. They had to contend with language barriers and teams like France waiting until the very last minute to enter.

In a diary post after the event, Cooper herself summed up their sacrifices at the event itself:

While the teams got early nights before matches, I would be typing the programmes on my desktop publisher till 2am and then get up at 7am to get the programmes to the printers. The phone would start ringing at 7.15am. While it was my greatest worry that the phone would not ring, I was not prepared for it to ring from dawn till midnight every day.

Debs was working similar hours typing reports and instructions on a dressing table, and just trying to oil the machinery to keep it going. While everyone seemed to be creating camaraderie between the teams, we felt terribly left out. My abiding memory of 2am in the bunker was of feeling lonely exhaustion.

After nine solid days of this we were so glad to see the final day dawn. Soon it would all be over. We were so tired that we had started to giggle and gibber pathetically – particularly worrying when reporters kept sticking microphones under your nose and asking for a sensible answer. Thankfully all the press and VIPs turned up, the standard of rugby was spectacular and the press reports glowed for days.

And the best team on the day won the cup. After the event we had to entertain the VIPs at the dinner and after the celebration was over, after three hours' sleep some of us got into our cars, and drove straight to our workplaces and back to work. Some vacation!

The sterling work of the organisers was appreciated by many of those who took part. Italian Federica Bortolato recalled:

I remember so much, so many emotions, so much disbelief to see that around the world there were so many other girls who were like us, that were confronting the idea that rugby was a sport for males only. I have memories of matches, thrilling anthems, energy and satisfaction. I came back from the tournament with the bag full of shirts, shorts and socks of opponents and with a heart full of emotions I'll never, ever, forget.

Spain's Isabel Perez Garrido has similar memories:

It was shocking to see the team from the Soviet Union selling souvenirs in order to be able to pay for their stay in

Cardiff. And I remember the final between England and USA at the big stadium, and the number 8 from England, Gill Burns being the kicker of her team. The 'third half' of every match was very friendly, full of songs and hugs and friendship between players from different teams; as was the final dinner.

Aside from being enjoyed by those lucky enough to represent their countries, the competition made a massive difference to the acceleration of women's rugby.

Prior to the event, only half of the teams who took part came under the umbrella of their national rugby unions. One of the most positive outcomes of the tournament then was that, within a few months, the Italian, Dutch and New Zealand unions all now welcomed women's rugby. By the end of 1992, of those teams taking part, only rugby in Wales, England and Japan was still organised by separate women's unions and much stronger affiliation was being supported.

The IRB, however, continued to refuse to recognise the 1991 tournament, a position they maintained until 2010.

The first women's rugby World Cup in 1991 may not have changed the world, but it certainly laid the foundations for the future of the women's game. This dedicated group of women should be held in huge esteem for their efforts.

The Scots come to the rescue

After the success of the 1991 event, players and organisers looked ahead to another World Cup with excitement. It had been agreed that this one would be held in the Netherlands three years later in 1994 to avoid clashing with the men's World Cup. It would have the support, it was hoped, of the IRB.

After all, Cardiff had proved that it was possible to host a major international event for women despite the obvious financial constraints. With three years in between there was plenty of time to try to bridge the gaps in relation to sponsorship and interest.

Some 16 teams initially agreed to take part, but just four months out the Dutch became embroiled in a string of rows and financial problems. In part this was due to the lack of support from the IRB, who would not allow the tournament to be awarded an official World Cup status. Without that, Dutch organisers feared that many unions would not send teams to the tournament and in the end the arguments that followed did see teams including Germany and New Zealand withdraw their entries.

News filtered out slowly but, facing the risk of major losses, the Dutch decided to disband the tournament and withdrew their hosting status just 90 days from when it was due to start. The remaining teams were devastated.

Scotland were unlikely saviours. They hadn't even been represented at the 1991 event, though many of their players had travelled to Wales to watch the final, and they had only played their first Test match a year earlier. But Sue Brodie, the SWRU chairperson, saw an opportunity and was determined to grasp it. Brodie had received the fax with notification of the cancellation. Later that evening she told her team-mates at Edinburgh Academicals (Accies) and, after training later in the pub, broached the idea of hosting a version of the event in the city.

The plans accelerated once it was clear there was plenty of interest from the teams who had been planning on travelling to Holland. Brodie and her newly formed organising committee decided the tournament would be called the World Championships so there could be no additional fallout with the IRB.

With less than three months to organise the entire event, the Edinburgh rugby community sprang into action. Free venues were provided in and around the city and sponsorship and support were forthcoming so the dedicated organising committee wouldn't be out of pocket.

That the women's game in Scotland was ready and willing to organise such a massive event at such short notice is testament to the determination of those involved, spearheaded by Brodie, who, like Griffin three years earlier, was not going to let a lack of funds and limited time stand in her way of helping the women's game take huge steps forward.

Women's rugby in Scotland was still relatively new – the Scots had played as a Select XV against England in 1992 and lost 70-odd nil – before inviting Ireland to play their first official Test game in 1993. Brodie played in the game, alongside some players who would become renowned Test stars in the Scottish team like Sandra Colamartino and Kim Littlejohn. Debbie Francis, who played with England at the 1991 World Cup, had switched allegiances and also featured.

Eleven teams agreed to come and take part in the hastily arranged World Championship.

Scotland were joined by France, USA, Japan, Sweden, Russia, Canada, Kazakhstan, England and Wales. Scottish Students XV also took part when Spain pulled out late.

The teams paid their own way, though Russia again arrived practically penniless. Brodie took to local radio to describe their plight. Once again support flooded in to ensure they were able to find accommodation and transport to get them to and from training and games.

Brodie's message in the souvenir brochure read as both a welcome and a manifesto for long-term change. She took time to point out that many teams were not present due to lack of support from their own national unions, including New Zealand and the Netherlands:

On behalf of the SWRU, I would like to welcome all participating players and officials to the 1994 Women's

Rugby World Championships. The organisation of this event, given the unusual circumstances of its change in venue from Holland to Scotland, has brought many people from the rugby community in Scotland together, to ensure that the best possible conditions for its competition could be provided in a very short space of time.

It has been a pleasure to be a member of an organising committee which has received so many offers of assistance, confirmation that women's rugby in Scotland has come a long way since its birth around the time of the Women's World Cup in 1991.

I am confident that the extreme efforts many people have exercised to put on this event will be rewarded with a display of the best women's rugby this country has ever seen. I am therefore grateful to the participating nations for taking up the invitation to enter this Championship (many have travelled a long way at great personal expense) and would like to wish them the best of luck in their endeavours.

However, while congratulating those that do take part, I would also like to remember those women who have been prevented from doing so. As enablers, each respective union must ensure that participation is encouraged at all levels, locally and internationally. As a first step, the conference to be held this fortnight must ensure that all women have control and proper representation in the organisation of their chosen sport.

I hope the determination displayed by all the players over the championship will carry women's rugby into a secure and flourishing international future.

Although the Test game was still in its infancy, the game at the highest level had accelerated quickly since the 1991 World Cup.

England and the USA were favourites to contest the final again, especially with New Zealand not travelling.

England had learned significantly from their experience three years earlier and the game in their country had continued to grow at pace. The summer before they had beaten Canada, Wales and the United States in Toronto to win the inaugural Canada Cup and the transformation in their technical standards within the space of a few years had been impressive.

Karen Almond still marshalled the team. Burns, who was by now a formidable leader, Emma Mitchell and centre Jacqui Edwards had become pivotal players in a team which had a brilliant pack whose scrum was already feared. They had also learned how to better pace themselves, making far better use of their squad than they had three years earlier to help them through tough knockout games.

The USA brought a strong squad with leaders like Candi Orsini, in her prime in the centre of a fast and electric backline, with talent like Jos Bergmann and full-back Jen Crawford expected to be particularly dangerous.

France had been beaten by England earlier in the year. With the rest of their games between the tournaments coming against Spain, the Netherlands and Italy, less was known about how they would fare, though a semi-final spot seemed likely.

Wales had run England close a couple of times while Canada had been boosted by their hosting of the first ever Canada Cup the year before across cities in the Greater Toronto Area. Although they had only one won game against Wales, the women's game had been given momentum and support and the significance of the Canada Cup would continue into the mid-2000s.

Ireland and Scotland were newcomers to the Test scene but had played each other twice in the lead-up. The women's game in Ireland had been growing slowly since the first teams had been established in the 1980s. By the time of the first World Cup there were about ten teams up and running there.

In 1992, the players were determined to get a national side off the ground. Led by Blackrock player Mary O'Beirne, the IWRFU was established with a significant focus put on establishing a domestic league structure.

With a number of Irish-qualified players playing a good standard of club rugby in England, the first Irish team who played Scotland on Valentine's Day in 1993 was made up of a combination of ex-pat and home-based players. The side was captained by Jill Henderson, who was playing for Waterloo in the north-west of England at the time.

Henderson had been one of the driving forces behind getting the national team set up in the first place and had got involved in every aspect – playing, helping to organise trials and finding coaches.

The match against Scotland was played at Raeburn Place – the world's second-oldest rugby ground where the first ever men's rugby international took place in 1871, a clash between Scotland and England. Henderson, interviewed recently, for Irish website the42.ie, said that first international was historic and has lived long in the memory:

> It was significant that we were having it there. It was a suitable pitch in Edinburgh on an international weekend, St Valentine's Day. That was really good and when we were organising things, I was travelling back and forth from home to arrange the trials and get the team together.
>
> I had to write the constitution and fit all the criteria so that the players met the international standards and requirements.

Ireland were coached by Alain Rolland, who would go on to become a renowned international referee. They faced a brand-new Scotland side, captained by scrum-half Sandra Colamartino, who scored both tries in a 10-0 win for the hosts.

The teams played again a year later with Scotland winning 5-0. The Scots also played, and lost to, the Welsh in the lead-up to hosting the event.

Although the Soviet Union had competed three years earlier, its dissolution meant that this time around Russia and Kazakhstan were represented at the competition. Kazakhstan arrived as a completely unknown force, having kicked their Test life off by playing Germany the year before. Most of their players came from the same rugby club, the Almaty Army's Rugby School.

Japan were welcome returnees given their popularity in Wales three years earlier, but they had not played a single Test match since, though they had been training ferociously and were desperate to grab at least one win.

Pool A comprised USA, Japan and Sweden. Pool B was England, Scotland and Russia. Pool C had France, Ireland and Scottish Students. Pool D included Wales, Canada and Kazakhstan.

There was good media coverage before the tournament. The profile of the game was clearly growing, despite the short notice that the competition was taking place at all.

The competition began with the USA bulldozing their way through their pool, hammering Sweden 111-0 and Japan 121-0 to sail through to the quarter-finals against Ireland, who had lost to France but beaten the Scottish Students.

England and Scotland met in the pool stages for their first ever Test match against each other, with a crowd of over 5,000 turning out at Meggetland to watch the historic game. England were impressive up front and, with players like Helen Harding marshalling the backs, went on to win it 0-26.

Both went through regardless to the quarter-finals. England were due to play Canada and Scotland to play Wales, who had impressively turned the Canadians over in their pool. Japan thrillingly beat Sweden, a win they had been building towards for three years, which meant they went through to play France.

The knockout stages were closely fought affairs. England cleared their hurdle by defeating Canada 24-10 at Galashiels with Gill Burns, Karen Almond and Maxine Edwards impressive, while Josée LaCasse scored a late try for Canada. England would face France in the semi-final after they had run amok against Japan with a 99-0 win.

Thanks to their next win over Scotland at Melrose, Wales joined England in the semi-finals, where they would face the USA. The 8-0 Welsh win over Scotland had been played at a furious pace. Wales struck a telling blow ten minutes from full time when Kim Yau scored a try after the full-back, Kate Richards, had come cleverly into the line. Amanda Bennett missed the conversion kick but did succeed with a penalty to seal the victory.

England's semi-final with France was closely run, with the English eventually coming out on top 19-6. The USA's journey to the final was much more straightforward. They hammered Wales 56-15.

The final was set up to be a clash between the USA's skilful and brilliant backs, and England's tougher and more powerful forwards.

First, though, hosts Scotland had to play Canada in the Shield Final, winning 11-5 in front of a delighted crowd. Coach Mark Francis, writing about the game in the media afterwards, reflected on an important moment for the women's game in Scotland:

Women's rugby as a whole tends to have a very low profile and it has been particularly low in Scotland in the past. I think this fortnight will have opened many people's eyes in Scotland. Before, during and for a little while after the tournament the attention that is paid is enormous and I just hope it can carry on from there.

Because it is such a new sport here the response has been surprising. The crowds have played an invaluable part, not least in the big matches against England and Canada. They provided a major boost to our game. The hope now is that sponsors will realise just how popular the game now is and will become in the future. We've had good support so far but more of the same will be needed to take us up to the next level.

England were confident going into the final, feeling they had got their tactics and general preparation right. They had decided to pay more money to stay at what they felt might be a lucky hotel in the city, the George Hotel, where the England men's sevens side had stayed the year before when they won the World Cup. They also better rotated their squad than they had done three years earlier.

The USA, reigning world champions, started as slight favourites, but England laid a marker down from the first scrum. Stephen Jones of the *Sunday Times* reported that England 'almost drove the Americans out of the stadium through the back entrance' as Burns scored an early try.

Later Giselle Mather, then Pragnell, who played in the centre for England in the final, recalled that though they were underdogs, she had been confident they would win In a conversation with a House of Rugby podcast she said:v

We played France in the semi-final on the Wednesday and on Thursday we had a recovery day followed by video analysis on the Friday. We had a brilliant team meeting and I left it knowing I would be a world champion that Sunday. The American backs were unbelievable, but they were technically shabby. We had done all the preparation.

England won 38-23, their power restricting the American backs to four tries forcing the US to run possession, even when it was ragged.

Carol Isherwood added:

> We wanted to starve them of possession. They were trying to play a seven-a-side game with 15 players. We played to the laws for 15 players. We did not play negatively; we played some good rugby and scored a really good try from long range. In the previous final we lost after winning 60% of the ball. This time we exploited our superiority.

The tournament remained illegitimate in the eyes of the IRB for years but has retrospectively been officially recognised as the second women's rugby World Cup.

It's astonishing that it happened at all. Had it not been for Brodie and her brilliant team, it could have been years before the IRB finally turned their support and attention to the women's game.

In the end, the interest in the event in Edinburgh meant they simply could no longer oversee a sport which left out women. In 1995 they hosted a vital event in Edmonton inviting representatives from around the world to form the first women's advisory committee, who would develop a plan for the women's game through to 2001.

It would prove to be the catalyst for changes that would soon see women's rugby become much more widely integrated into the sport's international governance structures and mark the acceleration of the grassroots game for women and girls around the world.

Chapter Five

The game gets organised

IT WAS clear that women's rugby could no longer be ignored. Although no governing body had yet truly embraced women's arrival at all levels, this in many ways, however, suited the early development of the women's game.

Part of the reason that Scotland was so efficiently able to pick the 1994 tournament up and run with it at such short notice was because they had already broken away from the WRFU the year before to form their own women's union, chaired by Brodie, which was independent from the Scottish Rugby Union. It meant those in charge could take decisions quickly and were free from the bureaucratic burdens that so often came with being part of a national governing body or federation.

Wales followed suit, resulting in the creation of both the Welsh Women's Rugby Union (WWRU) and the Rugby Football Union for Women (RFUW) in England. These groups had affiliations to the governing bodies which ran the game more widely in each country and were at times supported financially by them, but they were in reality responsible for the entirety of their women's and girls' games and for the most part, this arrangement suited both sides.

Though attitudes towards women's rugby were changing, the game was still too often treated with disdain or as a novelty. The separation between the official unions and the women's organisations, mostly run by volunteers, worked for everyone at the time. Despite the financial constraints, they were far better placed to adjust to the growing popularity of the game and to structure the sport in a way that suited it and not simply mirror what already existed for men and boys.

One of the criticisms of modern women's rugby is that as it has come more and more under the auspices of national governing bodies, it has become too rigid and has struggled to break free of structures which simply don't suit it and worse its growth is often stifled by organisations that see the women's game as a distraction, not a priority.

Eventually, the loosely independent organisations did formally affiliate and merge with the governing bodies in their countries, but huge groundwork had been done to put down roots that would be difficult, though not impossible, for those organisations to row back on.

The WRFU itself disbanded completely soon after the creation of the WWRU and RFUW, having done its primary job of getting the game off the ground across Great Britain and overseeing the emergence of real growth at grassroots and elite level.

In Ireland, the first game against Scotland in 1993 and their involvement in the World Cup the year after was the springboard for the growth of the IWRFU, the organisation I would join a decade later. The IWRFU was tasked with building a domestic game and a Test team less reliant on overseas players, something which boosted the team in the early years in terms of experience, but which made training and travel arrangements difficult.

A men's Six Nations had been going for well over 100 years, having started life as a Home Nations competition in 1883. With the format and traditions already established, it made sense at the time for the mostly amateur women's unions to piggyback on its structure and fame.

Discussions between those running the women's game in Ireland, Wales, Scotland and England were now regular and plans were put in place for a first ever women's Home Nations Championship in 1996. This would eventually go through various iterations, including the introduction of France, the drop-out of Ireland for a period and the arrival of Spain, whose place in turn was eventually taken by Italy so the competition could formally be run by the Six Nations organisation with matching men's, women's and men's U20 competitions.

The initial four teams went into the inaugural competition in 1996 with high hopes of building the game's profile off the field and continuing to improve standards on it. England, the world champions, were favourites for the title. Wales had only played a couple of games since the 1994 World Cup but, having finished fourth there after a semi-final defeat to France, went in with high hopes.

Scotland were quickly developing a reputation for their power up front. Ireland's squad included a large number of exiles and the competition pitted them against England for the first time.

The tournament kicked off in Dublin when Scotland were 0-21 winners. England headed to Leicester to take on Wales, with Gill Burns in superb form leading the team to a 56-3 win. Wales's only points came from the boot of Amanda Bennett.

Wales improved in their next outing, narrowly getting past Scotland 11-6, while Ireland impressively beat Wales 22-6 at Old Belvedere before going on to only narrowly lose to England 12-8.

Given Ireland had only played eight Tests going into the competition and had only won one – against Japan at the World Cup – these were decent results for a new team, though it would hardly be the catalyst for success. The Irish would have to wait another eight years before a win in the competition, although they did not take part in 2000 and 2001.

With England also beating Scotland, they became the first ever Home Nations champions. The launch of this competition coincided with the IRB finally waking up to their responsibilities to run a game for everyone. Having refused to sanction the 1994 World Cup as official, the international federation was preparing to host what *it* considered the first women's rugby World Cup, which would be held in Amsterdam in 1998.

The IRB had by now established a women's advisory committee, tasked with coming up with a five-year development plan for the women's game globally. The three overarching aims set out in the eventual plan were relatively simple:

1. To encourage the participation of women in playing, coaching, refereeing and administration
2. To promote women's rugby nationally and internationally
3. To integrate women's rugby into all relevant aspects of the IRFB's operation

Though written over 25 years ago, part of the plan's detailed SWOT analysis is still relevant today. It considered that among the strengths of women's rugby was the fact that those involved had few preconceived ideas that would inhibit its development, that the game was growing rapidly and had some novelty value which attracted new players, that it offered a contact sport for people of all abilities and that there was an increasing focus on women athletes that would help it to quickly develop.

Most of the weaknesses identified are, unfortunately in some parts of the sport arguably still applicable today:

The weaknesses of Women's Rugby (IRFB Development Plan 1996)

• An inequitably low share of resources is made available from the parent union – financially, technically and administratively

- Obscurity of the game generally and amongst women in particular
- Resistance to integration of Women's Rugby into the male game by the parent union
- Women playing a contact sport is contrary to the culture of many societies
- At present the numbers playing in countries is small, they are often spread out and the number of countries playing is small (24) and spread making contact and competition expensive
- Lack of depth in the number of administrators. The load falls on a few shoulders
- The image of rugby especially in non-traditionally rugby countries as a violent, brutal sport in which socialising and abuse of alcohol play a big part in the game
- A lack of information on rugby in society
- The media focuses on the novel and different rather than regarding the game as an accepted women's sport
- A network of contacts has not been established. Contact via national unions is inefficient
- Lack of grassroots development in pre-teenage and teenage women's rugby
- Differences in the level of acceptance and integration with governing body between countries which may create mismatches detrimental to International Competition
- There is a high level of competition for players from other sports
- Sport in general and rugby in particular is restricted in schools
- Retention of players as they progress from pre-teenage mixed rugby to teenage women's rugby and when they move from age grade to open grade rugby
- The lack of competitions

- The media's neglect of women's sport
- The small number of participants

And some of the threats the plan identified feel quite familiar to this day for many in the game:

- Non acceptance of rugby as a women's sport
- Media perception as a curiosity to get something different
- Own ability to communicate the game limited by the attitude of the parent body and a lack of resources
- Management of growth with the influx of women into rugby in growing numbers
- Lack of funds
- 'Lip service' from unions at all levels
- Complexity of game makes it difficult for people to understand
- More choices of sport for women to play
- Lack of support for salaried people who can follow up and who are accountable
- Mismatches as some teams improve quicker than others
- Lack of good coaching
- Women's working environments
- Sexism
- Management of professionalism

The plan set in motion several workstreams, all building to the 1998 World Cup, to which the IRB would invite 16 teams.

With a Home Nations Championship giving Ireland, Wales, Scotland and England regular games, FIRA, the administrative body for rugby union in Europe, was also looking at giving opportunities to other European sides.

There had been European competitions before. The 1988 European Cup was the first women's rugby European

Championship and the first multi-national women's rugby competition of any sort, albeit not a competition organised by FIRA. It was also the only occasion where a Great Britain side entered such a competition. The four individual nations were separated in all future 15-a-side competitions, including the first FIRA Women's European Championship in 1995, with France, Spain, Italy and the Netherlands also taking part.

The women's game in Spain, like in many other European countries, could trace some history back to the early 1900s. There are some historical reports that women played the game in secret in school but, like in France and England, it only began to take real flight in the 1970s when students took up the game at university. Among the students pushing the game forward was future international Isabel Perez Garrido:

> I started at university. I had been an athlete (sprint and heptathlon) since I was twelve years old, but I thought I should know more about the world of team sports if I wanted to be a better professional. And there it was, a new-born rugby team at my university. I heard about that, and I went to see a training session. There was a coach from New Zealand who was working in Madrid around that time, leading the session – his name was Laurie O'Reilly. What I saw appeared very enjoyable and I thought I was going to have a lot of fun with that. This was around 1989.

Teams began to be formed in the Barcelona area where two clubs, BUC and INEF, played each other regularly. Teams then started to spring up in and around Madrid and spread to the Basque Country and Valencia. By 1991, regional competitions had been formed.

Spain played their first international match on 2 May 1989, losing 8-0 to France. They planned to travel to the 1994 World Cup but a lack of cash forced them to pull out at late notice. So it was something of a shock when Spain won the first European Championship in 1995, defeating France in the final.

A second European Championship was contested in 1996 with Germany taking part for the first time. France reversed the tables and beat Spain in the final. England were champions once again in the Home Nations Championship, but the games were relatively close. Standards were improving as all sides looked to step up a gear before the World Cup. On the other side of the world, a traditional power of men's rugby was belatedly joining the ranks of the women's international game.

Women's rugby had begun to be revived in Australia in the early 1990s with games taking place in Newcastle and New South Wales. In 1993 the Australian Women's Rugby Union (AWRU) was formed. The union selected 'the Wallaroos' as the name for the newly formed international team, inspired by one of the oldest clubs in Australia, the Wallaroo Football Club, which was formed in 1870. The Wallaroos played their first Test game just a year later against New Zealand at the North Sydney Oval.

Joan Forno was the driving force behind the development of the game there. A Western Australia resident she had come across rugby when living in the UK and, when she returned to Australia in the early 1980s, she began working for the Australian Rugby Union (ARU) as a financial controller, a role she held for 16 years.

In the early 1990s, she was approached by the chairman of the ARU, Leo Williams, who was looking to start a women's rugby team. Forno threw herself into a supporting role, establishing the AWRU and becoming its inaugural president.

She was team manager for Australia's first World Cup appearance in Amsterdam in 1998 and was recently honoured by the ARU for her influential role in the growth of women's rugby, which culminated in Olympic gold for the Wallaroos sevens team in Rio in 2016.

In North America, Canada were itching to get back to Test rugby having not played a game since the World Cup. They had hosted the Canada Cup in 1993, a new international competition with England, Wales and the USA. On the back of so much international rugby happening in Europe, the Canadians decided to revive the event in 1996. They invited New Zealand, France and the USA to take part.

Having not taken part in the World Cup in 1994, because their rugby union would not sanction them to participate in an event the IRB hadn't approved, New Zealand had played hardly any games at all in five years, apart from a couple of matches against Australia. Despite this, they were miles better than everyone else at the Canada Cup, winning all three games with ease and taking the title. They were frighteningly good, posting massive scores – beating France 109-0, Canada 34-3 and the USA 88-3 – laying down a serious marker for the 1998 World Cup.

Their performances, spearheaded by their powerful wingers Louisa Wall and Vanessa Cootes, began a pattern that would frustrate so many international teams over the coming decades, especially England. Their lack of match practice did not inhibit their ability to win international tournaments. They were just too good.

Wall was a particularly outstanding talent. She had been a brilliant athlete and scholar at Taupo-nui-a-Tia College and played for the New Zealand netball team at 17 years old. In later life she became a powerful advocate for social change in New Zealand as an MP and a driving force behind legalising same-sex marriage. For now there was a World Cup to be won.

Sevens begins in earnest

If 1996 proved a busy year on the Test front, 1997 was another step up. International sides ramped up their World Cup preparation and a major moment in sevens rugby took place.

This year's Home Nations was won once again by England, but Wales ran them very close on the final day in Worcester with the hosts squeezing out a 24-22 win. Scotland continued their development with wins over the Irish and Welsh.

The FIRA European Championship event was ready for expansion. The 1997 edition moved to eight teams with England, Scotland and Ireland entering to join France, Spain, Italy, Germany and the Netherlands in Nice for the competition. England went in as favourites as the holders of both the Home Nations and World Cup titles.

The European tournaments would prove a rare opportunity for those teams who are now considered developing Test nations like Germany and the Netherlands to play regular rugby against more experienced teams. Although England and Scotland unsurprisingly reached the final, with England winning 24-8, the games were not significantly one-sided, save France's 58-18 win over Germany. In the years to come the gap would widen significantly.

The RFUW had been making serious strides away from the field and had recently appointed its first professional administrator when Nicky Ponsford was hired as a development officer. Her role was the first of its kind in the world, with funding secured by the then English Sports Council, who granted the RFUW £45,000 for the upcoming four years. Ponsford combined it with a successful playing career for Saracens and England.

Something else was also afoot in the game which would massively shift the trajectory of women's rugby. While 15-a-side rugby had dominated the early growth of the game, sevens was beginning to grow in popularity.

In countries where rugby was less developed, it had the advantage of being easier to understand and required fewer players. Tournaments involving lots of games could easily be played over a weekend, something particularly attractive for amateur players. The ability to play multiple games in a few days was also seen as a particularly good format for women, many of whom took up the game late in life and who benefited from playing as many games as possible, with rugby for girls in schools a rarity anywhere in the world.

There were already lots of invitational sevens events taking place around the world to which women's teams travelled to take part. In 1992, for example, a US selection called Atlantis, with plenty of international players, won Spain's prestigious Benidorm Sevens, beating a Saracens team which fielded a handful of established England players.

The Hong Kong Rugby Union already hosted the men's Hong Kong Sevens annually and was preparing to host the men's World Cup Sevens. To broaden the appeal of their events to a wider fan base, they sent letters to 16 women's teams in 1996 inviting them to take part in the Hong Kong Invitational Women's Rugby Sevens to be held the following year. The initiative – the first recorded international Test women's sevens event – would pave the way for the massive growth of the short form of the sport in the years ahead.

It was a huge undertaking with no real precedent. For many nations, the Hong Kong competition would see the debut of a women's sevens team at international level. Twelve teams eventually took part with Singapore, Fiji and Hong Kong entering the international arena for the first time. More established names like the Netherlands, Japan, England, Australia, Canada, USA and Scotland travelled to the Far East with a selection from the Arabian Gulf regional union.

New Zealand did not have an international sevens team at the time and wouldn't for several years. The Wild Ducks, captained by Anna Richards and coached by future World Cup-winning coach Darryl Suasua, would be their representatives. It was a self-funded invitational team made up of some of the country's top players. They were too good for everyone, steamrolling the USA 43-0 in the final.

New Zealand's players were almost too good for their own good. While an official New Zealand women's sevens team was established in 2000, the NZR's support for the team was totally inconsistent. They removed the country's women's sevens championships from the domestic calendar for several years from 2003 and offered minimal financial assistance but, since the teams were successful, there was very little public pressure applied on the NZR to up their support for women's rugby.

The nation's top sevens players instead signed up to play for representative sides like the hugely successful New Zealand Aotearoa Maori, organised and often financed by Peter Josephs, to see international action. It took the arrival of the World Cup Sevens for women in 2009 and a strong directive from the IRB for things to change in the approach to women's rugby from the top of the game in New Zealand.

The Hong Kong tournament didn't happen in 1998 – the 15s World Cup took precedence in Amsterdam – but it returned in 1999 and the final was played in a packed main stadium. It laid the foundations for the development of women's sevens to be accelerated and eventually formed the cornerstone of the IRB's bid to have rugby back in the Olympics.

As international rugby dried up for the year, there was one significant tour yet to come. England were preparing to play New Zealand for the first time, travelling there for a series of games and a Test match. The tour was expensive, and England's players had to pay a significant chunk towards it themselves, resulting in a number of key names dropping out.

The trip was not without its controversy.

When the England squad arrived in New Zealand, they said they were expecting to stay for three weeks, playing provincial games first before playing a one-off Test match.

That story is disputed by many in New Zealand, who say the Test match was always scheduled at the start of the tour. The consequence of the confusion was that England were barely on the ground for 36 hours before they had to line up to play New Zealand in Burnham.

England were hammered. New Zealand won 67-0. Though the tourists did go on to win their remaining tour matches, the result told the rest of the world that New Zealand would surely be the team to beat at the World Cup. It was a serious momentum-killer for an English team hoping to grab back-to-back world titles.

Unforgettable years for Scotland and New Zealand

Despite their disappointment in New Zealand, England were still favourites for this final Home Nations in 1998. Though Scotland had finished second in both previous versions of the event, England's organisation and increased funding meant they were a step ahead, at least on paper. The pace of Scotland's development as a Test nation since their inception, however, was remarkable.

Having played their first game against Ireland in 1993, their hosting of the World Cup just a year later highlighted the incredible can-do and progressive attitude of those running the game there. The enthusiasm was clearly infectious as on the field the team began to turn losses into wins.

As the 1998 tournament approached, the team was quietly confident. They were developing a formidable pack cornerstoned by young Donna Kennedy, who would eventually win more than 100 caps for her country. They also had smart talent out wide with Sandra Colamartino, Scotland's first captain and the scorer of both tries in the 10-0 win over the Irish in their first game, while Kim Littlejohn also proved a real handful on the elite stage.

Having run England close on a few occasions, and having been runners-up twice in the Home Nations, by 1998, they were ready to step things up. A 15-0 win in Dublin started off the competition well and although France were not officially part of the tournament, the home nations played them as part of the schedule.

Scotland beat them too – 19-3 at Raeburn Place – before travelling to Cardiff and winning 22-12.

Only one team now stood between Scotland and a grand slam.

Scotland and England lined up at Inverleith. Though the game was low-scoring, the reports were that it was an enthralling contest. England's best players included half-backs Emma Mitchell and Giselle Pragnell, whose assuredness kept them in the game after Scotland scored the opening try. Kim Littlejohn made the most of a knock-on deep in her side's half to score.

England were back on the scoreboard before half-time, levelling with a wonderful try after Maxine Edwards drew in the Scottish defence, helping Pip Spivey to sprint in for the leveller. Scotland's scrum was too strong though, and as they asserted some dominance up front, Paula Chalmers booted a penalty to win the match 8-5.

Recalling the games afterwards for Scottish website The Offside Line, Littlejohn described the achievement:

> It was just an amazing season. To get the three other games under our belts before meeting England – we couldn't have written the script better. It was the final match, at home, we had done so well, and we had to believe that we could do it. And we did. That was an incredible journey. It's one of these things where it's the combination of people, and the planets aligning as well – everything coming together.

Donna Kennedy, speaking to me about the game over 20 years later, also remembered it vividly:

> There was just a massive sense of belief that we could do this. England was always the big scalp to beat. They had a big brutal pack and had pacey backs, so we knew we'd be in a game. It was a huge win, and the elation was phenomenal. It was just a different feeling on that day to anything I've had since and it's still our only grand slam. It is such a special memory and the fondest I have in my career. Special times with special people.

As European sides finalised their preparation for the World Cup later that year, New Zealand and Australia developed their rivalry, playing each other five times between 1994 and 1997. New Zealand won them all but the outings were invaluable to Australia. They made their 1995 trip across the Tasman into a tour, playing games against provincial sides before both their Test matches.

The year before the World Cup, they travelled again, this time to Dunedin, with Australia's Selena Worsley later recalling how hostile the home fans were:

> I remember every single window in the town was about the All Blacks. Our game was a curtain-raiser and the middle fold out of the *Otago Times* was a cut-out shirt. When we ran out on the field there were already 40,000 people there. They booed us and you could hear a really loud rustling of newspapers as everyone pulled out their cut-out jersey!
>
> Melodie Robinson was playing for them, and she was holding me back from a scrum, so I went to hit her hand and she split my eye with a whack! It was memorable. That whole week wherever we went we were just getting

abused! They absolutely live and breathe rugby there. It was brilliant.

Neither side played again until the World Cup, but the experience of their games stood them in good stead. Both ended up ranked in the top five sides in the world by the end of 1998.

Amsterdam finally hosts the World Cup

After the false start in 1994, the Dutch rugby union got the go-ahead from the IRB to host the next World Cup in 1998. The games would all be held at the recently opened National Rugby Centre in Amsterdam. This time New Zealand would be the big threat.

The USA were considered dangerous but they had not progressed much results-wise between the two World Cups and had been thrashed by the Kiwis at the Canada Cup the year before, while England had been defeated by Scotland in the Home Nations earlier in the year.

The tournament was by invitation with 16 sides taking part. Australia and Germany were the only two sides playing in a World Cup for the first time. With the IRB on board, this time none of the players involved would have to double-job and be involved in the running of the event, all the better for preparing and focusing on the on-field action.

The hosts kicked the competition off with a tense and competitive game against Canada in front of around 1,700 fans. Canada's experience told, as they won 16-7. Canadian flanker Joanne Gardner stood out while the home side's diminutive full-back Wieneke Tielen was player of the match thanks to her fearless tackling.

Unsurprisingly for a 16-team tournament, there were some big scores posted on the opening day. England thrashed Sweden 75-0 with Vicky Brown scoring five tries. The USA beat Russia 84-0.

Ominously, New Zealand beat Germany 134-6, finishing with an astonishing 22 tries and 12 conversions against Germany's two penalties. Eight of the tries were shared equally between brilliant full-back Tammi Wilson, who had also played rugby league and touch rugby for her country, and right-wing Dianne Kahura. Wilson kicked five conversions for a personal total of 30 points.

Captain and hooker Farah Palmer issued a warning to the other teams after the game:

> We never ease up. That's not what we are about. In fact, we hate to concede points, but good luck to the Germans. They did not give in and deserved their two penalties.

The Germans amused the crowd by their show of delight on scoring their points, with players backflipping back to the halfway line.

Spain impressively beat Wales 38-18, the game a triumph for winger Isabel Perez, who ran in four tries. There were no huge upsets, though Ireland's loss to Kazakhstan was a mini surprise. The Irish lost 12-6 thanks to tries from Olga Kumanikina and Svetlana Zhernovnikova.

The quarter-finals pitted the USA against Scotland (USA winning 25-10), Australia against England (England winning 30-13 having pulled ahead from a 10-10 half-time score) and Spain against New Zealand (New Zealand winning 3-46).

The last quarter-final saw France particularly disappointed to miss out on a semi-final slot as they were beginning to develop a strong team. Full-back Annick Hayraud, a future national team head coach, was impressive and Estelle Sartini on the wing proved a handful. Ultimately Canada's tough defence stood firm to help them win 9-7, with prop Gillian Florence and hooker Moira Shiels outstanding.

The semi-finals were surprisingly one-sided. New Zealand's team was proving to be considerable with strength out wide like no one had seen before.

Louisa Wall and Vanessa Cootes were powerhouses while England were not helped by injury to their inspirational skipper Gill Burns. Either way, New Zealand were favourites and played like it.

Anna Richards told me afterwards that the Kiwis knew they'd be a handful:

> We were a really good team going over there. We had a very mobile pack and a lot of brains across the team for the game. Our starting backline – well all bar one was in the New Zealand touch team so we had a lot of skills out there and Daryl our coach had basically said play what is in front of you. He was confident in us to run the ball off our own line – he told us to have a go.
>
> We had all been hugely disappointed not to travel to the 1994 event and we had a group of girls who had been playing for a number of years and were waiting for this. We felt we wanted to prove a point that we were a good side and we were confident in ourselves.

England started strongly with two early penalties from Claire Frost, but New Zealand were relentless and by half-time the game was very much in their hands. They built a 10-6 lead after an opening try from Annaleah Rush, who went on to score the winners' first 13 points and finished with 24, including a second try.

England scored one try through winger Jane Molyneux but ultimately lost 11-44. Vanessa Cootes – nicknamed the 'Black Dot' by her team-mates because that's all anyone would see run with the ball when she ran off with the ball– was among the scorers in the second half.

England captain Emma Mitchell said afterwards:

> We did about the best we could against them for 30 minutes, when we had them rattled, but they are a great side and justify their status as the best in the world. Our goal has to be to come back stronger and aim to beat them next time.

In the other semi-final, the USA hammered rivals Canada 46-6, using all their previous World Cup experience to brilliant effect. They raced into a 31-3 half-time lead and ultimately achieved a victory by six tries, five conversions and two penalties. The result was sparked by dominant individual performances from full-back Jennifer Crawford, who had three tries, and outside-half Jos Bergmann, who added five conversions. Canada worked hard but struggled to match the physical strength and incisive running of the winners, with just two Moira Shiels penalties to take from the game.

So, to the final where New Zealand were unstoppable, winning the first World Cup of many thanks to a brilliant display of power and pace helping them to a 44-12 victory. Cootes grabbed the headlines with her four brilliant tries. On the other wing, Wall was also superb. The team was well led by Farah Palmer in the front row and organised by Richards at fly-half.

Russia, never far from controversy, finished bottom in 16th place by losing 3-23 to Sweden. An unfortunate incident occurred after lock Galina Chasovnikova was dismissed early in the second half for persistent high tackling. Chasovnikova went after referee Sean Mallon and failed to attend the mandated disciplinary hearing.

In a subsequent official communication, publicised by the IRB, it was recommended that 'the Russian coaching staff be charged with ensuring their players are coached in proper tackling skills. The very fact that all the players have a penchant for high tackling is a direct reflection of the coaching they receive.'

Was the first 'official' World Cup a success?

Crowds were certainly not massive and many players bemoaned being in hotels miles from anywhere, but with 16 teams, the event gave invaluable competitive game time to a large number of players. Crucially, the IRB footed the bill.

The one-location event also gave the games something of an intimate feel for the players. They still had to contend with varying weather that veered from biting cold in the opening days to 30-plus-degree heat as the days wore on. But despite the teething problems, it was something to build on.

As teams took home the lessons from the tournament, other competitions began to expand. In 1999, the Home Nations became the Five Nations with the official addition of France.

France were a welcome permanent fixture, bringing with them quality and experience and giving England, who despite Scotland's success in the competition the year before were still the team to beat, consistently tough competition. Their third-round game with England in that first year was unsurprisingly close. England pipped it 13-8 in Worcester and the win helped them to the grand slam, with France runners-up.

While Ireland had struggled to get results in the competition over the last three years it was still a surprise when the IWRFU decided to pull out of the competition after 1999 to concentrate on strengthening their domestic game. Spain would be invited to take their place.

Ireland also pulled out of the next European Championships, returning with the same format as the previous edition in 1997, but with Germany and Ireland being replaced by Kazakhstan and Wales.

While games were close at the 1999 event, France were the standout team. They took the title thanks to a 13-5 win over Spain. England, in a period of rebuilding after the World Cup, were beaten by the French in the semi-finals and Scotland again in the third/fourth-place match.

With most of the 15s action over for the year, attention was put back on the sevens with the Hong Kong Invitational back on the cards after initial success in 1997. This time the final would be played at the main stadium, handing women's sevens an unheard-of chance in the spotlight in front of over 20,000 fans.

The USA, having travelled internationally to play sevens for years, were determined to get to the final given the exposure it would give the women's game. They beat England in the semi-final, a game which may well have been the first international rugby match in which identical twins – Jane and Emma Mitchell – competed against each other (Jane for the US and Emma for England).

New Zealand, competing again as the Wild Ducks, loomed large in the final and they were once again too good, taking it out 29-0.

Having struggled to gain acceptance in many parts of the global game, the women's event in Hong Kong proved a significant catalyst for change. Recalling the final afterwards, USA coach Emil Signes said:

The fans raved about the game, and our players were recognised, and complimented, by dozens of fans as they left the stadium at the end of the evening. Furthermore, during the course of the next two days, several coaches, players, committee members and members of the media spoke to me with great admiration for the standard of play. Even commentator David Campese, who two years earlier had said women shouldn't be playing rugby, spoke positively of the game, and talking with him made it obvious he had watched the whole thing.

Back in Europe, a new-look Five Nations Championship was held in 2000. It was won by England, who achieved the grand slam while Spain got into the groove quickly and finished third.

As the world prepared for life in a new millennium, the women's game was about to face a decade of growing pains which ended in the biggest and best World Cup yet.

Chapter Six

Growing pains

ONE OF the great challenges in women's sport is whether the structure of major tournaments and events should mirror those of the men's game, particularly where a significant brand has already been developed and invested in.

In women's rugby, the development of most of the sport's major competitions trod a well-worn path. On the international stage there are the Six Nations and the World Sevens Series; in the domestic game we've got a Women's Provincial Championship in New Zealand, a new Super Rugby competition and a familiar-looking Premier 15s league in England, to take just some examples.

For the most part it makes sense to capitalise on the back of competitions which are already familiar to fans and the media, and this is exactly why an insurance brand recently funded a feasibility study into the possibility of a women's British and Irish Lions team. A women's Lions team is no new conversation though. Discussions about a possible tour go back to 2000 when the possibility of a joint tour with the men's event in Australia was seriously mooted.

The Telegraph delved into the story recently, setting out that England and Saracens players Emma Mitchell and Janice Byford had been involved in a serious proposal to get the event off the ground. Byford, Charles Richardson wrote, had written to Roger

Pickering, the secretary of the Lions' tour committee, setting out that along with Welsh and Scottish players Lisa Burgess and Kim Littlejohn, there were plans afoot to head down under.

Pickering replied positively and talks progressed to the point of discussions about logistics, travel and a draft itinerary involving a couple of Tests against Australia. The tour would need sponsorship backing or the players would have to self-fund, and there would need to be support from the ARU.

Byford made contact with Wallaroos team manager Stephen Swann and head coach Don Parry who were positive about the plans, but the decision makers higher up the ladder at the union were much more circumspect. Eventually plans were abandoned when Jeff Miller, the ARU's high performance manager, emailed Byford:

> We have discussed the possibility of the Lionesses touring Australia at an executive level and have decided that it would be impossible for us to host next year. Our Wallaroos are already committed to a series against England and financially this is all we can cope with currently.
>
> We appreciate your interest and approach, but we will gracefully have to decline your offer.

Byford and Mitchell tried again to get the tour off the ground again a few months later, having secured interest from sponsors, but the ARU once again declined the offer.

'It was extremely frustrating,' Mitchell told *The Telegraph* 20 years on. 'It felt as though the people in charge of making the decision had no regard for the women's game. They didn't take it seriously and saw it as an inconvenience.'

Eventually they admitted defeat, but the discussion about a women's Lions tour never went away and later in the book we find out what happened next.

But while it seems to make sense to use established brands and piggyback off their success, it's vital the women's game keeps in mind only what is right for women's rugby and that is not always a mirror image of what already exists in the men's game. We should not close off avenues to innovative competition models which might better suit a sport in its relative infancy.

By 2001, in Europe at least, developments for international women's Test teams were continuing to accelerate. The competition that would eventually become the Six Nations had already been through significant upheaval. It remained a Five Nations Championship in 2001 with Ireland again declining to take part.

England were strong and won all four games, only conceding 18 points in the process. France, Spain and Scotland all won two and lost two while Wales were rooted to the bottom without a win.

Although the next World Cup, to be held in Barcelona, was just a year away, the summer's European Championships in France were used by numerous sides, including England and France, to try out new talent. Both sent their 'A' teams.

Although 'A' teams have almost disappeared completely now, they were widely used in the early days of women's rugby, with many of the first few Home and Five Nations Championships hosting double-headers where the senior team and the 'A' team played back to back. Cost apart, it's difficult to fathom why this trend has fallen so far out of fashion.

With only a handful of sides now operating national teams at U20 level and domestic league competitions varying in terms of competitiveness, there are scant opportunities to test whether players can step up and cope with the intensity of international rugby.

Back then, the European Championships were excellent testing grounds to do just that. In 2001, 12 nations featured in the competition. For the first time matches were spread around several grounds in a region rather than being played at one location. The competition was tiered into two with the strongest eight teams in pool A and the lower-ranked teams in pool B.

Games were tight among the best teams. Scotland narrowly beat France 6-9 in the semi-final. They would face Spain in the final, who had also just squeezed past England 15-8.

Scotland had gone into the tournament with high expectations. They were playing well and resources were improving enough that they could train together much more regularly. There was no team competing that they hadn't beaten, and they sent the strongest team they had available.

But Spain – by now a highly experienced Test team – were confident too and looking to lay down a marker given they were hosting the next World Cup. Spain's acceleration had been impressive. They had already established themselves as a top European side.

The final in Lille was bound to be close. Having not conceded a try all competition, Scotland were just about favourites. They took an early lead as Jenny Dickson, the wing, dived over before powerhouse centre Rimma Petlevannaya scored again.

Paula Chalmers, the player of the tournament, added a conversion and a late penalty. Although the Spanish threw everything into rescuing the game, the Scottish defence held firm and they won it 15-3.

Apart from the delight at their win, the players expressed satisfaction that they had done enough to secure more National Lottery funding, which had been stopped the year before, Chalmers saying afterwards, telling *The Times*:

> Fortunately, the Scottish Rugby Union stepped in with aid, otherwise this would not have been possible. This is

going to raise the profile of the women's game in Scotland a huge amount, and it gives us something to show the girls when they come to the summer camps, to show what can be achieved.

There was another reason that England had sent some development players to the European Championships. They were about to embark on a tour to Australia and New Zealand later that summer and strength in depth would be key.

The tour kicked off in Australia with two Tests against the Wallaroos, one in Sydney and one in Newcastle. The second leg would see England play two Tests against the now-renamed Black Ferns, in Rotorua and North Harbour.

If they could feel confident travelling to Australia to play a side who barely played outside of World Cups, the New Zealand Tests would be fascinating. The hosts were unbeaten for ten years.

England, on the back of a Five Nations win and with their domestic game growing, were in good form. Shelley Rae and Paula George were key in the backs, while up front players like Jennifer Sutton and Claire Frost were dangerous.

Though they'd done well at the 1998 World Cup, Australia were still inexperienced on the Test scene and youngsters like debutant Louise 'Cookie' Burrows got their first taste of rugby at this level in the opening game against England.

England were too strong in the first Test in Sydney, winning 19-41, but Australia were fast learners and the second Test was much closer. England won 5-15.

The first Test against New Zealand, coached again by Darryl Suasua, was held in Rotorua.

It started well for the hosts when the brilliant Cootes stormed over the line with pace and strength just three minutes into the match, but mistakes and penalties started to build.

Going to the break 5-3 up, the Black Ferns added a second try when Exia Shelford produced an excellent step to outwit the defence. When Cootes followed up with a trademark run for another score, they appeared to have the game in the bag at 15-3.

However, they were unable to press on and England scored through Claire Frost and Rae's kicking made things very tight. Local media described the game as 'closer than expected' though the reality was that England, with greater time together and coming off the back of two games in Australia, were better prepared than ever to face the world champions. They lost 15-10 but were full of belief they could win the rematch.

Test two would be close again.

England started badly, conceding an early penalty that Tammi Wilson couldn't convert. A series of powerful drives from the Black Ferns' forwards put the visitors under pressure. Wilson benefited from a strong run by Anna Richards to score the opening try, which she converted herself.

Strong line-out plays and mauling allowed England to hit back immediately, helping Nicky Crawford to slide in on the right, but New Zealand hit back thanks to a nice try from Vanessa Cootes. Shelley Rae knocked over a penalty for England to make it 12-8 at half-time.

A thrilling dash by Feltham up the right was matched by a solid Cootes tackle, but England were building momentum. Rae scored a superb try from a line-out, weaving her way through the defence and somehow managing to stretch for the line to give her side the lead.

Annaleah Rush raced over to help New Zealand regain the lead but a sensational break up the left saw Feltham race away from the halfway line to score beneath the post with minutes left. England held on for a famous victory ending 17-22.

Geoff Richards, the England head coach, said afterwards:

The key was our self-belief. New Zealand's record is frighteningly good, but we had self confidence in our squad. It is probably the high point of women's rugby in England. It was a great match, and I am delighted for the players.

The win also gave other sides confidence given how dominant the Black Ferns had been since their arrival onto the Test scene. It was tough, but they were beatable.

Rae, one of the best kickers the game has ever seen, was later named the IRB Women's Player of the Year.

Going into a World Cup year, it seemed it would be a two-horse race. But France were determined to try to shake things up.

France finally arrive

Although France had done relatively well in the Home Nations Championship in the three years since they'd joined, they had yet to win a title.

Scotland were confident, now European champions to add to their previous Home Nations victory.

This time the teams would be playing for a first full Six Nations title and Ireland were back in the competition again after a period of rebuilding.

Unsurprisingly, the Irish struggled after two years out and were handed one of their most painful defeats in Worcester, losing 79-0 against England, still the highest margin of victory in the history of the fixture.

England had 50 by half-time with tries from hooker Amy Garnett, Assunta De Biase, Chris Diver (three), Nicky Crawford, scrum-half Jo Yapp and captain Paula George. The Irish put up sterner resistance in the third quarter but then the floodgates opened again to let in George, Crawford, Emily Feltham, centre Sue Day and a fourth try from Diver.

It would be over a decade before Ireland would actually beat England in the tournament.

France beat Spain in the opening round before travelling to Wales where they recorded a solid 20-0 win. The French team had players who were really hitting their stride at Test level. Hayraud and Sartini were prominent while the brilliant Nathalie Amiel was captain in the middle, providing outstanding leadership and experience.

Wales had a good team too. Full-back Naomi Thomas was pivotal while Mel Berry and Louise Rickard were real threats alongside the hugely experienced Jamie Kift.

But with Amiel pulling the strings, this French team looked like a different proposition.

Amiel's history in the French set-up is worth a book on its own.

She had started playing rugby in the 1970s. When she was 12 her mother registered her in a rugby team, given the sport was popular in the local area. She played with boys in Capestang and news of her talents and abilities spread throughout the small French women's rugby community.

She was selected to play against Great Britain at just 15 and allowed to play because the game in France was not governed by the FFR at the time and so there were no age restrictions. Another 55 Test appearances would follow, primarily at flanker, although she switched to centre towards the end of her playing career in 2002.

That particular Six Nations would be her last, so it was fitting that she led her side to eventual glory.

The crunch game, as ever, was the clash with England in the third round in Lyon. France pipped it 22-17. The path was cleared for them to take their first title and be crowned the first ever women's Six Nations winners, and with a grand slam.

All roads now led to Barcelona for another women's rugby World Cup in 2002.

New Zealand too good ... again

Although the game was growing and its profile was building, few players speak fondly of their experiences of the World Cup in Barcelona, away from the games at least.

The intimate feel of the previous event in Amsterdam was gone. Players were spread out across the Barcelona area and many had to travel miles to train. Interaction between the teams was rare.

Although New Zealand were probably favourites again, England's win on their home turf the year before had given the Black Ferns something of a wake-up call and forced a tactical rethink. A panel of leading New Zealand coaches such as Wayne Smith and Robbie Deans had been brought together to support Black Ferns coach Darryl Suasua and help the team to step up.

As part of the new focus, the players trained alongside the men's Super 12 development teams and played games against a handful of regional women's teams. Captain Farah Palmer would later declare the loss to England as the best thing that could have happened to them and a springboard for improvement.

Once again 16 teams competed. For the first time a pre-tournament qualification match took place to decide Asia's second representative. All the rest were invited by the IRB. There were two differences from 1998. The lowest-ranked European teams (Sweden and Russia) were replaced by teams from Asia (Japan) and Oceania (Samoa).

Hosts Spain were realistic about their chances with captain Mercedes Batidor telling the media beforehand:

> The World Cup is the pinnacle of a player's career and I am sure Spain will do well in front of its own public. I think finishing between fifth and seventh in the world would be a good result for us, but it will be tough work

because the other teams have made great progress, we will go match by match.

Spain opened the competition with a win, and a convincing one too, 62-0 against Japan.

Just like the last World Cup, New Zealand opened with a thrashing of Germany, this time 117-0 instead of 134-6. The opening round also saw big wins for Canada (over Ireland 57-0), England (over Italy 63-0) and the US (over the Netherlands 87-0). The one-sided nature of some of these results would play a part in the IRB deciding to curtail the competition to 12 teams from 2006 to enable other sides to build depth and make the overall event more competitive. They've curiously not made similar changes to the men's format, which has suffered similar imbalances.

The quarter-finals went relatively to form, though England stuttered against Spain, trailing at half-time before going on to win unconvincingly 13-5. The competition was set up for a grandstand finish with New Zealand taking on France and England taking on Canada for a place in the final.

The Black Ferns were efficient in their match, winning with ease, 30-0 in the end. Tammi Wilson scored 13 points at full-back, with Melodie Robinson scoring early too. With New Zealand down to 14 players for 20 minutes of the second half after back-to-back sin bins for Adrianne Lilii and Amiria Marsh, the stalemate continued, but when they returned, so did New Zealand's form. Dianne Kahura came off the bench to touch down and prop Rebecca Luia'ana put the seal on the win in injury time.

England, meanwhile, made up for their frustrating game against Spain with a huge 53-10 win over Canada in searing heat, finally showing the form that had pitted them as genuine World Cup contenders with a powerful performance in Girona. Sue Day had a hat-trick and England were far too good overall.

Gill Burns was still involved and having a huge impact, though the veteran of four World Cups would surprisingly not make the starting line-up for the final.

On the day of the final games, France won bronze, piling on the agony for Canada and winning 41-7. France were in part motivated by the fact the game would be the last for stalwart Amiel, who played brilliantly, scoring two tries. Estelle Sartini also had a fine tournament off the tee and France could be relatively satisfied with their third-place finish.

The final itself was watched by a crowd of around 8,000, though it felt less given the capacity at Barcelona's Olympic Stadium was over 55,000.

It was once again to be New Zealand's day, this time with a narrower result, 19-9. The victors played a more conservative style, having perhaps learned lessons from England's win the year before. Shelley Rae's kicking kept England in contention throughout a tight first half, but New Zealand eventually eased clear with tries from Monique Hirovanaa and Cheryl Waaka.

Rae cancelled out two Tammi Wilson penalties with one of her own plus her first drop goal of the tournament before adding a second penalty to edge England 9-6 ahead. But Hirovanaa put New Zealand back in front and Waaka extended their advantage to seven points. The Black Ferns managed to hold on for the rest of the second half despite the sin-binning of Victoria Heighway. Hannah Myers, a replacement, sealed the win with a penalty in injury time.

Alison Kervin, a pioneering female rugby journalist, covered the game for the UK press at the time reporting that the Kiwis deserved their win:

> New Zealand were the better side on Saturday; they were superior in the forwards and awesome in defence, as they had been throughout the tournament. They have not conceded a try and have had just 12 points scored against them.

At the end of the tournament, as the New Zealand team performed the haka to celebrate their victory and We Are The Champions resonated around the stadium, the England team clutched their silver medals to their chests and hugged one another.

To come so close to victory, and to lose in the final game, is a devastating blow, but to make it to a World Cup Final in the first place is a magnificent achievement. That England have made it to every women's World Cup Final says much about the dedication and commitment of those behind the game in this country.

Australia grabbed fifth place after routing Scotland 30-0 in their closing game. Charmaine Smith ran in a brace of first-half tries as the Wallaroos built a 13-0 half-time lead, with further touchdowns after the break from centre Sharon O'Kane and flanker Selena Worsley. The rest of Australia's points came via the boot of Tui Ormsby.

Afterwards, players would reflect on the venue and the decision to host the World Cup in Barcelona, a fantastic city but hardly one known as a rugby hotbed. New Zealand star Anna Richards said she hadn't much enjoyed the overall experience:

It was difficult. We were in the middle of nowhere in this little resort town. Our training ground was so far away it took the day to get out there and get back. We'd meet, bus for miles, train and have lunch, then come back and it was the whole day so the experience was just about having a really long day. The games would be one to two hours away and we were playing in different venues which didn't feel like it really worked. We didn't see any of the other teams apart from playing them. I can't say I enjoyed the 2002 World Cup at all, apart from winning the thing.

More history made, for better and for worse

For most sides, the World Cup marked the end of Test rugby in 2002, but there was one more historic moment that year. Scotland were due to take on Sweden and the game was to be held for the first time at Murrayfield.

In lining up at Murrayfield, Scotland would remarkably become just the first women's Test side in the northern hemisphere to play in their national stadium. The game took place as a curtain-raiser to the Scottish men's game against Fiji.

The match kicked off a good three hours before the men's game, giving little hope that fans were likely to turn out in big numbers, but it was at least an effort to make the Scottish game more inclusive. There was something still quite galling about Jim Telfer, then the Scotland Director of Rugby at the time, describing the moment as *allowing women to tread the hallowed turf* as though the country's national stadium only belonged to men and women could count themselves lucky to be let in at all.

The experiment did prove successful. A couple of years later the Scottish Rugby Union announced that Murrayfield could become the home ground for more women's Test games and Scotland went on to play there far more regularly.

Though women's Test games being played at national stadiums was already the norm in the southern hemisphere, the debate would rage for years on the other side of the world.

England didn't play at Twickenham until 2003, Wales had to wait until 2012 to play at the then Millennium Stadium while Ireland didn't play at the national stadium in Dublin until 2014, having to wait until after they had won the Six Nations and a grand slam to be given the opportunity.

Many believe it is better to sacrifice the atmosphere of a smaller, fuller stadium to get an opportunity for a nation's best women's players to play on the main stage, others believe the game should grow its fan base in smaller grounds first.

The reality is that a hybrid while the game is growing has worked best in recent years, with France highlighting that in a rugby hotbed in the south they can attract up to 20,000 fans, helping them when they hosted the World Cup in Paris in 2014 to attract bigger crowds to larger grounds.

Yet, while positive history was being made on one side of the world at Murrayfield in 2002, potential disaster struck on the other.

Despite their fifth-place finish at the World Cup, Australia had long been struggling for investment from the ARU. The organisation was not among the richest of governing bodies but were a year out from hosting the men's World Cup, where they were expected to make considerable profit. The media speculated that it could be as much as $45m (Australian dollars).

The ARU ran the elite women's game out of its high-performance unit. Just a few months after the World Cup, it announced it would move the whole programme into its community unit, alongside junior and school development programmes.

While the union argued that this would mean it would be able to focus better on the grassroots game, something badly needed given there were only around 1,200 registered adult women's players at the time, it effectively cut off the Wallaroos' funding at its knees, taking away $200,000.

The international programme ground to a halt for two years but the reality was even worse. Australia would not compete again until the 2006 World Cup.

Former Wallaroo Bronnie Mackintosh, a brilliant player who had retired earlier that year, told the media that the funding cut would in effect kill the women's game:

There'll be no tours, no development, no publicity and with us hosting the men's World Cup, that would have been a perfect opportunity to showcase our game.

It emerged after the 2002 World Cup that the ARU had not even wanted to fund the costs of sending the team to that event and had scrapped a build-up tour to New Zealand, as well as forcing the players to pay for their own World Cup training camp.

Local media quoted Stephen Swan, an ARU high performance manager whose contract was cut due to the changes, suggesting that the union didn't want to pay anything towards the World Cup but that they had come under pressure from the IRB.

> My understanding is that the IRB indicated to the ARU that that would not be a wise thing to do for a country that still, at that stage, had not signed the host city agreement for [the men's World Cup in] 2003. It makes me angry and also when I look at the USA, Canada, England, and even Wales who are setting up the proper infrastructure for women's rugby.

A couple of years later, the decision was reversed but it had already been reported internationally. The negative publicity was badly timed. The IRB was trying to persuade the International Olympic Committee (IOC) to make rugby sevens a new Olympic sport in 2008, with gender equality becoming increasingly important to bid processes.

Kathy Flores found herself in Australia some months later being awarded the IRB Women's Personality of the Year award and recalls addressing the issue:

> Truthfully, I think I might have been second or third in line for the award. I feel like they wanted to give it to the New Zealand team for winning the 2002 World Cup and they couldn't get them all there. That is serious – I recall getting told this in a roundabout way. So when they told

127

me to go down there to Sydney I really didn't know what it was about.

Well anyway, of course I had to mention what was going on in Australia in my thank you speech. I was introduced and went up to say a bit and I said I hoped the ARU would change their mind about their women's rugby funding. I was ushered back down pretty quickly after that.

Having lost their crown to France the year before and being beaten in another World Cup Final, England could have been excused for a lacklustre Six Nations. But with history to be made in their opening game, where they would play at Twickenham for the first time, they were not about to sit back.

Taking on France, England started their campaign in rampant fashion. They won 57-0 with a hat-trick each for Sue Day and Chris Diver in a match played as a curtain-raiser to the men's Six Nations game between the same teams.

Scotland beat Ireland while Wales also started well, thrashing Spain 44-0, their first win over the Spanish. It was thanks in part to a brilliant performance from Non Evans, the full-back who scored 15 points.

England showed no mercy as the rounds progressed, beating Wales 69-7 and Spain 69-0. As they marched towards a grand slam, Ireland recorded some history of their own. Having not won in any form of this competition since 1996 when they beat Wales, they travelled to Madrid desperate to break their unwanted streak.

By now I was working as a volunteer with the IWRFU. One of my jobs was to take a call from Mark Andrews after the away games so I could gather enough information to write a report to send to the media in the hope of generating some coverage. With results hard to come by, it was never a call I much looked forward to, but this time, as Mark relayed the details of the 0-16 win, I remember well how thrilled I was for the team.

Ireland, coached by Donal O'Leary, were starting to bring through real talent. Players like fly-half Sarahjane Belton and back-row Fiona Steed were as good as any in the world on their day in their positions. Belton kicked 11 points to add to a second-half penalty try to secure the win, in a game where a young player called Fiona Coghlan – later an outstanding Irish captain – came off the bench to win her first cap.

On the phone from the sidelines afterwards Steed, then Ireland's most-capped player, told me:

> It's absolutely amazing. It is the happiest I have ever been on a rugby pitch. I still think that it's just the start for us and although we have a tough three games left this is just the springboard we all needed for this season and for the future of Irish women's rugby. Two seasons ago Spain hammered us 42-0 when I was captain. That was the worst moment ever for me. To captain your country to a 42-0 loss, and it's ironic that Spain should again be the opposition when I feel the exact opposite tonight.

Still, the grand slam would be England's. A brilliant team was simply too good and too strong for everyone else.

Outside the Six Nations there was precious little other Test rugby to be played in 2003, though the Canada Cup would crank back into action in 2004 and, in New Zealand, exciting plans were being made for a novel end-of-year Test series.

With money tight but the NZR conscious of the fact their world champion women's team ought to be playing more games, they had come up with a relatively cheap way of getting some home matches played.

They would host and fund a World XV to play the Black Ferns in Auckland at the end of the year. The first Test would be played as a curtain-raiser to Auckland's NPC game against Northland at Eden Park while the second Test would be in Whangarei before Northland met Wellington. The World XV would be led by the former New Zealand coach Darryl Suasua and supported by Franck Boivert, a former USA women's head coach.

The NZRU would pay to fly 15 players from around the world, with the bench for the World XV team to be made up of promising young uncapped New Zealand players including future stars like Justine Levea. Suasua got together a good squad including Non Evans (Wales), Oka Autagavaia (Samoa), Estelle Sartini (France), Susie Appleby (England), Paula Chalmers (Scotland), Bronnie Mackintosh (Australia), Selena Worsley (Australia), Gillian Florence (Canada), Gill Burns (England), Phaidra Knight (United States) and Leslie Cripps (Canada).

New Zealand won the first Test 37-0 but the second was closer at 38-18. Though the concept was never picked up again, it kept the world's top players in the spotlight.

Women's rugby was growing. Games were becoming more regular on the international stage and the standards of domestic leagues were starting to improve. However, the game still suffered from an image problem.

As New Zealand were putting on a show against the world's best, the Women's Sport Foundation published a report in the UK which said that 17% of people didn't think that women should even be playing rugby, the same percentage as boxing.

As history tells us, all women's sports have faced questions about the necessity of their existence, but the physical nature of sports like rugby brings extra challenges. Public opinion was often divided over the years as to what was or wasn't appropriate.

Sexism has always therefore been part of the story of women's rugby. Players, even to this day, have to face criticism that has nothing to do with their ability and all to do with their sex. It is a challenge which feeds into every aspect of the game.

At grassroots level, where women's teams often contribute equally to the playing numbers and finances of their clubs as their male counterparts, women still often get the worst pitches, the worst kick-off times and are allocated the most inexperienced referees.

Around the sport itself sexist attitudes are rife. As recently as 2019, Scottish Rugby had to issue encouragement to clubs and teams to vet guest speakers at events after the president of the Glasgow University men's rugby club resigned for allegedly making 'disgustingly sexist' remarks at the university's 150th anniversary rugby club dinner.

He was said to have uttered inappropriate jokes about the female president of Scottish Rugby, Dee Bradbury, 'keeping her clothes on' at the event. Another speaker also suggested the women's team 'strip down' before the season started.

It's been painful too to watch the abuse and commentary thrown the way of female broadcast and media talent thanks to pathetic anonymous posters online who struggle with the idea that women could possibly know anything about rugby.

We are thankfully mostly past the days – although not everywhere – when women playing rugby was met with outright hostility and farcical myths about the impact on their health and well-being.

But while many carried on disapproving, the game continued to grow.

South Africa emerge

The 2004 Six Nations was once again a battle between France and England. This time the French, with the advantage of a finale against England on home soil, came out on top and took the grand slam. The last game was tight. France edged it 13-12 in front of over 7,000 fans in Bourg-en-Bresse, the spiritual home of French women's rugby.

Ireland were bottom again, but one-point defeats against Spain and Wales suggested they were not far away from a permanent breakthrough. Wales, meanwhile, announced that a few months later they would head to South Africa to play a historic two-Test series.

These would be South Africa's first ever Test games and the culmination of painfully slow progress in a country where rugby, for men at least, was hugely popular.

As Dr Hendrik Snyders sets out in his chapter in the recent academic text *The Professionalisation of Women's Sport: Issues and Debates*, women had been involved in rugby for decades in South Africa but their inclusion was largely wiped out of history.

> Matches between groups of men and women, such as the so-called 'Suffragettes v. Mere Men' in 1909, are forgotten moments and deemed of no historical significance.
>
> Similarly, the intervarsity between teams of the University of the Western Cape and Hewat Teachers' College (1968) and the University of Stellenbosch's Sharp Girl Rugby Competition of the 1980s continued to be viewed as aberrations and as comical or 'gay interludes'. This state of affairs is the result of 'the obsession with formal histories and almanacs that record only games that have been officially sanctioned' and that promotes the perception that women's rugby emerged 'spontaneously from some kind of vacuum'. Women in rugby, therefore, remained 'historically invisible' and relegated to 'shining in the reflected glory of male rugby players'.

It was not until 2000 that the union hosted its first women's national 15-a-side tournament, with eight teams taking part. In 2003 the South African Women's President's XV competed against the England Women's Development team.

In their first proper Test against Wales a year later, they proved more than a match for their more experienced counterparts, losing narrowly 8-5 at Port Elizabeth. South Africa had taken the lead through winger Ronwin Kelly, but Wales hooker Jenny Davies recorded her first international try before the break to even the score at half-time. Wales added a penalty from the boot of winger Stacey Saunders after the break and could have added further points but a couple of tries were disallowed.

The squads then flew to Pretoria to play a second Test at the Loftus Stadium. It was another incredibly tight affair with Wales pipping it 15-18, getting one over the men to become the first ever Welsh rugby team to complete a successful Test series in South Africa.

After that series wrapped up, Canada prepared to host their fifth summer cup tournament. This time it was called the Churchill Cup and the Canadians hosted New Zealand, England and Wales at an event to be played across Edmonton and Calgary, with the finals taking place at the Commonwealth Stadium.

Coming right in between two World Cups, the tournament was a useful opportunity to see how the world's top teams were progressing. Though there were no runaway scores, New Zealand were still clearly out in front and beat everyone comfortably, including England 38-0 in the final.

As 2005 loomed some vital plans were being worked on off the field.

England were keen to host the 2006 World Cup and were preparing a serious bid. With support from UK Sport and the RFU, the RFUW were in negotiations with the IRB and were confident that they would have a strong chance of winning hosting rights.

Having held the previous World Cups in Barcelona and Amsterdam though, the IRB were keen to move the competition outside Europe, even though so far it had yet to be held anywhere that could be considered a hotbed of rugby. With respect to those two great cities, neither could really offer much of a springboard to attract massive crowds to build momentum or any sort of legacy.

There was disappointment for England then when the IRB chose Edmonton in Canada to host the 2006 event. Syd Miller acknowledged at the time that the decision was indeed about moving the tournament to a new continent:

> Since the first tournament in 1991 WRWC has been the catalyst for the tremendous growth of the women's game worldwide.
>
> The move out of Europe is therefore another example of the growing global popularity of rugby. The IRB has made every effort to ensure that its tournaments are hosted throughout the rugby world and this announcement means that all of our major regions will have hosted an IRB tournament between 2003 and 2007.

Importantly, the organisers would once again foot the bill, not just to get the teams there this time, but also for transport and accommodation costs. They also reduced the event to 12 teams in an effort to increase the tournament's competitiveness.

With 18 months to go, the 2005 Six Nations was another chance for teams to develop their squads. France were crowned champions for a second successive year thanks to beating England at Imber Court.

Wales were poor, finishing bottom having lost to Ireland. The Welsh performances, fuelled in part by a new selection policy that meant only Wales-based players could be picked, would come back to haunt them when the IRB came to choose the teams who would take part in the World Cup.

Once again there were no qualifying tournaments. Instead, teams were invited to take part in the World Cup based on performances at the World Cup in 2002 and in international matches between 2002 and 2005. This would lead to anger and frustration among the teams left. It was Wales who were the most badly affected, with the place they had hoped would be theirs going to Samoa.

The world's two leading teams had a chance to gauge where they were a year before the World Cup when England headed back to New Zealand for a two-Test series. England warmed up for the Test games with a 53-0 win over a side with limited experience, Samoa, before facing the Black Ferns at Eden Park.

England suffered through a lack of attacking opportunities and poor defence while the Black Ferns raced out of the blocks. New Zealand scored 18 points to England's three in the first half, touching down for three tries and a penalty, while England's only points came from a penalty from Saracens fly-half Karen Andrew. After the restart the Black Ferns continued in the same vein with the game ending in a five-try demolition, 33-8.

England fell to another defeat in the second Test, 24-15, though with a much-improved performance. Numerous players made their debuts, including Tamara Taylor who would go on to win over 100 caps.

New Zealand, it seemed, would still be the team to beat in 2006 in Edmonton.

Women central to an Olympic strategy

Having failed in a bid to have rugby included in the 2008 Olympics, the IRB once again tried to get sevens into the London Games in 2012. It headed the shortlist of five sports as possible contenders for inclusion. The IRB had a strong supporter for their bid in Dr Jacques Rogge, the IOC president, a former Belgium rugby international.

Gender equality was a crucial part of the picture taken into consideration. At that stage, though, the IRB were only bidding for men to be part of the Games. There was no official world circuit or established international sevens tournament for women. Though many teams travelled to play in events around the world, they were not IRB-sanctioned.

The game had failed to capitalise on the success of women's teams at events held in Dubai and Hong Kong, so it was no huge surprise then when the IOC rejected the bid again.

The good news for women's rugby was that the outcome forced the game's decision makers to properly include women in elite sevens competitions, starting with the World Cup Sevens in Dubai in 2009 and culminating in the Olympics in 2016, with a brand-new women's World Sevens Series sandwiched between.

The year 2005 was also notable for action in the developing nations. Uganda and Rwanda played their first Test matches and the Uganda Women's Rugby Association was formed. For the world's 12 best teams though, it was all about Edmonton.

Chapter Seven

Baby steps

WITH THE World Cup looming, the 2006 Six Nations would lay down an important marker for the five teams competing that would travel to Canada.

After their disappointment in New Zealand, England needed to get back on track. Their growing profile, coupled with investment from the National Lottery, was beginning to put pressure on them to win more titles.

Wales too had a point to prove. Smarting from their omission from the World Cup made them highly motivated, something that would propel them to strong performances over the coming two years.

Discussions had begun for the women's competition to be brought 'in-house' and run under the overarching organisation who ran the men's Six Nations. That would likely mean Spain being sacrificed in favour of Italy. It was a controversial proposal, unfair on a Spanish team that added plenty to the competition and who had players full of promise. Those like Inés Etxegibel, Berta García and Bárbara Plà were a match for anyone on their day.

Frustrated at their likely omission and with limited opportunities to play international rugby now on the horizon, Spain would turn in their poorest performances that year in the championship. Among them was the opening fixture in Dublin.

The 2006 championship got off to a historic start when Ireland beat the Spanish 25-10 for their first ever home Six Nations win. Tania Rosser scored first before Orla Brennan grabbed a brace. When the highly experienced Ulster back Suzanne Fleming dotted down, Ireland made sure of the points before captain Sarahjane Belton rounded it off despite Spain's consolation penalty try.

England's win over Wales and France's win over Scotland were felt to be business as usual and the top two sides headed towards a pivotal fourth-round clash in Paris. England turned in one of their best performances to win 0-26 to pave their way for the title.

The Welsh performances were much improved. Led by Mel Berry, the backbone of this particular Welsh team was impressive. Jamie Kift and Non Evans were involved, while Liza Burgess brought decades of experience. They beat Scotland, Ireland and Spain to guarantee at least a third-place finish, their best ever. Then they welcomed France to Pontypridd in a huge final weekend fixture that ended in a historic victory.

The 11-10 win was marred by a horrible injury to Evans, who was stretchered off with a double break to her leg causing an hour's delay to the game. It sent a firm message that Wales surely should have been at the World Cup.

France led 7-0 early on but the hosts hit back with a penalty from Philippa Tuttiet and were handed a numerical advantage on the stroke of half-time. France were reduced to 14 players as Clotilde Flaugère was sent off for punching. France briefly extended their lead through the boot of Estelle Sartini, before Tuttiet added her second penalty of the game and Mel Berry crashed over in the corner to hand Wales victory.

The result handed England the title before a ball was kicked against Ireland in their final outing, but they were after a first grand slam in three years and the perfect pre-World Cup boost. They led 24-5 at the break, with tries from Vanessa

Huxford, Amy Garnett, Vicky Massarella and Helen Clayton. Ireland's only score came from winger Nuala Ni Chaidhain and England's extra points came from Karen Andrew.

Ireland scored again through Joy Neville but the game was wrapped up when Clayton crossed for her second before youngsters Michaela Staniford and Danielle Waterman later got on the scoresheet.

Spain bowed out with their worst finish, rooted to the bottom of the table. It may have been understandable that the women's competition could generate additional publicity and resources by joining up with the men's event, but the removal of Spain left a sour taste. It continued a pattern whereby those running women's rugby felt it right to follow a path established to suit the structure of the men's game rather than its own.

Spain were undoubtedly a better team than Italy, who had struggled to compete against bigger teams, though the Italians could point to the fact they'd finished ahead of Ireland at the 2002 World Cup.

The decision dealt a hammer blow to the 15s game in Spain. To this day the Spanish team struggles to gain any meaningful Test games between World Cups, particularly after the demise of the European Championship. Italy, though improving, have never seriously gone on to challenge for a title.

Before the World Cup, though, the 2006 European Sevens champions would be decided. In their first appearance at the tournament, Wales would emerge winners with a path to victory which included defeating Switzerland 32-0 and Germany 20-7 before falling to England 7-0 in the pool stages.

They kicked off the knockout stages with a 10-3 quarter-final win over Spain before downing the Netherlands 29-0 in the semi-final. With England pushing over Ireland 21-0 in the semis, the stage was set for a Wales v England finale.

Having lost to England in the pool stages, Wales were out to prove a point. Mel Berry grabbed Wales's first try in the opening half to put them 5-0 up at the break, but an English reply was not long coming, and they secured seven points shortly after the restart.

Clare Flowers crossed for Wales with three minutes to go. With players like Naomi Thomas in outstanding form – she was later named player of the tournament – Wales held onto the lead to secure victory. It topped off an excellent season: second in the Six Nations and European sevens champions.

Over to Edmonton

With key European events done and dusted, 12 teams looked ahead to Edmonton.

The profile of the women's game was on the rise. TV and wider media coverage was improving. The World Cup organisers had secured broadcast deals and would be showing all the games online.

Greater media coverage did bring some negativity, though. England's Sue Day was prompted to write a letter to *The Observer* before the competition taking issue with an article by editor Brian Oliver, who was critical of the standard of the women's game.

As the vice-captain of the England women's rugby team, the reigning Six Nations champions, I read 'A Man's World' with interest and agreed with a lot of the sentiment. Undoubtedly the women's sporting world needs to do more to sell itself, raise its profile and to demonstrate to the kids out there that it is a fulfilling and inspirational place to be.

I would take issue with certain suggestions made, however, not least from your own sports editor, Brian Oliver, who said: 'It's too simplistic to blame the media, who do not coach, develop and fund champions.' I agree that it is too simplistic – there are many other factors, including funding, opportunity, perception and quality of coaching. But if the system in place to bring through the female stars of the future is flawed, then the media's attitude to it is equally so.

The women's sports that get the most coverage seem to be those inextricably linked to the men's events – tennis, athletics, horse racing. Look at the coverage of my own sport. The England women's team fly out to the World Cup at the end of the month as second favourites. Each individual in the squad trains as a 'professional'. We have skill, determination and entertainment value to rival the men, and if you are reporting sport simply on its merits, then surely we would have seen news of our achievements.

I am realistic enough to understand that it will probably take decades (at least) to begin to compete with the history that goes with hundreds of years of male-dominated sport. However, it would be nice to see the British media do their bit towards ensuring that women's sport actually is reported on its merits.

Meanwhile, in the sport's ongoing work to develop female referees, the match officials at the 2006 World Cup also included more women than ever before; 12 in total.

By the 2014 World Cup, all the referees at the tournament would be women – a decision not without its detractors with many coaches speaking out about standards and a desire to have the best referees in the world refereeing showpiece tournaments, not just the best female referees.

However, in part because of those early opportunities, standards have improved enormously. Referees like Joy Neville, Sara Cox, Hollie Davidson and Nikki O'Donnell are hugely respected in the game and highly sought-after referees across both the men's and women's game.

The structure of the competition was complicated. The IRB opted to run a cross-pool league system, with pool A playing pool D and pool B playing pool C. The pool games were spread across Ellerslie Rugby Park and St Albert.

Hosts Canada were disappointingly thrashed by New Zealand on the opening day. The 66-7 result was exactly the sort of scoreline organisers had been trying to avoid by reducing the size of the competition.

New Zealand had only been in the country a few days but looked totally at ease with some brilliant tries, including two within seven minutes from wingers Claire Richardson and Stephanie Mortimer. Julia Sugaway scored a brilliant individual try for Canada but that was as good as it got for the home crowd. Richardson ended with a hat-trick while Amiria Marsh, the full-back, was the outstanding player on the field.

Canada's Sarah Ulmer summed up her thoughts afterwards, giving the media an honest perspective:

> I was personally excited to get New Zealand first before they'd had a chance to play more games and get that cohesion going and build. Unfortunately, it looks like they didn't need to get that cohesion! I would be more worried if we had performed well, and we had lost by that margin but we performed poorly.

Scotland beat Spain – Rhona Shephard scoring a great try to help put the Scots clear. South Africa made their World Cup debut against Australia, who astonishingly hadn't kicked a ball since the last World Cup but who were still too good. Tricia Brown had a hat-trick but Ruan Sims dotted down four times to take out a comfortable win.

Continuing the opening round of games, France had no problem against Ireland with Estelle Sartini outstanding at 10. England played USA, who were more physical than expected, and there was a surprising 0-0 score at half-time. Finally Kim

Oliver set the ball rolling with a score and England won, but failed to get a bonus point.

In round two, Canada needed to beat Spain to keep in the hunt for the knockout phases. This time they were impressive. Heather Moyse was excellent in particular as they ran in 13 tries. Maria E. Gallo scored five of them and the result put Canada back in contention for a semi-final spot. Moyse was a pivotal player for Canada and is often described as one of the country's best all-round female athletes. She would go on to win Winter Olympic gold medals in 2010 and 2014 and it was her power and pace which so often was the hallmark of Canadian rugby victory.

New Zealand then took on Samoa – the first time the two sides had played in a women's Test game. It was a remarkable game given that all of the Samoan players played their rugby in New Zealand, but even with the benefit of knowing exactly what to expect they couldn't do much about a relentless team in black. Amiria Marsh had a hat-trick in the first half and New Zealand won 50-0.

Scotland won their second game with a win over Kazakhstan, getting a bonus point thanks to Rhona Shepherd getting a try in the last play. The USA beat Ireland, Phaidra Knight getting two of the four tries in the 24-11 win. Australia were then beaten by a stronger, fitter and more experienced French team while England looked more at home against South Africa, scoring 12 tries in all, with Sue Day, captain for the day, getting four.

New Zealand were now guaranteed a semi-final spot. After that it was a matter of three of the next six teams needing to get as many points as possible in round three.

There Ireland picked up their first win with a victory over South Africa while Spain provided the shock of the pool stages by beating Samoa in their final match. Isabel Rodríguez's score in the final minutes sealed a 14-12 win. The USA beat

Australia but, by missing out on another bonus point, they lost out on a semi-final spot.

Canada needed a big win against Kazakhstan and they duly delivered. Moyse scored after just 60 seconds and from there on they never looked back. The brilliant full-back finished with a hat-trick.

Would it be enough? The last two games would determine their fate.

New Zealand and Scotland faced off as two undefeated sides. Donna Kennedy was winning her 93rd cap and Scotland needed at least a point from the game. At half-time this looked possible. New Zealand had rested many of their big names and led just 6-0. But in the second half, Marsh and Mortimer made the game safe at 21-0.

Scotland could still progress if France could beat England in the final game of the day. Sue Day set up Danielle Waterman however for an early try and the tone was set. England's pack dominated, Day added two more tries and there was no denying England their 27-8 win. Scotland were out of the World Cup on points difference.

The semi-final line-up was New Zealand against France and England against Canada.

The New Zealand game was disappointingly one-sided. The Black Ferns had scored 21 tries and conceded just one going into the game and their momentum was just unstoppable. Marsh scored her fifth of the tournament from full-back within a minute. Though France got one back quickly – it was 15-5 after ten minutes – Huriana Manuel was especially good in the centre and the match ended 40-10 with New Zealand safely into another final.

The England v Canada game had much more drama. Though Canada began the tournament badly, they had improved considerably. Backed by a small but vocal home crowd, they were confident this could be close.

England started well when a Catherine Spencer early break led to a try for Charlotte Barras. Karen Andrew made it 8-0 and England looked to be gaining the upper hand. Heather Moyse staged a vital defensive intervention when Kim Shaylor was prevented from scoring another and then it was Moyse's turn to cause trouble for England when her brilliant break in the second half led to a try from Julie Foster.

Barras grabbed her second followed by Moyse again with a great finish to keep Canada in the game. It was now 20-14 and Canada were pushing late on to get the converted try they needed to win.

Moyse was now a danger every time she got the ball. With 79 minutes played she broke into space and looked like she was heading for the line. It took an incredible tackle from Kim Shaylor to stop her. Without her intervention England would have been playing for bronze, but they managed to see out the final minute.

The final itself was played in the Commonwealth Stadium, a magnificent arena, but, with a capacity of just under 60,000 and a crowd of just a few thousand, it looked empty as England and New Zealand played out a fantastic 80 minutes.

England dominated possession in the first half but were 10-3 down at half-time. The New Zealand points came after a brilliant finish from Monalisa Codling, who latched onto a kick from Amiria Marsh, and a conversion and penalty by Emma Jensen. Karen Andrew kicked England's points.

New Zealand then dealt England a hammer blow, scoring almost immediately after the kick-off in the second half when flying wing Stephanie Mortimer scored straight after the break. A penalty try, a touchdown by Helen Clayton and Shelley Rae's amazing conversion from the touchline with less than three minutes left closed the score to 20-17, but Amiria Marsh eluded England's desperate cover defence to claim the crucial score in the corner.

Emma Jensen missed the conversion, but it didn't matter. New Zealand were ahead 25-17. Within seconds, the celebrations were underway for the Black Ferns. They had achieved a 14th straight World Cup match victory and a third world crown to send captain Farah Palmer into retirement with. England rued their inability to convert their early dominance into points.

The final itself was an enthralling contest, well worth watching on YouTube for the sheer physical nature of the contact and the skill in which some of the tries were scored out wide. It was no consolation to England afterwards that the media widely described the game as the best women's rugby game in history. The year would end, as so many World Cup years had, with New Zealand champions again.

Sevens gets serious

The IRB published a new strategic plan after the 2006 World Cup, coinciding with a raft of global developments in the women's game. Now desperate to accelerate women's sevens so another Olympic bid could be tabled, this time for Rio in 2016, the IRB announced that women would be included in the World Cup Sevens for the first time alongside the 2009 men's competition in Dubai. Sixteen teams would be able to take part.

The news meant there would be some significant decisions for the world's leading women's nations to take. Throw the kitchen sink at sevens, straddle your best players across the two formats or keep going with 15s on its own and run a standalone pathway for sevens?

For other countries, the news marked the first serious jumping-off point for plans and investment in their women's game. Fiji immediately formed a women's rugby union (the FWRU) with the primary intention of competing in Dubai. It was a significant step forward given how New Zealand had totally dominated women's rugby in the Oceania region, though Australia were on the verge of making their mark.

It also forced leading rugby nations like New Zealand to take investment in the women's game seriously. An IRB directive determined that the World Cup should be properly prepared for, with likely investment from new sources if the sport was to be included in the Olympics. The NZR had chronically underinvested in women's rugby, seeing it as a drain on financial resources and having little external pressure to change things given how the Black Ferns seemed to win everything regardless.

It was to be England's year again in the 2007 Six Nations, though Ireland's progress continued. Italy, in their debut year, unsurprisingly struggled.

England trounced Scotland 60-0 in the opener before Wales snuck past Ireland 10-5 and France welcomed Italy to the competition with a 17-37 win. The Irish continued to show progress, narrowly losing 10-13 to France at home. England were back at Twickenham, this time facing an improved Italian team who lost, but only 23-0.

Back-to-back wins for Ireland followed – over Scotland and Italy – handing them their best table finish of fourth. But with England irrepressible, the grand slam title was theirs again.

The 2007 championship was notable for the handful of players who made record-breaking appearances.

Scotland's Donna Kennedy became the first women's player in the world to win 100 caps and Wales star Louise Rickard wrote her name into the history books by becoming Welsh rugby's most-capped player with her 93rd appearance in their 24-0 defeat of Italy in Rome. Another Welsh player, Liza Burgess, continued to defy time. She played in the championship some 20 years after captaining the first ever Welsh team against England.

It would also prove a landmark year for Wales off the field as the WWRU fully merged with the Welsh Rugby Union, who took over the running of the women and girls' game from the grassroots to elite.

In further indication that the game was being given a bigger platform, the IRB hosted a major conference in London sandwiched between the Six Nations and that summer's European Championship. Its remit was to look at the development of the women's game overall. All 12 unions who had contested the World Cup and a number of developing nations were invited.

The conference explored all aspects of the women's game from the 2006 World Cup to regional tournaments, the strategic plan for women's rugby and the 2009 World Cup Sevens in Dubai.

After several years of low-key tournaments with the major nations absent, the European Championship returned in 2007 with its largest ever numbers. Sixteen teams competed in two pools, including four Six Nations countries, plus Spain. England and France were again represented by 'A' teams and Wales sent a development squad. Pool B was also of interest with four nations making their 15-a-side debuts: Finland, Luxembourg, Romania and Serbia.

England and France both started well, with two victories in their respective pools. England, coached by former Welsh player Amanda Bennett, were relatively untroubled, beating Russia 62-0 and Italy 41-11. France had a slightly tougher time of it, first seeing off Sweden 12-0 and then beating the Netherlands 27-8.

England booked their place in the final after a brilliant game with hosts Spain ended in a 22-22 draw. They were set to face France, who had edged Wales. The final was exciting, with England winning it thanks in part to two tries from captain and prop Rochelle Clark in Madrid.

France led 12-7 at half-time with Clark's try sandwiched between a brace of tries by full-back Aurélie Groiseleau, the first from 30 metres out and the second after a clearance kick from newcomer Katy Daley-Mclean (née Mclean) failed to find touch. But there was to be no victory for the French. Tries from Georgina Roberts, Clark and Claire Allan saw England recover to be crowned European champions.

Hosts Spain ended up third with a 37-0 defeat of the Netherlands in the third-place play-off, scoring seven tries in the process through Bárbara Plà, Isabel Rodríguez, Paila Medín, Berta García and Agurtzane Obregozo. Inés Etxegibel converted one of them.

As one European competition ended, another would soon get underway with the next edition of the European Sevens Championship in France. It took on even more importance this time with the prospect of the World Cup Sevens on the horizon. Regional sevens competitions were being taken more seriously and more top players and teams than ever before were involved.

The championship began with 12 teams each contesting the Division A and Division B tournaments over the two previous weekends in Croatia and Bosnia respectively highlighting the massive growth of the short form of the game across emerging rugby nations.

The top ten sides then met in France. The hosts were the eventual winners, beating England in the final. The 19-5 final victory was, in fact, France's second over England on the same day. The two sides had met in the last round of pool matches in the morning, with the hosts running out 15-12 winners to top the pool. It was England's second successive final loss in the competition following their 10-7 loss to Wales in 2006.

As the summer ended, there was major news for the grassroots women and girls' game in England when the RFUW announced it had been awarded £1.4m of funding from Sport England. The investment was to be spent on supporting club and coach development and would allow the RFUW to appoint ten new club and coach officers across the country to improve standards.

There was a common misconception among opposition international teams that the English players were professional and that it was impossible, and often unfair, to be expected to compete with them.

While it's true that England were better resourced than other teams and National Lottery funding supported players, particularly close to major competitions, the reality was that the RFUW, then led by Rosie Williams, were simply very well organised. Though they were supported by the RFU, their relative independence meant they were well placed to apply for and secure standalone investment for the game. Numbers at grassroots level continued to soar.

Now there are few standalone organisations running women's rugby. The game is run almost fully within IRB (now World Rugby) and recognised national governing bodies, but in those early years the separation between women's and men's unions often proved beneficial. There are many who bemoan that they jumped too soon.

Wales is a case in point. When it moved under the banner of the Welsh Rugby Union (WRU), Wales were on the up and on the verge of breaking through, going on to win a historic triple crown in 2009 on the back of a European Sevens win. Within a few years, their results were spiralling, their development team was scrapped, their U20 team no longer existed and they failed to capitalise on their progress at sevens.

Former player Gemma Hallett, part of the 2009 team, became a vocal activist, accusing the WRU of being an 'old boys club' and of mismanaging the women's game.

In an impassioned blog posted after another disappointing Six Nations in 2020 she said:

I believe the WRU has failed its women players. There's no doubt the girls playing in this year's Six Nations tournament (and every campaign before it) have done so with utter commitment, professionalism and a total desire to perform and win.

Unfortunately, these players are a product of their current environment developed by the WRU and the environment has failed them.

In 2008, the Welsh Women's Rugby Union was moved from being an associate member of the WRU run by its own executive committee to be embedded fully into the Union. We were moving, or so we thought, towards a promising future that would gain equality, grow the game and raise standards.

In 2013, the global buzz of rugby sevens becoming the game almost saw us lose our 15s team altogether but there was no structure in place and far too much resistance.

Seven years later and while the WRU has well and truly missed the curve on this one, they still dither and talk of targeting a World Series position.

The WRU, for their part, pointed to the growth of the grassroots game in recent years in Wales and a strategic focus on sevens. In response to continuing pressure, the WRU recently announced new investment, including contracts, into its national programme.

The reality is that while merging with their national unions ultimately became essential for the largely amateur bodies running women's rugby, the women's game would cease to be run by those who understood it inside out. It led to sharp growing pains and public flare-ups, as happened most dramatically in Ireland in 2012 thanks to a disastrous trip to France, in 2017 after their poor World Cup and in 2021 after their failure to qualify for the Olympics or World Cup.

In Asia, where the game was starting to take hold, 2007 ended with Kazakhstan beating China 34-5 in the final of the Asian Rugby Football Union Women's Championship.

The title was not a surprise. More than half of Kazakhstan's squad had played at the World Cup in Canada and they had a couple of standout players including flanker Anna Yakovleva and Anastassiya Khamova. China would shortly switch their focus almost entirely to the sevens game.

Canada, who came fourth at their own World Cup the year before, played a handful of Tests against the USA and ended the year with a two-Test tour of Scotland, winning both. The tourists featured impressive players like Jen Kish and Mandy Marchak, both of whom were on the verge of becoming big-name sevens players.

Peaceful coexistence

The international women's game was now beginning to split in two directions. Investment and interest in the sevens game, thanks to its own World Cup and the possibility of the Olympics sat alongside, were competing with the growth of the 15-a-side game.

The qualification path for Dubai brought an immediately obvious upside. Countries that had shown minimal interest in the women's game were now emerging. Unlike the 15s World Cup, there would be no automatic qualifiers. All national teams would have to qualify via regional tournaments.

And, unlike the men's tournament, the Arabian Gulf did not pre-qualify as hosts. The qualification process allocated two slots for Africa, two for North America/West Indies, one for South America, three for Asia, six for Europe and two for Oceania.

The South American qualifiers were first out of the blocks in January 2008. While the women's game had a foothold in the region – the South American Sevens Championships had been up and running since 2004 – the prospect of the World Cup gave it extra momentum with the 2008 event doubling up as a qualifier.

Brazil had already won three regional titles and went into the competition, which also featured Colombia, Venezuela, hosts Uruguay, Peru, Paraguay and Chile, as firm favourites. They breezed through the competition and made history by becoming the first side to qualify.

Australia were next to get up and running, getting their first ever international sevens team together for training to prepare for their qualifiers in Samoa later that summer. That event involved nations from across the Oceania region, including Australia, New Zealand, Samoa and Fiji, with just two advancing to the World Cup.

The Australian management scouted far and wide for talent, inviting several national touch rugby players to be part of their squad, recognising that talent transfer in sevens would be likely swifter than the 15s game and tapping into the pool of exceptionally skilled athletes across similar disciplines. It would later prove an inspired choice. Players like Bo de la Cruz and Nicole Beck, both ex-touch rugby players, enjoyed immediate success.

While much of the world was focusing on sevens, Europe's leading teams were preparing once again for the Six Nations. No team had ever won three grand slams in a row, but England were well placed to do it having been building impressive strength in depth and transitioning to new head coach Gary Street and captain Catherine Spencer.

Though England would indeed come out on top, the tournament was really about what happened beneath them. Ireland continued to build and Scotland continued to decline. The Scots' tournament came to a disappointing end with a loss to an Italian team who were still acclimatising to life at the top table.

France, on paper a match for England, were equally disappointing. They went down to their largest home defeat to England before losing to Wales for the second time in three years. Their final result was third place. Wales recovered from an English hammering in their opener to finish in a well-deserved runners-up position once again.

England kicked it all off with that 55-0 win over Wales, Claire Allan grabbing three in Cardiff and handing Gary Street the perfect start in charge. The game was played alongside an U20 match which England also won with a promising young player called Natasha Hunt also getting a hat-trick.

Ireland opened with a 19-0 over Italy, while France were comfortable against Scotland, winning 43-15 with Céline Allainmat scoring two tries.

England were rampant in Rome the following weekend, winning 76-6 to make it 131 points in two games, though Italy had bravely taken the lead through a rare women's rugby drop goal, this one from fly-half Veronica Schiavon.

They would face France next in what was fast becoming the annual championship decider. France had just beaten Ireland 26-17 and Wales had bounced back from their first-round hammering impressively, beating Scotland 23-6 in a game where Louise Rickard would score two tries in her 97th Test match.

Spain, now out of the competition, did see some action on the same weekend, losing 22-5 to England 'A'. Lía Bailán scored but Spain succumbed to a strong young English side. High-quality games would be harder for the Spanish to come by in the years ahead as the disappearance of 'A' teams and the formalising of the new Six Nations structure made it nigh on impossible to find top sides to play regularly.

Away from home, a brilliant England performance against France was enough to suggest that the grand slam would be theirs with a record 0-31 win. Claire Allan scored early, kicking off a game that would be relatively one-way traffic. Just Scotland and Ireland now stood in England's way for a historic return.

Scotland lost to Ireland despite leading 0-3 at half-time through Sarah Gill, going down 13-3 thanks to tries for Joanne O'Sullivan and captain Sarahjane Belton. Wales continued to build impressively with a 27-5 win over the Italians.

England were 34-5 winners over Scotland next out, the Scots putting in a decent performance. Heather Lockhart became the first team to breach England's try line so far in the championship. Wales remained on a collision course with France for second place, coming from being behind 10-3 to Ireland, who scored through Joy Neville and Marie Barrett. The Welsh team rallied with another try from Louise Rickard and fine kicking from Non Evans. It was confirmed that Wales and France would square off for second after the French team recorded a 35-6 win over Italy thanks to impressive performances from Caroline Ladagnous and captain Estelle Sartini.

It was set up for an exciting finale. England would host Ireland seeking a grand slam, Wales and France would clash for second spot, while Italy and Scotland would be aiming to avoid the wooden spoon.

It was a landmark weekend.

England grabbed the headlines thanks to a 17-7 win over Ireland in Sunbury. The Irish made Gary Street's team work incredibly hard for every point. When Claire Allan scored in the first minute it seemed like it would be an easy home win, but England led just 10-0 at the break after rising star Katy Daley-Mclean, who had burst onto the Test scene the year before, added a penalty.

England only stretched further ahead in the last ten minutes when Sarah Beale scored and Alice Richardson converted, but Ireland wouldn't leave empty-handed, crashing over late on through Yvonne Nolan.

Down at Taffs Well, a tight game was playing out. There was no free-flowing rugby at this one. Michaela Reed kicked the only points of a 3-0 Welsh win, handing them a second-place table finish for the second time in four years. Wales also fielded their first U20 team. The immediate future seemed bright.

At the other end of the table there was delight for Italy, grabbing their first win in the championship. This one had plenty of tries, Italy winning it 31-10. A converted try and two penalties from fly-half Veronica Schiavon and another try from Flavia Severin saw Italy race into a lead. Though Jilly McCord scored for Scotland, it was nowhere near enough and their 2008 Six Nations ended in disappointment.

Dreaming of Dubai

The World Cup Sevens was now just over a year away and though no nation had any sort of settled sevens pathway, plans were being quickly assembled for qualifiers and preparation tournaments.

England announced that they would face New Zealand in a one-off game alongside the men's London Sevens event in the summer. It was part of their build-up for the 2008 European Sevens Championship, which would determine the six sides who would qualify from the region for the World Cup Sevens. The summer's other qualifying tournament was in Oceania. All the rest would take place later in the year.

European sides headed en masse to the Amsterdam Sevens in May, another opportunity to try out players at a decent international level. England, France, Spain, Sweden, Ireland, Scotland, the Netherlands and Wales were among the teams involved.

So few sides had dedicated sevens players that the teams were made up primarily of the best and most likely candidates from the Test 15s team. It was clear that coaches and management were going to have to make tough choices about who played what to get a better understanding of the ability of leading players to criss-cross the international sevens and 15s arena.

The teams who did best in the long term were those that decided early on to operate almost fully separate playing pools, crossing over only at major events like World Cups. But, as the 2009 World Cup approached, most nations neither had the investment nor the talent pool to do so.

One of the few that did was England. As they were winning the sevens title in Amsterdam, another England squad was cruising through the FIRA European Championship in 15s, also being held in the area. The competition hosted both first and second tiers of the championship in the same country, with the top sides being placed in Pool A and the second sides in Pool B.

England were too good in Pool A, comfortably winning their way through to the final where they played Wales – a clash between the top two ranked sides in Europe at the time. It was tight. England won 12-6 thanks to the boot of Katy Daley-Mclean, while Non Evans contributed the Welsh points. Ireland finished third thanks to a thrilling 22-22 draw with France, while in Pool B, Russia finished on top ahead of the likes of Germany, Finland and Romania.

In a pattern that was becoming familiar, the action then tracked back to sevens. England faced the New Zealand Aotearoa Maori at Twickenham in an exhibition game and won 14-10 against a Kiwi team featuring the likes of Anna Richards and Selicia Winiata. England's winning score came from Gemma Sharples.

The summer would belong to the 15s game, though. England were set to host the Nations Cup for the first time, welcoming Canada and the USA, though the organisers had hoped to include France and Wales too. There would also be an U20 tournament featuring Canada, England and Wales.

England dominated both tournaments, first winning the U20 title with a side featuring rising stars including Emily Scarratt and Natasha Hunt and coached by former World Cup winner Giselle Mather.

Africa rises

Though South Africa was undoubtedly the continent's leading women's Test team, the arrival of the World Cup Sevens and the possibility of an Olympics helped to grow the African game steadily from the late 1990s on.

There was already regular 15s action between Kenya and Uganda since the two sides played annual Tests as part of the Elgon Cup. The competition was normally played over two legs, one in each country, though finances have often dictated its regularity. Uganda won the inaugural women's title in 2006 before it was cancelled in 2007. It returned in the summer of 2008 with renewed impetus, given many of the players were hoping to feature in the World Cup Sevens qualifiers taking place later in the year.

The games were pleasingly tight. It opened with an 18-7 win for Uganda, the 'Lady Cranes', thanks to scores from Fortunate Irankunda, Rachel Kakaire and Asha Sonko, Kenya's only score coming from a penalty try. The return leg brought a win for the Kenyans, but the 15-13 result still handed the title to Uganda on points difference.

South Africa were slow to get out of the blocks, struggling to find a way to capitalise on the momentum behind rugby as a sport in the country overall, but they highlighted some strategic planning with the formation of an U20 team to play a game against the USA, just a couple of years after featuring on the global stage for the first time at the World Cup. The idea was that the 2008 U20 team would form the core of a side to play at the 2010 World Cup, though in reality they would only play a handful of times over the next few years.

With Brazil already qualified for the World Cup, Africa's qualifiers, from which two sides would go through, were held that September in Kampala. Seven national teams plus one invitational side met for the competition. South Africa won outright with Uganda qualifying by virtue of finishing runners-up. Kenya finished third with Tunisia fourth.

The two sides would join Brazil in Dubai. Next to earn their tickets were England, the Netherlands, Spain, Russia, France and Italy, who were all about to qualify through the European Sevens held in June in France.

The European qualifiers were split across a number of events, with 33 teams all involved in the effort to get to Dubai. The main event was the final 16-team competition from which six teams would progress.

France, England, Spain, Wales, Italy, Netherlands, Sweden, Russia and Portugal were all in attendance. Joining them were Romania, Finland, Israel, Germany, Moldova and Andorra, who had battled through various other competitions across Europe earlier in the year to make it. The Czech Republic took the place of Scotland, who pulled out.

England were clear favourites, having decided to prioritise the World Cup Sevens over the Test 15s game for a year, something that would contribute to them losing to Wales for the first time the year after in the Six Nations. France too were dedicating more and more resources to sevens. They would have a poor 2009 Six Nations on the back of that decision with their worst ever finish.

Australia and New Zealand also safely made it through, guaranteed a place thanks to coming through the Oceania competition a few months before. There, Australia, New Zealand, Samoa, Fiji and Niue had competed in a tournament played alongside the men's qualifiers in Apia Samoa.

While there was no surprise at the two sides who emerged as the victorious qualifiers, Australia's performances laid down a marker that they would be serious World Cup Sevens threats with their first ever wins over New Zealand. They beat them twice over the two days of the competition, 15-5 during the pool stages and then 22-15 in a tight final.

They had to come from behind in the decider after Selicia Winata scored. Debby Hodgkinson levelled it up. She then set up a score for Ruan Sims but New Zealand's Victoria Grant made it 10-10 going into the break. Sims and Grant would score again to keep it neck and neck before the brilliant Nicole Beck raced away for the win.

Australia's policy of scouting for talent across a variety of sports would pay off.

The influx of players bringing experience from elsewhere into the squad added competition for places and they had no fear of New Zealand, who, despite losing twice, were still most people's favourites for the World Cup, though England were touted too.

In a North America and West Indies qualifier, Canada and the USA came through as expected, winning the regional qualifying event in the Bahamas ahead of Trinidad and Tobago, Guyana, Jamaica, Barbados and the Cayman Islands. Canada won the final 14-19.

Finally there was Asia, where nine women's Test sides would compete alongside the men in Hong Kong to contest their three allocated slots. With Kazakhstan having been crowned Asian 15s champions earlier in the year, they were expected to qualify alongside Japan and China. But out of nowhere came Thailand, who prior to the competition had barely registered in rugby terms at this level. They produced a huge shock to qualify ahead of Kazakhstan.

The Kazakhs and China were expected to meet in the final but Japan and Thailand upset the formbook, Japan edging Kazakhstan 5–0 in their semi and Thailand beating China 14–7 in an equally tough last-four match.

Japan won a tight final 17-12. In the crucial play-off for the third qualifying spot, China beat Kazakhstan 17-5 to join Japan and Thailand in the 16-team draw. The full list of teams was now complete.

All that was left was for those sides to take part in as many build-up competitions as possible and for decisions to be taken by leading 15s nations about how to marry the two disciplines and manage their players to be competitive in both.

Unsurprisingly, 2009 proved another seminal year for the game.

Chapter Eight

No going back

FOR AUSTRALIA, one of the upshots of their successes over the New Zealand sevens team in the summer was that, as well as finally getting a results monkey off their back, the players who had been involved in the qualifiers came back into the 15s programme fitter and stronger than ever before.

A 15s Test series was about to be held in Australia for the first time since 1998. The sides would compete for the Laurie O'Reilly Memorial Trophy. New Zealand had won it handily the year before with 21-10 and 29-12 victories.

The new-look Wallaroos squad included nine players from the summer's sevens wins over New Zealand. With an average age of 23, they were surely better placed than ever to compete against the team that had so far proved too experienced and too good at this level.

New Zealand were blooding players too, bringing newcomers like Selicia Winata and Stephanie Te Ohaere-Fox into a squad captained by the experienced Melissa Ruscoe. Half of the players had won the World Cup in 2006 but all signs pointed to a series that might be much closer between the sides than ever before.

The first game was disappointing as a contest. New Zealand were far too good and won it 37-3, but the time together over the days between the two games helped the hosts to gel. The second Test was much better. The Black Ferns triumphed 22-16 but not before a proper challenge.

The gap between New Zealand and the rest was closing, but only ever so slightly.

Australia had, however, found their feet at international level. Through sevens, they had seemingly found a route to being successful at the very top of the sport. They were unearthing and developing some outstanding athletes.

Debby Hodgkinson had been part of the Wallaroos for a number of years but her power on the sevens field was highly impressive. Within a year she would become the most decorated player in women's rugby, winning accolades including the IRB Women's Personality of the Year, Australia's best sevens player and player of the tournament at the World Cup Sevens.

All that was to come. For now, as 2008 came to a close, there was one more important off-field development. The IRB appointed its first ever Women's Development Manager. Su Carty, a former president of the IWRFU, was hired to work with member unions to grow their women's games at a time when the IRB estimated there were around 200,0000 registered players worldwide.

While the appointment was welcome, the fact that it took the IRB well over a decade from organising their first women's rugby World Cup to appointing someone internally to focus solely on the women's game, was an indication that though progress was being made, the pace of change was at times glacial.

Game adjusts to a new era

With the 16 sides now determined for the World Cup Sevens, decisions had to be made by those nations who planned to run programmes for their top players in 15s. What was the best way forward?

With England and France juggling players who were also due to play sevens in Dubai in March, the Six Nations was primed for upsets. Dramatic results duly came in the opening rounds of the tournament.

Ireland had never beaten France when they welcomed them to Ashbourne on a bitterly cold night in front of 3,000 enthusiastic fans. A tense first half saw no score at all but France, missing a handful of regular backs who were involved in sevens preparations, grabbed a score early in the second half when some fine mauling up front made space for Cathy Langenfeld in the corner.

Ireland, without the strength in depth of many Test sides, had been developing a squad backboned by real togetherness. Players like Niamh Briggs, Fiona Coghlan, Lynne Cantwell, Tania Rosser and Joy Neville came up through the ranks at the same time and were starting to look like seasoned Test stars.

The Irish pack got them back into the match, mauling their way through multiple phases. Fiona Coghlan crashed over and Niamh Briggs converted to give them a 7-5 lead. Caroline Ladagnous missed a long-range penalty in the dying moments, handing Ireland their first ever win over the French and sending the vocal Irish crowd into overdrive on the sideline.

England started with a business-as-usual big score over Italy, winning 69-13 with Fiona Pocock grabbing three and Emily Scarratt two. Wales put Scotland to the sword 31-10, Non Evans taking 16 points from her boot.

Though England were also without World Cup Sevens players for some games, their pack was formidable. No one seriously expected them to lose their first game since the 2006 World Cup Final down at Taffs Well. But Evans had been kicking superbly for the Welsh and her boot would be at the fore to help her team to a first ever win over England.

She opened proceedings with an early penalty to give Wales a 3-0 lead but England scored against the run of play when wing Pocock intercepted a pass to race to the try line. Katy Daley-Mclean added the extras. Mel Berry, who had thrown the intercepted pass, soon made up for it. She took a fast penalty close to the England line and dived over for a try, but Emily Scarratt put the visitors 12-8 ahead just before the break.

Evans missed two kicks at goal but Wales were boosted when Scarratt was sin-binned for a professional foul. Eventually the pressure told as Wales made use of the spaces out wide to send replacement winger Aimee Young over in the corner for an unconverted try.

England looked to have snatched the win in the last minute when Daley-Mclean sent a penalty through the posts, but Wales worked their way back upfield, winning a penalty which Evans duly slotted to end 22 years of losses to England.

Evans spoke emotionally after the game about what the win meant:

> If I hadn't kicked that last penalty, I would have considered retiring.
>
> I missed a few during the match, but I would never have forgiven myself if I hadn't made sure of that last one.
>
> I've been playing for Wales since 1996 and we've never come that close to beating them before. We felt really confident coming into the match and a few of the senior players said to each other 'it's now or never'.
>
> This win puts us in a good table position, now we want to build on that by beating France away from home in two weeks' time.

Ireland carried on their good form with a 17-35 win over Italy. France beat Scotland 25-12, the game notable for a standout try-scoring effort from Lucy Millard who was fast becoming one of the best centres in the tournament.

The Irish and Welsh winning runs would come to a halt in round three, however.

Though Ireland had never beaten England, there was some pressure on Gary Street's team after the loss to Wales. Ireland started brilliantly when Niamh Briggs, a converted Gaelic footballer, kicked a penalty. Winger Amy Davis gave the Irish a 10-0 lead after a great break from Joy Neville from the base of a scrum.

With England losing Amy Garnett to the sin bin, a huge upset looked on, but England stayed composed and Emily Scarratt raced over to reduce the arrears to 13-5 at the break. A fitter and stronger England team went on to dominate the second half. Centre Alice Richardson's passing was prominent and she set up Alex Matthews for an early try, with the same player scoring again to help England into a 17-13 lead. From there it was all England. Catherine Spencer scored and Fiona Pocock latched onto another Richardson pass to secure a 29-13 win.

Wales were now the only unbeaten team left in the competition, but France put paid to that at home, beating them 27-5 and ending their hopes of a grand slam title thanks to scores from Clotilde Flaugére and Laetitia Salles. Scotland, meanwhile, did their hopes of avoiding a wooden spoon the power of good with a narrow 13-10 win over Italy. Tanya Griffiths got two tries for the Scots.

The match that really mattered for the destination of the title would be England v France in the next round, as ever. In the end it was something of a disappointment for anyone hoping for a close score. England were in total control at Old Deer Park in west London with a 52-7 win.

The result did mean there was a chance the title could go to Ireland and Wales on the last day – Ireland beat Scotland and Wales beat Italy in the fourth round – but in reality the title was England's due to their superior points difference. England duly wrapped it up with a massive 72-3 win over Scotland, winning their fourth title in a row.

Wales ended the tournament with a triple crown, their first, thanks to a 13-10 win over Ireland. They finished second in the table, just ahead of the Irish, who also recorded their best finish. France, after a poor championship, squeaked past Italy 10-14. Fourth place was their lowest finish. The competition had thrown up plenty of surprises.

Despite the loss to Wales in round one, England captain Catherine Spencer said winning the championship in 2009 meant a hell of a lot in her book *Mud, Maul, Mascara*:

> It meant more to me at the time than any other of my six tournament wins. Of the six, it was the only one that was not a grand slam. It means so much because we nearly lost it. Nearly losing something really does help to make you understand whether you really want it.

With an exciting Six Nations ending, developments came off the pitch too.

England were announced as the hosts of the 2010 World Cup beating interest from other countries including Germany, South Africa and Kazakhstan. While the World Cups in Amsterdam (1998), Barcelona (2002) and Edmonton (2006) had been a modest success, they were peculiar places to host major rugby events, especially for a growing part of the game.

The change of strategy from the IRB for 2010 was welcome and vindicated when England not only hosted the best World Cup yet but set a blueprint for all the World Cups since.

For now, there were qualifiers and warm-up games to be played.

As part of their World Cup build-up, the Black Ferns announced that they would be heading to England for the first time later that year, for the first Tests between the teams since

2006. New Zealand had only played four Tests in the three years since. All were against Australia. The New Zealand players had begun to become frustrated by the lack of investment in a Test schedule. England, still their main rivals, had played handfuls of games by comparison.

The RFU recognised the importance of assessing their team's progress against New Zealand and the 2009 tour was largely funded by them, not the NZR. The English union funded the Black Ferns' trip again in 2011 before paying for England to travel to the other side of the world in 2012.

As one former Black Fern told me:

> England kept New Zealand women's rugby afloat in that era. We have a lot to thank the RFU for, when our own union refused to put their hands in their pocket, able to get away without too much backlash despite, or maybe even because of, our success.

That lack of investment would eventually catch up with the brilliant Black Ferns. But not yet.

History made at the first World Cup Sevens

Overlapping with the 2009 Six Nations, 16 women's teams headed to Dubai in March to take part in the first ever World Cup Sevens. It's hard to quantify just how important this event was to the IRB.

Having been twice rejected by the IOC for a place in the Olympics, everything was thrown at Dubai to show that rugby sevens, with a burgeoning men's and women's competitive scene, was ideal for the Rio de Janeiro Games. With Sweden's highly influential IOC member Gunilla Lindberg leading a commission to attend the World Cup in Dubai, everything needed to go well, from the standards on the field to the operation off it.

The IOC would be thorough in their due diligence, probing the IRB's governance models and their investment model and pushing them as to what rugby could really add to the Olympic schedule that wasn't already there. The IRB also had to show that the World Cup Sevens was not a one-off. If sevens made it into the Olympics there would need to be a sustainable path for the sport to develop, especially for women. That required them to invest heavily in the years ahead in the women's World Sevens Series, a commitment maintained to this day.

Lindberg could hardly have attended a better event.

The results in the men's competition were wild. All the big guns were knocked out before Wales won a thrilling and shock title. The women's competition was enthralling too, the final going into extra time, where a golden score would win it.

With no world rankings system, there was no scientific way of telling who should have been favourites going into the women's competition but England, having won their last six tournaments, were up there. New Zealand were also just simply expected to be brilliant – they always were – and Australia had laid down a marker the year before by beating them.

As the women's game was opening its eyes to sevens on the world stage, a truism of the shorter form of the sport was becoming clearer. With so few players on the field and so little time on the clock, anything could happen. The game could turn on a bounce.

The format of the World Cup Sevens was simple enough: four pools of four, with the top two in each advancing to the quarter-finals. The pool rounds all went to form, France and Australia emerging from Pool A, England and the USA from Pool B, Spain and Canada from Pool C and New Zealand and South Africa from Pool D.

The knockouts were where it got truly exciting. The USA dispatched France, who had been beaten by the Netherlands in the pool stages, in a relatively routine 19-0 win. Tries were scored by Jessica Watkins and Christy Ringgenberg. New Zealand saw off Canada 33-12 with the Black Ferns team starring Carla Hohepa, who was a huge threat in space, and Linda Itunu, who brought the power in the tight exchanges. South Africa snuck past Spain 15-7 before the first upset. England went down to Australia.

The match was hotly anticipated. Australia had done well in the pool stages but had dropped a game to France. An exciting England team captained by the experienced Sue Day had high expectations given their form going into the event.

Since their wins over New Zealand in Samoa in the qualifiers though, women's sevens had quietly been stepped up in Australia. Though they weren't playing as regularly as England, coaches were given funding to help prepare the nation's top players. They had developed as a close-knit group.

They went into the England game somewhat apprehensively. Their loss to France had knocked their confidence, with Selena Worsley, who carried on playing through to the final despite dislocating her shoulder in the pool game against China, reflecting afterwards to me:

> When we lost to France, we were then put up against England in the quarter-final, and we knew that that was not a good thing! There was massive disappointment after the pool loss. Our coach asked us why everyone was gloomy, and we said well we didn't want to face England. He gave us a different perspective. He said he was glad; he'd come here for us to be the best, so we'd have to beat the best. He was right. We said bring it on – here's our opportunity.

The match was tight. England grabbed an early try. Heather Fisher thought she'd scored again, only for England to be pulled back for a penalty. The game, as so often happens in sevens, turned on its head. Australia were extremely physical and a late try by Rebecca Tavo won it 17-10 for them, leaving England devastated and the Aussies through to face South Africa.

The tight nature of the games carried on into the semi-finals. New Zealand had a tough time over the USA, squeaking into the final in front of a massive crowd to secure their place in the final game. The USA were hardly a surprise package. They had always had exceptional athletes and the sevens game was likely to suit the pace and power at which they liked to play, but this was tighter than anyone expected.

Huriana Manuel put the Kiwis in front early on before Christy Ringgenberg made space for Amy Daniels to score. New Zealand scored again just after the second half and despite a late US score, it ended 12-14. South Africa had enjoyed a great tournament and Australia's place in the final was by no means a given. Their semi was exciting too, with the Springboks eventually succumbing 10-17.

By the time the final match came around, the stadium was full. Over 40,000 people were ready to watch the first ever women's World Cup Sevens final. In the crowd were members of the IOC, ready to witness an exhilarating and exhausting game between two huge rivals.

New Zealand were expected to win. They had all the experience on the big stage, albeit in 15s, but Australia, drawn together from a raft of sports from touch rugby to netball to basketball alongside the core of experienced Wallaroos, were more than a match.

Led by the indomitable Cheryl Soon, Australia raced into the lead with tries to Nicole Beck and Debby Hodgkinson seeing them go 10-0 ahead. A yellow card for Rebecca Tavo helped New Zealand back into it, tying the game through scores from Justine Lavea and Carla Hohepa either side of half-time.

It remained that way to full time. Sudden-death extra time would decide who the inaugural winners would be.

With 36 seconds gone, New Zealand couldn't stop Shelly Matcham and she stretched over the line for a try that sealed a 15-10 victory and sparked jubilant scenes as Australia were crowned world sevens champions. Worsley picks up the story:

> It was so tight. Everyone on the field was so focused. You don't fall apart, you don't panic. At full time we were absolutely rooted because a few of us, Debby [Hodgkinson], myself and Alex [Hargreaves] had played every minute of that day and our job was to play direct to create space for the rest, so we were totally stuffed because of how we were playing up the guts and when the full-time whistle came, we just collapsed on the ground. Shezzy was brilliant as captain. We had a minute's break before extra time, and she was picking us up and shouting over the crowd that we'd got this.

> It is indescribable how that felt at the end of the whistle. It was euphoric. It was bizarre. The night we got back we went and hired a place down at Bondi beach and the whole team was there and it was brilliant. Unforgettable.

It could hardly have been a better showpiece for the watching Olympic committee members. The victorious captain Cheryl Soon was about to play an even bigger part later that year in securing rugby's place in the Olympics.

Back to 15s

Though the 15-a-side World Cup was only a year away, the qualifiers for the event were only just up and running as the Dubai tournament came to an end for the world's leading sevens players.

The pathways to qualification were not as open as the IRB had initially promised. When confirming England as hosts, the international federation said that there would be a global and expanded qualification process. However, when the full details were published in early 2009, it was clear that many nations would not have a chance to take part.

Qualification tournaments would take place in just two regions, Europe and Asia. In Oceania, two nations would play off in a single game for one place. Aside from that, the IRB would determine who else would qualify.

In Europe, England, France, Wales and Ireland were guaranteed a place by virtue of their Six Nations standings and previous finishes. Scotland had to fight it out with Spain, Italy, Germany, Russia, Netherlands, Belgium and Sweden for one of the two remaining places from the continent.

There were two qualifying pools. Scotland duly sealed their place, topping a pool that included Russia, the Netherlands and Belgium thanks to a final-round 38-18 win over the Dutch with Lucy Millard touching down for three tries. The Dutch failed to qualify despite the impact of Dutch winger Kelly van Harskamp, who scored seven tries in her team's 100-0 win over Belgium. Van Harskamp would go on to become a key name in the first professional Dutch sevens teams set up a few years later.

There was high drama to come in the other pool which featured Italy, Sweden, Spain and Germany. The pool was expected to come down to a shoot-out between Spain and Italy; one side with the benefit of recent Six Nations experience, the other still smarting from their exclusion.

Sweden had featured at the 1991, 1994 and 1988 World Cups but were not part of the 2002 and 2006 editions and had only played a handful of Tests in the years going into the qualifiers, which they would host – their first home games since 1997. They caused a huge upset on day one by beating

Italy 16-14, thanks to a try at the death from debutant Jennifer Lindholm, with star player and captain Ulrika Andersson-Hall also kicking two penalties.

Spain proved too strong for Germany in the other game on the opening day, scoring 11 tries to run out 74-0 winners. Back-row Bárbara Plà grabbed a hat-trick, setting up a winner-takes-all game against the Swedes. The crux game was hard-fought and exciting, with Sweden, the underdogs, showing that their win over Italy hadn't been a one-off. The vocal crowd in Enkoping were treated to another shock home win.

There had been little to separate the teams throughout and the score at half-time was 3-3. Ulrika Andersson-Hall kicked the hosts ahead with a 15th-minute penalty before Marina Bravo replied for Spain. Early pressure from Spain in the second half gave Bravo the chance to put her side ahead but the Spanish lost a player to the sin bin and Andersson-Hall added another penalty. Spain then lost Berta García to the sin bin and the pressure ultimately told, resulting in a try for Rebecka Lind and an 11-6 win to leave the hosts, quite literally, jumping for joy at the end of the game. Sweden were through.

Elsewhere, with the World Cup on the horizon, there was a busy international calendar for the sides planning to head to London the following summer. The most exciting development was perhaps the return of the Nations Cup in Canada featuring the hosts, England, South Africa and France.

Canada, fourth at the previous World Cup, were not shy about setting out their own ambitions. Scrum-half Laura Stoughton told the media beforehand that they didn't want to just compete at the World Cup but win it. Featuring the nations that finished second to fifth at the last World Cup plus Africa's strongest side, the Nations Cup promised to be a real test for everyone involved.

In the end England were too good, winning all their games, but there were some important pointers as to World

Cup form. South Africa were outclassed but not disgraced and the emergence of Zandile Nojoko gave them a fly-half of truly international class. Canada, going in with such high hopes, had a disappointing tournament, finishing fourth. They raced into a good lead against South Africa before falling away and lost to France.

France were good in patches, beating Canada and almost beating the USA. The Americans showed up very well. Having not won since 2006, they played well against England and beat South Africa and Canada before drawing with France.

England remained head and shoulders above everyone else, winning even when not at their best, and could take real momentum going into their two-Test series against New Zealand that summer. But before the arrival of the Black Ferns, there was other welcome development news.

Carol Isherwood entered the record books again, this time being appointed the first female official on the IRB's overall rugby committee. It was a shockingly late appointment in reality and highlighted just how male-dominated rugby's top table was, even in 2009. Isherwood would prove an inspired addition.

Further autumn Test games were confirmed to be played at major stadiums. France would play Canada at the Stade de France for the first time while England would play at Twickenham on the same weekend.

The World Cup qualifiers carried on too. Australia beat Samoa in a one-off Test to secure their spot. Kristy Giteau, the sister of Wallabies star Matt, made her debut. Kazakhstan became the twelfth and final team to qualify after an emphatic 43-5 defeat of Japan in the final of the four-team Asian tournament.

Kazakhstan had gone in as favourites and overwhelmed Hong Kong 58-14 to reach the winner-takes-all showdown with Japan in front of a big crowd which included former

Japanese Prime Minister Yoshiro Mori, who made the trip to Singapore to support his country's women and their dream of World Cup qualification.

Kazakhstan were ultimately too strong. The win meant that they would join three-time defending champions New Zealand, hosts and 2006 runners-up England, bronze medallists France, Canada, USA, South Africa, Wales, Ireland, Scotland, Sweden and Australia at the World Cup the following year.

Their qualification also ended a year of firsts for women's rugby in the region. Earlier that year the first women's international sides from Iran, India and Malaysia had taken to the field, competing in the Asian Sevens. Laos fielded a Test team at 15s for the first time and Cambodia were also fielding at the same level.

There was also a first in Africa in 2009. Egypt formed their first national sevens side and competed in the North West Africa Women's Rugby Sevens tournament in Ghana. The tournament, won by Tunisia who would compete at the next World Cup Sevens, included women's teams from Morocco, Ivory Coast, Nigeria, Togo, Burkina Faso, Egypt and hosts Ghana.

For Egypt, like many sides in Africa, there were massive challenges to overcome given the cultural barriers that sometimes made it impossible to accept women playing sports like rugby. Some players couldn't even play due to family restrictions, many were required to have a chaperone outside the family home and there were obvious financial restraints.

The year would end with top-quality Test 15s games and major news on the Olympic front.

With such a successful outing in Dubai, the ante was stepped up to persuade the IOC to choose rugby for the 2016 Games. In Lausanne in early summer, the IRB had delivered a successful presentation, supported by Cheryl Soon, Australia's impressive World Cup Sevens-winning captain. On the back of it, rugby sevens and golf were put forward as recommendations by the executive board to the IOC membership, ahead of squash, softball, baseball, roller sports and karate, with a final decision to be taken in Denmark later that year.

Soon was involved in Denmark again, alongside Kazakhstan captain Anastassiya Khamova. The IRB delivered a 20-minute presentation that helped secure a comprehensive 81-8 vote in favour of rugby's inclusion in the Olympics for the first time since 1924, when it had appeared as a men's 15s event.

The decision would change the face of women's rugby forever. New revenue streams would begin to fund professional women's international sevens teams and with a new World Sevens Series on the horizon, women's rugby standards would skyrocket by 2016.

That was all to come though. For now, there were important 15-a-side Tests to be played.

New Zealand's trip to England was highly anticipated in 2009.

They arrived in London having played just four Test games since winning the World Cup in 2006. England by contrast that year alone had played nine Test matches.

There would be a Test game at Esher, a game against England A at the same venue and a final Test game at Twickenham, where the match would be played after the men's England v All Blacks match.

The first two games were played in a four-day window. New Zealand once again defied their lack of Test practice and won both. The first was close, New Zealand winning it 16-3. The second, against England A, was a 48-3 rout. Players like Carla Hohepa and Kendra Cocksedge starred, while newcomer Kelly Brazier was impressive.

The game at Twickenham though was a different kettle of fish. England finally got one over on the Black Ferns, winning 10-3, just their second victory over their great rivals and a massive boost just a year out from their home World Cup. They did it in front of a good crowd too, some 12,000 people staying on after the men's game.

The Black Ferns took a 3-0 lead, but England then came alive. Catherine Spencer got a try after a neat pass from Katy Daley-Mclean, who also converted. It was the first try New Zealand had conceded on the tour so far. Emma Jensen had England scrambling from a quickly taken penalty, but with England starting to dominate up front with Spencer and Maggie Alphonsi making their mark, Daley-Mclean dropped a goal to make it 10-3. Fiao'o Fa'amausili ran hard for the visitors but England stood firm and, when Anika Tiplady missed a tough shot at goal, England held on for a rare win over the Black Ferns.

There would also be an upset in France, with Canada ending an 11-year losing streak against the French, having only ever beaten them once. The game was also notable for the debut of Andrea Burk, who played well at full-back. The teams played again at the Stade de France and France got their revenge, winning 22-0.

Wales, meanwhile, ended a great year on a high with a 56-7 victory over Sweden in Swansea. Non Evans scored 21 points in the nine-try win to help the year's triple crown winners on a comfortable afternoon.

Cuts and losses

There were several important milestones on the way to the World Cup.

The year 2010 started with a two-Test series between the USA and Canada in the Atlanta Cup in Florida. Canada won the first Test 18-8 having come from 8-0 down at half-time, while the USA snuck the second 10-11, Vanesha McGee scoring the winning try.

With five of the teams competing at the World Cup later that year and no clashing sevens commitments this time, the 2010 Six Nations would have even more importance attached.

After the frustration at their loss in Wales the year before, England were looking to exact revenge in round one. They got it with a clinical 31-0 win over the Welsh. Prop Catrin Edwards showed well for Wales but tries from Heather Fisher, Kat Merchant and the ever-impressive Emily Scarratt were enough to see them home.

Ireland beat Italy 22-5 but the story of the round was in Scotland, where Lucy Millard would help her team to a rare win over the French. Millard was player of the match, handing new coach Gary Parker a perfect start to his tenure.

The Scots couldn't keep the momentum going in round two against Wales, where France would also bounce back to beat Ireland and England would overcome Italy. The championship was once again heading for a final-round shoot-out between France and England. It would also bring a shock result for Wales against Italy.

The France v England game was a nail-biter. England won it away from home 10-11 to secure a grand slam. Amy Turner's try had given them a 5-3 half-time advantage and the home side had Claire Canal sent off on the half-hour mark. Despite their numerical advantage, England conceded a second-half try to Céline Allainmat that put France ahead 10-8 before Daley-Mclean kicked the final points of the game with a 64th-minute penalty.

Aurélie Bailon's last-minute 45-metre penalty fell just short of the posts as England held out to record a record-breaking fifth consecutive Championship title.

At the other end of the table, Wales were beaten by Italy, handing them the wooden spoon just a year after winning the triple crown.

The build-up to the World Cup ought to have shown women's rugby in its best light, but the financial disparities between the men's and women's games were instead brought into the public spotlight.

In New Zealand, there was dismay when the NZR announced they would axe the women's National Provincial Championships, a move publicly criticised by current and former Test players. New Zealand captain Melissa Ruscoe spoke out saying the decision was 'a kick in the guts' that would make it difficult for players to perform at the World Cup.

NZR general manager of professional rugby, Neil Sorensen, said that the women's provincial competition was not the only victim of necessary cost-cutting, as if it made it more acceptable for players heading into a World Cup year:

> The central funding for the women's competition has been removed for 2010, along with a bunch of other initiatives that we've cut for 2010, like the Junior All Blacks and participation in the Pacific Nations Cup.

Canada too were in financial strife, with players long having had to pay their own way to represent their country. Star player Heather Moyse had given the game a new spotlight after her successful turn at the Winter Olympics in the two-woman bobsled and the team's plea for financial backing burst into the media.

Writing for Scrumqueens.com at the time, former player Meghan Mutrie observed:

> Although the Canadian women are ten positions higher than their male counterparts on the IRB World Rankings, they receive limited funding because the IRB's financial commitment to each nation is dependent on where the international men's program places.
>
> Because of this, since the 2006 World Cup, the Canada women's rugby side has operated on a pay-to-play basis,

with each tour averaging a cost of $3,000 (£2,000) for each athlete. For players who have been on the roster for the past four years, the cost of representing their country (2–4 events per year) totals roughly $36,000 (£23,000). And that number is growing.

With two more events planned before the 2010 World Cup in August, the players will be asked to dig into their own pockets again, for at least another $6,000 (£4,000).

A planned tour to New Zealand had to be cancelled with neither nation now able to financially back its team and the Canadian team issued a public plea for support. The appeal went well and the team raised $150,000 towards their World Cup preparations, but it was a dire situation for one of the world's best teams to be in.

World Cup preparation carried on for others.

South Africa beat Kazakhstan in a one-off two-Test series in Dubai before following it up with an eye-catching win over Scotland. Canada and the USA played another Test series and there were training games between Ireland, England, Wales and Scotland.

A London World Cup was almost here.

Chapter Nine

A game-changer in London

HAVING LOST out to Edmonton in 2006, England – where the women's game was still run by the RFUW – were determined not only that they would host the World Cup in 2010, but that they would host a bigger, better and more player-centred tournament than ever before.

While many players found the experience of Edmonton improved on Barcelona, there was continued frustration at the strict criteria set out by the IRB about how host nations delivered the tournament, with much of it more suited to a professional sport rather than one still in its infancy.

The criteria, which included forcing the hosts to hold knockout games in national stadiums, might have been intended to give the game the best platform possible for its showpiece matches, but in reality, it meant games being played in massive, empty-looking and empty-feeling grounds, hardly conducive to presenting the game at its best.

When England won the bid, the RFUW team led by Rosie Williams saw a different model working better for the women's game and, though it would require tough conversations with the IRB about locations and structures, the competition would look and feel vastly different to anything before.

Two major changes were introduced which became an important part of future World Cup models. The first was that the pool stages would be held in a single venue with back-to-back pitches and games, with all the players staying in the same venue nearby. The second was that the final would not be held at a national rugby ground, but at a smaller ground which had a much better chance of selling out. Not only would that deliver an improved atmosphere, but it would almost certainly look much better than a mostly empty Twickenham for a global TV audience.

The organising team explored numerous locations before settling on Surrey Sports Park in Guildford, still a building site at the time. The decision brought immediate benefits. The site had been subject to almost £40m of investment from the University of Surrey and was due to officially open just a few months before the World Cup. As the venue's first international tournament, the buy-in from those running the facility as a result was enormous. They were all-in in their support to help England deliver an excellent tournament.

The other major plus was that the single site enabled Williams and her close-knit team to secure a deal with Sky Sports to show 13 live games and the knockout matches. Sky brought on board its leading rugby union commentary team at the time with Alex Payne, former international stars Will Greenwood and Tyrone Howe, Will Chignell, Martin Gillingham and Johnnie Hammond all involved. They were complemented by several well-known women's rugby faces and the coverage gave the women's game a profile it had never enjoyed up to that point.

Media interest still felt indifferent in the year before the tournament, though there was great support for the game in certain corners.

Had you not been involved, been a big fan or been covering it, you would hardly have known the competition was taking place.

It was frustration with this lack of coverage that led me to launch Scrumqueens.com in 2009. Along with my partner

Sarah, whose agency Make it Clear provided back-end and technical support, I spent a few months gathering content and encouraging other passionate fans and writers to come on board, most notably John Birch, who remains one of the best reporters on women's rugby today. The website was well established by the time the World Cup kicked off with a match between Canada and Scotland. I had other like-minded volunteers on board and I was lucky enough to have a ringside seat for both pool and knockout stages.

What unfolded was a festival-style event, higher in quality than anything that had gone before. As it built towards the final games, so too did the media interest, culminating in a tense and close final.

It felt a hugely different experience to anything international women's rugby had seen before. It was relaxed, fun and, crucially, the standard had clearly improved.

Williams and her team did a superb job both in battling with the IRB to agree a brand-new approach and in ensuring that the competition was thoroughly enjoyable for the athletes taking part. Though Edmonton had provided a positive player experience, the scant crowds and profile had not made it feel like the pinnacle event it was.

Williams herself reflected on some of those key decisions:

> We always wanted a single venue, and we were very lucky to find Surrey where we were able to also host the teams, which was an added bonus. We had looked elsewhere – places like Brunel, even Eton College, and looked at whether they would work for us and certainly it took us a while to find the right place. It's not just about finding the perfect venue either – you have to find one that delivers you the event within a set budget and that from my point of view was the main issue as we searched initially.

We wanted the players also to be around each other as much as possible as well. In the women's game you often get teams on tours going in and out of a venue quickly and not getting that time together, so we wanted them to experience the long-term friendships and bonds that comes from World Cups.

A real highlight for me one day was sitting on the hill between the two pitches and actually getting to watch the games and enjoy it – I was surprised to find myself with no job to do because everything was being run so well. Everyone bought into the concept that this would be the best World Cup ever.

Of course, a smaller venue had some constraints and when we sold out quickly it meant some fans couldn't come. Like everyone else I would love to have been able to help build a massive stand out there for the games and get as many people as possible in, but for a variety of reasons we couldn't and what we focused on then was getting everyone really close to the action which we did.

The tournament structure saw three pools of four teams. At the end of the pool stages the teams were seeded based on the position in which they finished in their respective pools and points scored during the pool stage.

The three pool winners and the best runner-up went through to the semi-finals. The other two runners-up and the best two third-place finishers went into a competition for fifth place, while the bottom three teams competed for ninth place.

Central to England's strategy to hosting a successful World Cup was a sold-out final at the Twickenham Stoop, a 14,800-capacity stadium which was home to Harlequins. A sell-out required England to get to the final and almost certainly they would have to be up against New Zealand. It was the final everyone expected and the final the RFUW had invested in by paying the substantial costs for the Black Ferns to come and play in England in the lead-up to the event. Both squads looked primed going into the competition to get there though England, at home, and with a far superior build-up, might have just been favourites this time around.

England had in fact had their best run-up to any World Cup, playing 38 Test games since the World Cup in 2006 and backboned by the experience of Danielle Waterman, Maggie Alphonsi, Rachael Burford, Tamara Taylor and Catherine Spencer, all playing in their second World Cup. Emily Scarratt had already been marked out as a future star at just 20 years old, having scored 16 tries in her first 18 games for England.

New Zealand coach Brian Evans chose a squad used to big games but not used to many. They'd played a paltry six games since the 2006 World Cup Final and, perhaps unsurprisingly considering their lack of ability to try new talent, the group that travelled to London featured numerous players with previous World Cup experience. Monalisa Codling had already played in three World Cups while five more players were seeking a hat-trick of titles in 2010.

Amiria Rule (née Marsh), a star in Edmonton, was named initially but suffered an injury just a few weeks out from travelling. Evans replaced her with Anna Richards – a three-time World Cup winner and perhaps the greatest Black Fern ever, but at 45 years old she was the oldest player in the competition and one who had not been training with the squad in the lead-up. Her impact at the competition would be remarkable, playing a hugely decisive role right up to the final minute of the final game.

Pool A pitted New Zealand, Australia, South Africa and Wales together. Pool B had England, Ireland, USA and Kazakhstan. Pool C featured France, Canada, Scotland and surprise package Sweden.

Of the pack chasing England and the Black Ferns, France were expected to push hard for at least a semi-final slot despite remaining maddeningly unpredictable, as they'd shown earlier in the Six Nations, losing to Scotland but almost stopping England from winning the grand slam. Winger Fanny Horta was in great form going into the competition while the vastly experienced Sandrine Agricole would be key too.

The USA, coached by former World Cup winner Kathy Flores, the only female head coach at the event, would certainly target a semi-final slot. They brought a raft of experienced players like impressive forwards Jamie Burke and Phaidra Knight, as well as Ashley English in the backline.

Australia's success in Dubai also made them a real threat. The majority of their World Cup Sevens team travelled to the UK including Cheryl Soon, Debby Hodgkinson and Alex Hargreaves, while the inclusion of Kristy Giteau, sister of men's player Matt, generated interest and profile.

On form, Canada were certainly capable of topping their pool. They'd recently beaten France and went to the competition on the back of good preparation and game time. Winger Heather Moyse was back in the team having been the top try-scorer four years earlier. She brought speed, big-game temperament and profile.

South Africa were captained by the inspirational Mandissa Williams, who had led her team to their first away Test matches earlier in the year when they'd beaten Kazakhstan and Scotland. There were nine players with previous World Cup experience in the team with Zandile Nojoko fast becoming a handful out wide.

Scotland had had a mixed year starting with the momentous win over France but then suffered two losses to South Africa. With Donna Kennedy coming out of retirement to help add experience to the team, they had a sniff of making it out of their pool in a good place, though it would be tough. Kennedy went into the competition on a remarkable 110 caps. Having officially retired after Edmonton but persuaded to rethink her plans for the next year's Six Nations, she announced her retirement again a year later. Her decision to play in the World Cup was a huge boost for the Scots.

Ireland had been steadily improving and, though the opener against England offered a daunting start, they were expected to compete for a runners-up spot in their pool, though realistically they would have been looking for a top-six finish overall. Joy Neville was a key player going into the tournament with her ability from number 8 proving key to Ireland's progressing fortunes. They were also in something of a transition, with Philip Doyle returning just two months before the competition to be head coach.

Kazakhstan were not to be underestimated in that pool, coming into the competition as Asian champions and with limited pressure on them. A powerful, physical team, who would end the competition with two red cards and ten yellows, the Kazakhs were frankly horrible to play against with the experienced Anna Yakovleva leading a bruising pack. They also had the formidable Olga Rudoy, playing in her fifth World Cup at 47 years old. Rudoy had been a mainstay since the 1994 World Cup, having only taken up rugby at the age of 30 under the guidance of Valeriy Popov, the Kazakhstan national team coach. She epitomised her hardy team.

Had the World Cup been a year earlier, Wales would perhaps have been more confident despite their tough pool, where they would face all three southern hemisphere teams. But 12 months is a long time in sport and Wales had gone from triple crown champions to wooden spoon holders in the Six Nations. The prospect of facing New Zealand in particular would be very tough.

Sweden were undoubtedly the surprise inclusion. With nothing to prove, they were capable of making life difficult for teams who were expected to beat them comfortably. Led brilliantly by Ulrika Andersson-Hall, they were also expected to travel with a noisy and passionate band of supporters.

A success from the off

The opening day of the competition was a success before the games even started due to a campus festival-like feel and full sidelines, a huge relief to organisers who might have had some anxiety about how this brand-new format would be received by paying fans. On the field, the rugby was largely competitive. The improvement in quality from four years earlier was evident from the off.

Australia and New Zealand began Pool A with two dominant performances. Australia had barely played since the previous World Cup – just five Test matches in four years – but their talent out wide, with several World Cup Sevens winners, was too much to handle for Wales. Though a far more experienced Test nation, the Welsh team's bumpy year left them low in confidence. Nicole Beck, Sharni Williams, Tricia Brown and Cobie-Jane Morgan all starred as the Wallaroos cut loose through the backs. Wales were impressive up front but they lost 27-12.

New Zealand dominated South Africa 55-3 with standout performances from Casey Robertson in the back row and Carla Hohepa on the wing. It was the start of a sensational tournament for the speedster.

As the games carried on throughout day one, it was clear the competition venue was a triumph. The opening day sold out, there was plenty of room for fans to move from pitch to pitch, the rugby was highly entertaining and a large number of the games were being broadcast on television sets around the world.

Hosts England got their World Cup off to a good, if somewhat nervy, start against Ireland in front of a big crowd later in the day. Over the 80 minutes, Ireland met England head-on up front, making the home team work until the final minutes to get a bonus point. Fiona Pocock started the scoring in the 27-0 win before a superb finish from Maggie Alphonsi sent the hosts 12-0 up into the break. Tries from Amy Turner and Alphonsi gave England a bonus point in the second half. In the same pool, USA hammered Kazakhstan 51-0 with Christy Ringgenberg in good form alongside wing Victoria Folayan.

Perhaps the biggest surprise though was in Pool C where Sweden almost caused the upset of any World Cup by pushing France all the way in their opening match. The Swedes, appearing at the World Cup for the first time in 12 years, were expected to be something of a bonus-point rollover for the French, who started well with an early try for Sandra Rabier. Swedish captain Ulrika Andersson-Hall kicked a penalty, and it was neck and neck from there almost through to half-time, to the delight of the small group of noisy Sweden fans.

Andersson-Hall, one of four survivors from the last Swedish World Cup appearance in 1998, kicked her side into a 6-5 lead before France went back ahead with a try and the Swedish captain reduced arrears with another penalty. France made it 15-6 when Claire Canal scored her second, but they had to hold on to sneak the win. Andersson-Hall afterwards described it as one of Sweden's best ever games:

> I think we showed we are in this tournament and that we actually can pick up some points. We are disappointed that we lost, the girls were crying afterwards because it was such a good game and we were hoping for maybe a draw or a win, but I mean it was a very good start of the tournament for us and I'm very pleased and very proud of the girls.

In the other pool game, Canada got their campaign off to an impressive start with a 37-10 victory over Scotland, for whom

Lucy Millard was a threat. Heather Moyse was dangerous throughout as the Canadians made clear that their game against France would surely be pivotal in this pool.

With there being just three pool matches and no quarter-finals, the second round of games was vital. Key match-ups included Ireland v the USA and New Zealand v Australia, with the other games likely to go to form.

The Pool A games promised much and they delivered. South Africa piled on the pain of a tough year for Wales with a hard-fought 15-10 win, leading 10-0 early on with players like Zenay Jordaan and Zandile Nojoko in brilliant form. Non Evans threatened to get the Welsh back into it and Elen Evans scored but the South Africans had done enough to notch their first win.

The Australia v New Zealand game had been much hyped in advance but the reality was that despite Australia's stunning sevens success, they had nowhere near the guile or the experience as the Black Ferns in the 15s game. It showed, with the Kiwis winning 32-5 in an exciting if somewhat disappointingly one-sided game. Hohepa, a standout throughout the competition, was brilliant again, as was Victoria Grant. Though it was far from the best of New Zealand, the reigning champions showed they were building nicely into the competition.

In Pool B, England thrashed Kazakhstan with a 12-try 82-0 win, but it was Ireland's game against the USA which brought the pool to life. It was always going to be a key game in this pool and, with Ireland having lost their opener against England, a win was needed to keep any hopes of a semi-final spot alive. Despite being played at the same time as the New Zealand v Australia game, the match drew a great crowd on pitch two with highly vocal support for both sides.

Ireland scored early through Joy Neville, winning her 50th cap, before the Americans levelled through Jamie Burke. Niamh Briggs was flying for Ireland at full-back. She was a real threat in open play and her try gave her team a half-time lead. Neville's second try and another from Tania Rosser gave Ireland a bonus point and, though Vanesha McGee got one back, Ireland's 22-12 win was thrilling for Philip Doyle's side.

Pool C was exciting too. France beat Scotland 17-7 with the Scots putting in an impressive performance despite the loss. They failed to come back from early tries from Elodie Poublan and Marie Charlotte Hebel, though they did score a superb try from Lucy Millard. With Canada beating the Swedes 40-10, it nicely set up a top-of-the-pool clash in the final round between themselves and the French. Canada had impressed with players like Kelly Russell and Mandy Marchak in good form, helping the team to a second bonus-point win.

The final round of games in Pool A was unlikely to do much to affect the standings. New Zealand duly put Wales away 41-8 with Kelly Brazier truly arriving at the tournament with a hat-trick. Australia were miles too good for South Africa, winning 62-0 with seven different try-scorers. New Zealand topped the pool and went straight into the semi-finals. Australia would have to wait to see if they'd done enough for a best runner-up slot.

The final games in Pool B were decisive too. England beat the USA 37-10 with Danielle Waterman scoring a few gems, while Ireland beat Kazakhstan 37-3, Joy Neville getting a brace of touchdowns.

In Pool C, the match that mattered was Canada v France. Finally the French put together an 80-minute performance, winning 23-8 thanks to scores from Lucille Godiveau, Claire Canal and Cyrielle Bouisset. In the other game, Scotland beat Sweden 32-5 for their first win.

The results meant that New Zealand were the top-seeded side going into the semi-final. They earned themselves a knockout game against France, while England would face Australia. Canada, Scotland, Ireland and the USA would battle

A game of barette in progress in Paris in 1925 (Credit: Topical Press Agency/Getty Images)

The shirt worn by the Wivern players on their historic tour of Europe in 1985. (Credit: Kerri Heffernan)

Wales' Liza Burgess and England's Carol Isherwood pictured after the first Test match between the two countries in 1987 (Credit: Colin Elsey/Colorsport)

Victorious USA players celebrate with the World Cup at the Cardiff Arms Park in 1991. (Credit: Howard Boylan/Allsport/Getty Images/Hulton Archive)

USA players celebrate after winning the World Cup Final in 1991. Pictured left to right, Mary Sullivan, Patty Jervey, Cassie Law and Krista McFarren. (Credit: Kerri Heffernan)

Irish players Aoife Rodgers, Joanne Moore. Deirdre Fitzgerald, Trina Watt before their first Test match against Scotland in 1993, wearing kit that was far too big for them (Credit: Anne Parsons)

Gill Burns on the charge against Wales in the Home Nations Championship in 1996 (Credit: Tony Marshall/ Alamy)

New Zealand star Louisa Wall hands off England's Paula George during the World Cup semi-final in Amsterdam in 1998. (Credit: David Rogers/Allsport)

Scotland celebrate in France after winning the European Championship with a win over Spain in the final in 2001.
(Credit: Denis Charlet/AFP via Getty Images)

Paula George leads the celebrations for England after ending New Zealand's ten-year unbeaten run in Auckland in 2001. (Credit: Scott Barbour/Allsport)

Canada's Heather Moyse evades the tackle of Kazakhstan's Svetlana Klyuchnikova at the 2006 World Cup in Edmonton where Moyse was a standout player. (Credit: World Rugby)

Farah Palmer leads the celebrations for New Zealand after beating England in the World Cup Final in 2006 (Credit: World Rugby)

Wales players Mel Berry, Louise Horgan and Naomi Thomas celebrate with Non Evans (#15) after she kicked the winning points in a Six Nations game against England in 2009 in Cardiff. (Credit: Stu Forster/Getty Images)

Australia's Cheryl Soon is hoisted high after Australia win the 2009 Rugby World Cup Sevens in Dubai, beating New Zealand in the final. (Credit: World Rugby)

Maggie Alphonsi fends off Ireland's Niamh Briggs during pool play at the World Cup in England in 2010. Alphonsi's profile rocketed in England after the event. (Credit: World Rugby)

Irish stalwarts Joy Neville, Fiona Coghlan and Lynne Cantwell lift the Six Nations trophy after winning a first title and Grand Slam in Italy. (Credit: Dan Sheridan/Inpho)

*France celebrate beating England at Twickenham in 2013
(Credit: Paul Harding/Alamy)*

*Canada's Magali Harvey races away to score a wonder try in the World Cup semi-final against France at the Stade Jean Bouin in Paris in 2014.
(Credit: World Rugby)*

it out for the fifth to eighth-place finishes, while the bottom four spots would be contested by South Africa, Kazakhstan, Wales and Sweden.

The World Cup wasn't the only event in international women's rugby going on in the area at the time. As the semi-finals loomed, Japan arrived in the UK to play some games and take in the finals. Having played in three of the first four World Cups, the Japanese women's team had been amalgamated into the overall Japanese Rugby Union and started a long-term plan to turn around their fortunes and become the powerhouse team of Asia again, a title now held by Kazakhstan. They arrived in the UK and played Richmond and Saracens with the aim of building experience and qualifying for the next World Cup.

Back at the World Cup and England and New Zealand were clear favourites to reach the finals, although the semis did promise some intrigue.

France had been playing in fits and starts at the event and, as underdogs, they often pulled off their best. Sandrine Agricole was key in the centre and had been playing well, but the French had been drifting in and out of games. If the Black Ferns could start strongly, the win would surely be theirs.

New Zealand had been impressive, though by their own standard, had also yet to put together a complete performance. If things looked relatively slick on the field, the players told a different story about the organisation off it. The team was forced to play in white for the semi-finals because the NZR hadn't provided enough black shirts to cover the entirety of the competition.

The Black Ferns' programme had never been properly invested in by the New Zealand union and the players were (and still are) able to rattle off multiple experiences which highlighted how poorly they were treated, often using it as motivation and drawing them closer together.

England had pressure on them going into the game against Australia, a potent attacking side but who were expected to struggle in the tight exchanges against the far more experienced hosts. Maggie Alphonsi and Heather Fisher had become high-profile stars as the tournament had progressed. Both got widespread media exposure for their impressive play in the back row and there was a much-improved media build-up to the two games.

In the event, New Zealand were ominously good against France, nothing short of totally dominant on the way to a 45-7 win. Hohepa scored early with her back-three partner Grant in brilliant form, and she grabbed a second just before Huriana Manuel added a third to knock the wind out of the French. Though the result was decisive, it also meant that going into the final, the Black Ferns had barely been tested. England were about to take a tougher route to the final.

England coach Gary Street had made some changes to his side to play Australia, starting with highly talented Alice Richardson in the centre to counter the mercurial Wallaroo backline. Tries in the first half from Catherine Spencer and Danielle Waterman did just enough to get England through, as they added a penalty in a tense second half to make it 15-0.

The game though was most memorable for a wince-inducing tackle from Australia's Nicole Beck on England's in-form winger Fiona Pocock. It was an incredible hit but Pocock was badly hurt and stretchered off with an injury it would take her years to recover from. It features, even now, on big-hit compilations on YouTube. England though were through to the final, though not unscathed. Heather Fisher was also injured, meaning Street lost two key starting players going into the final.

With the semi-final action having moved to the Twickenham Stoop, there were seeding games to play out back at the Surrey Sports Park. With the final looming, Australia wrapped up third place with a 22-8 win over a disappointing France. Third place was a superb return for Australia, who barely played Test 15s rugby and who were mostly relying on the experience of the World Cup Sevens the year earlier. Players like Sharni Williams would go on to become Olympic champions while the likes of Cheryl Soon and Tricia Brown were lynchpins.

Soon reflected:

> We came here, we made history. First would have been nice, or top two, but after our loss against England our goal was to finish third and we achieved that, so we are very pleased with the result.

Impossible to call

For those of us who had watched every kick and every tackle of the tournament, the final was impossible to call.

England would have the advantage of having the majority of the 13,000-strong crowd behind them, but New Zealand were proven winners. Winning World Cup Finals against England was second nature by now.

England had been stretched by Australia more than had been anticipated but they took a more powerful scrum into the final. Big-name players like Katy Daley-Mclean, Danielle Waterman and Maggie Alphonsi were all delivering and they'd conceded just two tries in the entire competition.

New Zealand had hardly been tested at all. In the lead-up to the final I interviewed the brilliant Black Fern full-back Victoria Grant and asked her what the hardest match she'd faced so far was. She struggled to recall a single game where the going had been tough. In the end she came up with Wales, a side who were dogged against them but who were hardly a threat, going down 41-8.

They had seen off sides with alarming ease. Renne Wickliffe, Grant and Hohepa in the back three were among the finest attackers in the world. In front of them, Anna Richards had stepped back in as if she was never away and was directing play nicely. Goal-kicking was probably one rare weakness – the duties being shared among Kelly Brazier, Emma Jensen and Rebecca Mahoney, but none of them were hugely consistent.

The day of the final arrived exactly as the organisers had hoped. It was a clear day weather-wise and the stands were packed. A crowd of around 13,000 greeted the teams. Even better for the sustainability of the game, they were paying punters with tickets costing upwards of £20 a seat.

The passion was evident even before the kick-off. England fronted up to the Black Ferns' pre-match haka as the two teams met for the third consecutive World Cup Final.

It was a nervy start for the home team with England's most experienced player, Amy Garnett, dropping the kick-off. Danielle Waterman was forced into a try-saving tackle on Black Fern centre Kelly Brazier just three minutes in.

England were forced on the defensive for much of the first half as New Zealand launched wave after wave of attack. The home team, backed by the huge crowd, held on. Two missed penalties – one from Brazier and one from Emma Jensen – helped keep New Zealand off the scoreboard despite their total dominance.

As England battled to get into the match the Black Ferns were reduced to 14 when Richards was binned for not rolling away on the deck. The tide looked to be turning in England's favour as they finally had some possession deep in New Zealand's half. Katy Daley-Mclean missed a kick at goal but England finally had a foothold in the game with some jinking runs from Waterman getting the crowd and her team-mates going.

New Zealand were finding life at the breakdown tough with Sarah Corrigan, the Australian referee, pulling them up repeatedly for infringements. When Mel Bosman joined

Richards in the bin, England were attacking against 13. The Black Ferns, with their backs to the wall, played brave rugby, despite being two players down. They held onto possession well enough until Richards came back on.

Then their first score, which had been threatening all half, came. The try itself was straightforward enough with the ball moving wide quickly to winger Carla Hohepa and the lethal finisher made no mistake in getting across the line safely. Brazier's conversion gave the Ferns a 7-0 lead. They finally had something to show for their overall dominance in the half.

Daley-Mclean, disappointingly for the largely English crowd, missed a straightforward attempt at goal just before the break and the sides turned around with the Black Ferns a try and a conversion up.

England made a better start to the second half with Daley-Mclean getting them on the scoreboard almost immediately with a penalty. The best passage of the match followed as Hohepa blazed down the right wing after a ball squirted loose from a ruck. Jo McGilchrist, the England lock, managed to get a hand on her in a spectacular footrace and make a vital cover tackle. England somehow recovered possession as the Black Ferns were flat out in attack and kicked it clear.

Brazier kicked a penalty to edge the Black Ferns 10-3 ahead but New Zealand lost their skipper to the bin as Melissa Ruscoe was carded for being off her feet. With the crowd on tenterhooks, suddenly England were right back in it and attacking in New Zealand's 22 with a series of scrums. The home side were patient and were rewarded when a brilliant drive helped free the ball up and Charlotte Barras dived over in the corner.

The crowd roared wildly when Daley-Mclean nailed the touchline conversion. The game was tied up ten a-piece. Brazier, though, settled New Zealand's nerves with a well-struck penalty of her own minutes later. The game was set for a thrilling finale as New Zealand took a slender lead into the final ten minutes. England threw everything they had at the Black Ferns but the defending champions wound down the clock expertly.

It was a devastating result for England, even worse that they'd had such long periods of the game playing against 14 players. Tears rolled down the face of captain Catherine Spencer, who had been replaced late in the game.

New Zealand coach Brian Evans couldn't contain his pride in his team after the game, praising the hosts too:

> It's been brilliant. I think the English have done an awesome job. The tournament's been really good – the crowds at Surrey Sports Park – and now it's been great here. It's been a huge success.

On his Black Ferns, he added:

> They're incredible people first and foremost. They get together and they pass on knowledge, and they enjoy themselves – that's the biggest thing I notice. It's interesting watching how much fun the Black Ferns have. Winning helps that but I think they create that for themselves anyway.

After the competition, Carla Hohepa was named IRB Women's Personality of the Year 2010 while Anna Richards would finally retire – this time a four-time World Cup winner:

> It feels awesome, it feels kind of surreal. It was an awesome atmosphere and kind of a strange game with all the sin-binnings. It was a weird game actually, but nice to come out on top. I thought we had the better first 15 or 20 and then England came back when we had a couple of sin-

binnings. It was a real ebb and flow game; a real typical final. Winning a fourth World Cup – it feels really good.

For England, the result was a bitter blow. As Stephen Jones wrote afterwards, when it came to the occasion they had worked towards for so long, they rather 'froze':

> In the end, the final was so exciting that it sat easily on the shoulders of the rest of a memorable tournament. It was never a classic, and it must be admitted that when it came to the occasion for which they had worked for so long, England froze.
>
> It must also be said that New Zealand's dominance of this tournament continues, because this narrow victory means that they have won the World Cup on the last four occasions, with England getting ever closer but not quite managing to stop them. It was New Zealand who were holding the territory at the end and Kelly Brazier, the centre, missed with a penalty in the last few seconds which would really have rubbed it in. New Zealand looked suitably joyous and England suitably horror-stricken.

Jones was honest too about the weaknesses he felt the final had thrown up:

> If the tournament showed the women's game in a good light, then the final showed up one of the major problems. New Zealand committed arguably the most appalling stream of illegalities ever seen in a major rugby match. They lost three players to the sin bin at various stages of the game as the Australian referee courageously stuck to her guns when awarding a torrent of penalties when New Zealand infringed, particularly at the breakdown and after the tackle.

The problem in women's rugby when playing against what amounts to cheating is that very few players have the length of kick to punish offenders. England's kicking game was awful, with even Katy McLean misfiring. New Zealand knew they could infringe in what would be easy kicking range in a men's match and they also knew that England had no one to punish them by pegging them back with long punting.

All that apart, the competition had been an undoubted success and set the blueprint for the next two World Cups, where France and Ireland would follow the path set out by Williams and her team at the RFUW.

The competition proved too that, marketed well, the women's game had an audience. The event was broadcast to 127 countries. Sky Sports were excellent and dedicated host broadcasters and the final attracted what was then easily a world-record crowd for the women's game.

The exposure also catapulted several players to significant new heights. Hohepa was the undoubted star of the tournament with her pace, skill-set and vision resulting in seven tries overall, including one in the final. Alphonsi also became much better known with her incredible tackling earning her the moniker 'Maggie the Machine'. She soon became a regular on TV in the UK.

New Zealand returned home champions, but not much changed for them in terms of financial and resource support from their union. Over the next few years, instead of flourishing as four-time World Cup winners, the Black Ferns programme struggled. The lack of necessary support would catch up with them four years later.

For now though, much of the game's focus would shift to sevens.

Chapter Ten

Sustained growth

THE 2010 World Cup had been a success and had proved that if structured and marketed well, there was a growing untapped support market for the women's game. Now a significant acceleration in the development of sevens, in anticipation of the Olympics, was happening across the world.

For many countries, the influx of fresh investment and the ease with which international sevens teams could be established, often without any dedicated pathways, made it an attractive option for the development of their women's games.

Even in the earliest of days, many national governing bodies openly prioritised sevens over 15s, seeing it in part as an easier and more cost-effective way to support the women's game.

Their central investment was reduced because the majority of international sevens programmes started to receive new investment in bulk from Olympic agencies. Canada's 'Own the Podium', for example, came on board to support the women's sevens programme from its earliest days.

Australia was another case in point. Despite sevens funding coming largely from the Australian Institute of Sport, the governing body was able to point to the successful World Cup Sevens and that team's ongoing development as evidence the women's game there was being supported. Meanwhile, it was developing no meaningful high-performance programmes for the Wallaroos Test 15s team.

To those outside the game, it appeared that women's rugby in Australia was in rude health. The reality was that the national 15s team barely played at all between tournaments and scant attention had been paid to developing pathways and structures. That would all come later, but for now the ARU could point to their brilliant sevens players as proof of their dedication to women.

It's hard to believe now, given the development of the 15s game at the highest levels, that as teams prepared for a first women's World Cup Sevens, there was a real concern that some international programmes would ditch their 15s teams altogether and focus entirely on sevens.

This idea prevailed at the highest levels. In 2013, I spent some time freelancing and writing content at IRB international sevens events in Las Vegas and Houston. Senior staff from the international federation suggested confidently that sevens would simply 'become' the game for women.

I was horrified. While the sevens game has brought huge positives for the development of the women's game – particularly in how it has trailblazed professionalism and developed the game in countries that had little to no appetite before – it is clearly suited to a particular type of player or athlete. It doesn't lend itself easily to rugby's best and most unique selling point, that it is a game for everyone.

In an era where women and girls fear judgement more than ever when it comes to participation in sport, what better sport is there than rugby, where tall, small, big and petite players are not only welcomed but embraced. I once coached a group of teenage girls and the smallest girl on the field spent the entire session beaming.

I asked her afterwards what she'd found so fun. She said it was just great to be able to play something and fit in as she'd been told she was too small to play the sport she'd first chosen at school.

Another teen, who was overweight, was the star of the session. Amazing footwork and strength made her impossible to tackle. She loved the game too and has gone on to become a key player at a leading club. I loathe comparing sports – all participation is great – but those anecdotes are hardly novel. The idea that those girls might find only the game of sevens open to them is unthinkable.

The best asset the 15s game had in the early years of sevens development, where investment was all flowing in one direction, was the lure of major competitions like the Six Nations and World Cups, and in particular the ability of nations like France to attract massive crowds and secure strong broadcast slots. For, while sevens has exploded, it remains a long way behind in its ability to match the lure of a live Test 15s game between a team like France and another top side like England.

The attitude of the IRB officials I met in Vegas clearly reflected live conversations however and there was already significant concern among top 15s players, coaches and fans that their progress would be jettisoned in favour of a faster and fancier cousin which could offer the possibility of the Olympics and professional playing contracts.

In a blog after the 15-a-side World Cup in London, Kristy Giteau wrote about her observations of the differences between the Australian men's and women's set up and expressed concern about the rapid development of sevens compared to the 15s game:

> Physio and strappers ... CHECK ... food given prior and post games ... CHECK ... ice baths scheduled ... CHECK ... five-star accommodation and flights booked ... CHECK ... kit supplied ... CHECK ... management team provided to ensure every demand is catered to ... CHECK.

Welcome to the world of men's rugby.

Being a sister of a Wallaby has definitely exposed me to the luxuries that men have bestowed on them. I have watched my brother play in some amazing tournaments, travel and experience once in a lifetime memories and he is the greatest advocate of his sport. This led me to strive to be the best I can be in my chosen sport, which happened to be the same – rugby!

Training at 6am before work … CHECK … booking and purchasing your own plane ticket and accommodation … CHECK … apply for leave that I have accrued from doing weekend work prior to tournaments … CHECK … chip in some money to cover the cost of food throughout a tournament … CHECK … wear cheap singlets in an attempt at a playing kit that can be worn at a tournament so we look united … CHECK … Welcome to the world of women's rugby!

Giteau went on to discuss the other rewards of playing the international game – the experiences, the memories and the friendships – but left no doubt about her views on the development of the women's 15s game in her country while pointing out that sevens was providing a massive chance for the sevens and 15s games to be treated equally, with investment and promotion ahead of the Olympics already riding high.

It was already clear that cash-strapped unions, who stood a chance of competing for an Olympic medal, would see sevens as the major priority and nations like Canada and Australia were up front about it.

Canada had appointed John Tait to coach their 15s and sevens programmes after the World Cup and Rugby Canada said on his appointment that, through funding from their Olympic agency, they were targeting a medal in Rio and a spot in the finals in the next World Cup Sevens in 2013.

Pro rugby emerges

Canada was among the first out of the blocks in laying down a marker around professionalising and structuring its sevens programme.

In early 2011, Tait announced that he was taking 50 players to a camp in Las Vegas before choosing a squad of 12 to take part in the Hong Kong Sevens in March. Canada quickly became the team to beat in the international sevens game, stealing a march on everyone with their organisation and ability.

On the 15s front, the Six Nations was about to get underway again with England aiming to defend their title. In New Zealand, after public pressure from present and past players, the women's National Provincial Championship was confirmed as returning the following year.

Unsurprisingly following a World Cup year, it was to be a transitional year in the women's Six Nations, with significant changeover in personnel among the players and coaches. England were too good again, winning the grand slam and a sixth successive title and conceding a remarkable eight points in five matches.

Captained by Katy Daley-Mclean with Catherine Spencer having retired from the role, it was an impressive bounce-back from England after the disappointment of the World Cup Final. Gary Street's team did enjoy more consistency than others with few retirements. Most players were determined to have another crack at the World Cup in 2014.

It was an improved tournament for Wales, who moved off bottom to finish fourth, sandwiched on points differential between Ireland and Italy, who also recorded two victories in the 2011 championship. Those two wins made it Italy's most successful season since joining the Six Nations and showed they were moving in the right direction after failing to qualify for the World Cup, having lost out to Sweden in the European qualifying tournament.

Scotland, led by ex-international Karen Findlay, had a tough competition, finishing bottom and suffering an 89-0 loss to England.

England's runaway success was hardly something for the game overall to celebrate. It highlighted that they were so far ahead of every other team in Europe that it was at times almost embarrassing. It couldn't be good for anyone, including England, for the competition to remain so one-sided. France were always a good bet for a close game and they were at times wonderful to watch, but their inconsistencies remained a frustration.

Italy were clearly improving and they had finally learned how to beat the big teams. Findlay had a huge rebuilding job to do with Scotland, highlighted by the fact that, including a warm-up game against Spain, they lost five out of their six games in 2011 by record-breaking margins.

Ireland were genuinely a bright spot, finishing in a well-deserved third, though it was long clear that while the Irish were well coached and were developing a core of experienced and talented players, they sorely lacked development and investment and were choosing from an extremely narrow playing pool.

Unlike everyone else in the top four there was no 'A' or U20 team for up-and-coming Irish players to gain experience before being thrown into the heat of the battle. In addition, there was no Nations Cup or FIRA tournaments, or indeed any internationals at all outside the Six Nations. The Irish performances despite all of this were fast becoming impressive, but it was success based on frighteningly shallow foundations, something that would become obvious in years to come when they struggled to build momentum from big performances and wins.

With the Six Nations done for another year, Canada's early sevens focus looked to be paying off. The team looked impressive on the international sevens front. Players like

Jen Kish, Mandy Marchak and Ghislaine Landry were fast becoming stars. Captained by Marchak, the Canadians headed to Hong Kong, for an event where all the games were played in a day but where they were too strong, beating France in the final 28-14. The Hong Kong event also featured a raft of other emerging women's sevens teams – Russia, the Netherlands and the Philippines all competed alongside the likes of the USA, France and China.

Australia had already confirmed that their primary focus for the year would be on sevens. They had several training camps organised and plans for the national team to compete at the Gold Coast and Noosa Sevens.

Behind the scenes, the IRB were moving forward with plans to launch an inaugural World Sevens Series for women the year after. In Europe, too, focus began to sharpen on the short form of the game.

For the 15s European Trophy that summer, England and France sent their 'A' teams. Another group headed to the European Sevens as nations began the process of decoupling or managing groups of players to compete in both formats.

In the 15-a-side Trophy, Spain pushed England all the way, losing just 5-3 in the final with rising star Sarah Hunter getting the crucial try for the English. France were third. Also taking part were Italy, Sweden, the Netherlands and Russia, while Finland's appearance was their first since 2007.

The European Sevens also attracted a wide range of teams with Germany, Moldova and Romania all involved along with the big guns. England won the title in Bucharest, again beating Spain in the final. Their side was coached by a team including the former England star Susie Appleby.

There would be a Nations Cup that summer, hosted by Canada, who were joined by England, South Africa and the USA. It was preceded by an U20 Nations Cup involving the same four teams.

But a seismic decision was about to be taken in sevens. The first professional contracts were handed to a team with an Olympic dream.

The Dutch jump in

If it was something of a surprise that it was the Netherlands who were the first to go pro, it's worth remembering that the pioneering Dutch had a long women's rugby history.

They had been playing international rugby longer than anyone. They and France played in the first ever Test match. On the sevens front they'd finished runners-up to Spain in the previous year's European Championship, were runners-up again in Las Vegas and finished third in Hong Kong in the weeks before the announcement of their professional team.

As other more established nations were still making plans, the forward-looking Dutch reached an early funding agreement with their Olympic association and put together an innovative talent identification programme. Starting with a blank sheet, they made an appeal to Dutch athletes to attend a series of nationwide talent trials, initially targeting players involved in football, athletics and judo. It's an idea that hardly seems new today, but the Dutch talent-transfer programme was the first on such a scale.

Soon a squad came together with names who would soon become familiar on the sevens circuit including Linda Franssen, Inge Visser, Annemarije Van Rossum, Lorraine Laros, Pien Selbeck, Kelly van Harskamp and Tessa Veldhuis.

With the Dutch up and running and Canada establishing themselves on the world circuit as the team to beat, the IRB organised a three-tournament IRB Challenge series, the first taking place at the end of 2011 in Dubai with two more in Hong Kong and London in 2012.

At the first event, held alongside the 2011 Dubai Sevens, Canada defeated England in the final to win the cup. The second event in March 2012 saw England lift the title. Then, hosting the final event in London themselves in May, England beat the Netherlands in the final.

The trial event went on to become the women's World Sevens Series. The results were used by the IRB to determine the core sides for the inaugural event the next season. Australia, Canada, England, Netherlands, New Zealand and USA were confirmed as the core teams taking part in the first four rounds of the new circuit, with the venues confirmed as UAE (Dubai), USA (Houston), China (Guangzhou) and Netherlands (Amsterdam).

By the end of 2011, although New Zealand were yet to make a mark, the blueprint for the future of international sevens – professional contracts funded largely by Olympic associations and a World Sevens Series league run by the IRB – was set.

There was also growing evidence that the influx of new money into the women's game was encouraging new international teams to be established. India hosted its first international event that September, welcoming the women's Asia Sevens. Also involved were Kazakhstan, China, Japan, Hong Kong, Thailand, Singapore, Malaysia, Korea, Laos, Chinese Taipei and Iran, making clear that there was more commitment than ever among emerging rugby nations to the women's game.

Though sevens took centre stage for most of the 2011 summer, three major competitions were yet to play out that year: an U20 and senior Nations Cup in Canada and another highly anticipated Test series between England and New Zealand in England.

Of the mere seven countries who fielded teams at U20 level at the time, England, led by former Welsh player Amanda Bennett, were by far the best. In the space of the five months leading into the Nations Cup, England U20 had beaten France, Scotland and Wales. Heading to Canada they were motivated to become the leading side in the age group by beating the other three: South Africa, USA and the hosts. They had no problem in all three games and ended the competition with their 100% record secure.

Their senior counterparts were also favourites in their event, though that competition would be more dramatic. The USA almost sprung an upset in the opening game. England were forced to rely on an 87th-minute injury-time try from Rowena Burnfield to win 15-11. Canada, featuring numerous returning sevens stars, including Ghislaine Landry who touched down three times in the game, had no problem dispatching South Africa 52-17. The experience stood the Springboks in good stead. They remarkably overturned the USA in their next outing, a reminder that if they had regular games, they had all the talent to beat the best teams.

It was without doubt the biggest win in South Africa's history, their first against one of the world's top-six teams, and it was based on no little determination, with two late tries by wing Janine Felix securing the victory. With England beating Canada 22-10, it meant that the pool games had largely been competitive. The Canadians and English would meet again in the final.

England won it 41-19 to retain the title. It was a game that was also memorable for hooker Amy Garnett becoming the first English women's player to reach 100 caps, following in the footsteps of Scotland forward Donna Kennedy and wing-cum-second-row Louise Rickard of Wales.

As the competition ended, an exciting new announcement confirmed plans for the world's top two teams. Having lost four World Cup Finals in a row to New Zealand, the England set-up knew something needed to change if the same story wasn't going to play out in France, who had been awarded the 2014 hosting rights. It resulted in a historic announcement that the teams would play three back-to-back Test series in 2011, 2012 and 2013.

England would host three Tests in the autumns of 2011 and 2012 before heading to New Zealand for the final series in June 2013. The agreement was heralded as a massive step forward for the women's game. Previously there had been limited regular competition between the world's top two teams.

The NZR made no pretence that had it not been for the RFU, the series wouldn't be happening. General manager of professional rugby Neil Sorensen said the union was 'grateful' to the RFU for making it possible:

> We have not only achieved a regular programme against quality opposition, but we have also been able to create a fantastic touring opportunity for these teams funded in large part by the RFU which demonstrates the respect that is held for our world champions.

The Test series later that autumn would be massive for England, who were in need of belief that New Zealand were beatable. To further support their development, they'd also lined up two Test games in France, handing Gary Street the enviable position of being able to further build depth to his squad.

By comparison, neighbours Ireland hadn't played since the end of the Six Nations and there would be no more game time for them in 2011.

A glimpse at the future

The first autumn game in 2011 was an uncapped friendly between France and England in Marseille, with the French coming out on top 14-5 in miserable conditions. Both sides featured experimental line-ups ahead of the capped match a few days later at the Pierre de Coubertin Stadium in Châteaurenard.

France again came out on top in the second match, something of a blow to England's preparation for their New Zealand Tests, even though both featured some new faces.

French fly-half Aurée Bailon was key in poor weather once again, while the England performance was notable for the debut of Alex Matthews, who would go on to become a key player in sevens and 15s for her country.

With New Zealand arriving on English shores, Street recalled all his big guns for the first meeting between the two leading nations since the World Cup Final, 14 months before. The games would be the first for the Black Ferns since then. England had the luxury of a Six Nations, Nations Cup and the warm-up games in France to prepare. New Zealand also had a new coach, with Grant Hansen having taken over from Brian Evans.

There would be three Tests in a week. It was a huge challenge, particularly for the travelling team and, unsurprisingly, England drew first blood at Twickenham with a 10-0 win. Maggie Alphonsi scored the only try of the match in the 30th minute with captain Katy Daley-Mclean adding the conversion and a second-half penalty.

England, who had also run out 10-3 winners when the sides last met at Twickenham in November 2009, enjoyed the better of the possession and territory in a traditional tight battle between the top two teams in women's rugby. New Zealand had their chances with wing Renee Wickliffe pulling off a great attack out of nothing, only to lose the ball with the line in sight after a try-saving tackle from Emily Scarratt.

The teams would meet again a few days later in Esher, with both forced into squad rotation. This time England won comfortably, 21-7, in a fine performance, with Alex Matthews starring.

The final Test ended in an 8-8 draw but England had won the series, vindication perhaps for their investment decision and a dawning of reality for New Zealand. Alarm bells were rung back home about their fortunes after their first ever consecutive losses.

Former captain Farah Palmer described the results in the *Otago Daily Times* as a 'red flag', writing a powerful column:

> If a tree falls in the forest and no one is there to hear it, does it make a noise? The Black Ferns have fallen at the hands of arch-rival England in a three-Test series, with two losses and a draw, and there hasn't been much of an uproar.

Pointing out that this was the first time the national side had experienced consecutive losses, and the first time since 1991 the team had remained scoreless in a Test match, she asked:

> Is this something to be concerned about? Is this a glitch or a gaping sore? The performance of the Black Ferns against England is a red flag to the players, team management and the NZR that resources allocated to women's rugby have reached a critical level. And by resources, I'm referring to leadership, as well as funding.
>
> For the last few years, resources for the women's game have been cut, redirected, rationalised, diverted, put on hold and minimised, and yet the Black Ferns continued to win ... If the NZR was wondering how little the women's game could survive on, I think it has found it. The Black Ferns have hit rock bottom and perhaps the outcome in England is a blessing in disguise. Now, at least, we know how little we can get away with before the team suffers.

The warning from Palmer – who has since become the first woman to be elected to the New Zealand Rugby Board – would go largely unheeded at the NZRU. England somewhat bankrolled the Black Ferns' Test programme in the lead-up to the next World Cup and the national team hadn't quite yet felt the impact of the apathy from their union. It would come.

Though another Six Nations where England would be favourites loomed in 2012, the march of the pro sevens game carried on. The USA were the latest team to offer a number of players contracts with around eight relocating to Chula Vista, where they would have access to the Olympic Training Centre.

Canada had also begun a programme of centralisation. Its top players were relocating to Rugby Canada's new Centre of Excellence in Langford, British Columbia.

At the first major event of the year the Canadians collected their fifth major title in a row. The result at the Las Vegas Sevens meant it was a year since Mandy Marchak's team had even lost a game. The tournament was a warm-up for the second leg of the IRB's Challenge at the end of March in Hong Kong with a notable strengthening of the sides taking part. Australia, Brazil, Canada, China, England, Hong Kong, Japan, Netherlands, Russia, Spain, Tunisia and USA all entered.

The event would clash with the final round of games in the Six Nations, forcing England to take tough choices about selection. A few international teams were yet to have fully separated out their squads.

It hardly mattered though as England's dominance of European 15s rugby continued. A seventh consecutive Six Nations title followed a 23-6 win over Ireland at Esher in the final round. They were pushed all the way by a gutsy effort from the rapidly improving Irish and the game was tied 6-6 at half-time, but two tries late in the second half was enough to secure another title. Remarkably England also ended the tournament as the first side to win the competition without conceding a try.

Away from top spot, the competition placings were important. With England and France already qualified for the

World Cup by virtue of their top-six finish in 2010, the two next best sides across the 2012 and 2013 Six Nations Championship would qualify direct for France 2014. The remaining teams entered a qualification tournament. Ireland in third and Wales in fourth at the end of the Six Nations made them good bets to qualify.

However, the story of the 2012 Six Nations was nothing to do with England winning another title. It was all about Ireland, a dramatic trip to France, an ugly public fallout for their union and the determination it would plant in the Irish players' minds about what they could achieve.

Farce in France

Ireland's Six Nations got off to a rocky start, with their game against Wales called off just over halfway through because of a frozen pitch. In round two, they were due to travel to France.

Since the IRFU had taken over the running of the women's game, there had been some positives for the national team – access to a wider pool of coaches and facilities, for example – but there had been no increases in playing opportunities, the depth of the country's playing pool was still worryingly shallow and the investment in and around the team's infrastructure reflected their amateur status.

With the game due to be played in Pau, just 85km from the Spanish border, the IRFU's travel schedule for the team, all of whom were travelling to play a Test match for their country after a week in their day jobs, was gruelling. They had to fly into Paris, get a coach across the city, and get the TGV down through the country to reach Pau. The Irish men's team, meanwhile, who were also playing in France that weekend travelled on a chartered flight.

Paris being Paris, the Friday afternoon traffic was horrible. The team missed their train and ending up stranded in the

French capital just 23 hours before kick-off. Coach Philip Doyle recalled for the 42.ie:

> I was flipping my lid with the IRFU. All along we wanted to fly direct to Pau but were told we couldn't and now we were in a race against the clock to get there, worried the game might have to be cancelled. I was fuming.

The players gathered together and booked an overnight train to Pau. It was packed and chaotic, with the players spread over numerous carriages and the train not pulling into Pau until just a few hours before the match. The trip took 23 hours from Dublin.

Remarkably, with little to no sleep, Ireland gathered themselves and lost the game by just a point, 8-7, their closest ever result against the French. For a team that was growing in stature on the field, it was a galvanising moment.

'It was certainly a turning point,' Doyle reflected afterwards. 'The attitude then was that if we can get through something as traumatic as that journey, then we can get through anything.'

The fallout in Ireland came quick. The IRFU were forced to apologise for their treatment of the team and promise that it would never happen again after a series of negative stories in the media and a torrent of public criticism. It would not be the first time the IRFU would be forced to apologise for its handling of the women's game, but little ever seemed to change.

The end of the Six Nations coincided with the Hong Kong Sevens. While England were winning a 15-a-side title in Esher, their sevens squad won in Hong Kong, beating Australia 15-10 in a final in front of a huge crowd. England had broken Canada's chokehold on the circuit, which handed them a boost going into the final series event which they'd host in London.

That event would also prove a success for England, who beat the Dutch 34-7 in the final, who had in turn upset France and Australia on the way here. It was a reminder that despite their lack of experience, the Dutch investment in their sevens programme was starting to bear fruit.

Though New Zealand had barely featured on the recent international sevens stage, investment from their Olympic agency meant they were quietly making plans for a return. Sean Horan had been appointed the first full-time paid women's sevens coach in the country. A massive recruitment drive as part of the national Go4Gold programme had been held.

New Zealand would finally begin attending invitational international tournaments in the latter half of the year to ready for the first World Sevens Series which would start in Dubai at the end of the year. Meanwhile at the Amsterdam Sevens, Canada bounced back, winning the final against the USA, for whom youngster Bui Baravilala was a standout.

The summer of 2012 also brought a raft of 15s activity. England won the European Championship again, playing out a thrilling final against France, winning 29-15. Italy finished third, while in Division B, Sweden were the victors over the Dutch. It was an important clash with the finalists earning a place in the World Cup qualifying tournament the following year.

Japan also returned to the international scene, running out 61-15 winners over Hong Kong in a curtain-raiser to the men's Asian Five Nations encounter between the two rivals at the Prince Chichibu Memorial Stadium in Tokyo. Japan wing Chikami Inoue scored four tries in the victory, with flanker Chisato Yoko and replacement Keiko Kato both adding a brace.

England announced over the summer that they were to finally integrate fully with the RFU, with the RFUW to be fully merged into the overall governing body. It was one of the final mergers in the international game and most women's programmes were now fully integrated into overall governing body responsibilities.

The high point of the summer was surely New Zealand's return to the international sevens stage. Horan took a talented team to Fiji to play in the World Cup Sevens qualifiers, which they and Australia played in despite already being qualified for the World Cup.

Notable new faces included two high-profile netballers, Portia Woodman and Kayla McAlister, who had impressed in the open trials that had taken place around the country. In their first international sevens outing since 2010, New Zealand swept past all before them, beating Australia in the final which ended 35-24 – a sign of their probable dominance on the world stage when the time came.

Several other World Cup Sevens qualifiers played out globally with England, Spain, France, the Netherlands and Ireland cementing their places via the European Sevens circuit and Canada via the NACRA Sevens.

The end of the year would be busy on the Test front with the Black Ferns, now shorn of some leading players due to sevens, due to play England three times again after their series loss the year before. France and England would also play a one-off match.

The USA were also kickstarting an autumn tour series, travelling to play France twice and Italy once as they began an attempt, led by coach Pete Steinberg, to get back to the top of the global rankings. The three-Test programme presented one of the toughest tours the Eagles had ever embarked upon. Outside of tournaments such as the World Cup, no previous overseas tour had included more than two Test matches. This time they would play three Tests in a week.

They started with a win, beating the Italians 34-20 in Rome in the first Test between the two sides. The USA next headed to France and, in front of a big crowd, lost 13-0 at Stade

Marcel Garcin, with young French full-back Jessy Trémoulière starring. An even bigger crowd awaited at the Stade de France with the final Test being played as a double-header with a men's match. France came out on top 27-3.

All eyes were now on England and New Zealand. Could Street's side back up their series win of a year ago? Would New Zealand, buoyed by the return of their National Provincial Championships and the wake-up call of 2011, be able to travel and win?

England shaded the first Test in Esher, a highly physical game which ended 16-13 with Alice Richardson and Emily Scarratt pivotal for the hosts. A 17-8 win at Aldershot just a few days later meant England were able to back it up with a third successive win over the world champions. The Black Ferns looked off the pace and nowhere near as conditioned as an England side with far more games under their belt. A well-deserved series win became a whitewash at Twickenham a few days later. This time England won 32-23 in a highly entertaining match in front of a big crowd.

There was some consolation for New Zealand when their sevens team took the first official World Sevens Series opener in Dubai in December. They were hugely impressive considering they'd made just sporadic appearances as an official side since 2009, sweeping to victory in fine form. They were held only by Russia, against whom they could only manage a draw.

The tournament was also notable for the performances of Russia and South Africa. Russia were quietly building a reputation as one of the most improved sides in the world, taking the scalps of Canada, China and Netherlands before drawing with eventual winners New Zealand and eventually winning the plate after a narrow loss to Spain.

Head coach Pavel Baranovsky's team was still in its infancy and ruffling some feathers may have been Russia's aim before the tournament, but the hosts of the upcoming 2013 World Cup did far more than that. Through the likes of the exceptionally talented Navrat Khamidova, they quickly became the team to watch. What was even more impressive about Russia's rise was that the team were only able to train for about five months a year outdoors.

South Africa were also a surprise package in Dubai, reaching the final and showing they were also continuing to make real strides in the sevens game.

The 2013 World Cup Sevens would see numerous sides prioritise sevens over and above 15s. The result of that would contribute to a real shake-up of the world order.

Chapter Eleven

Watershed moments

THE LAUNCH of the women's World Sevens Series, bankrolled by the IRB, was significant for obvious reasons.

It gave the women's sevens game an official circuit that could be built upon. It gave the game a chance to develop so that by the time the Olympics came the standard would be much improved. It developed and championed high-profile stars. It brought bona fide professionalism to women's rugby, where many players had contracts and were able to focus fully on training and playing.

And it had an immediate knock-on impact on the 15-a-side Test game.

The first World Sevens Series in 2013 included two rounds which directly clashed with the Six Nations, Houston in February and China in March. England, as a core series team, had a tough decision to make. When they named their Six Nations squad, it was clear what they had decided to prioritise. A large chunk of their players – 17, including their entire likely starting backline – were removed to be part of the sevens programme.

England's decision was controversial. It was designed not just to establish themselves as a force on the series, but also to give them a chance to win the World Cup Sevens later that summer in Moscow. But, given England's dominance of the

Six Nations – they'd won the last seven titles, six of which had been grand slams – their decision to strip their squad of such a large bulk of experience opened the door for others, especially France and Ireland.

Undoubtedly England had great depth, but the French and the Irish were calling on full-strength squads. Though the English pack would be something close to full strength, it was a golden and rare chance at glory for someone else.

Ireland headed into the competition on the back of a competitive domestic interprovincial series which had been moved in the calendar to give the country's best players a chance to play a higher level of rugby leading into the Six Nations. They'd finished third the year before and almost toppled France away after the debacle in Pau. While they too were involved in sevens and would travel to Russia, they were not shorn of any players for the Six Nations. Instead, they were rather reaping the benefit of their sevens involvement which was giving their players more chances to play than ever before.

The re-emergence of the Irish Exiles, which reformed to add depth to the national set-up, was also timely. Several players emerged through the pathway including Sophie Spence, who had become a real force in the second row. With their toughest games against France and England being played at home, this was an 'if not now, when?' moment for Ireland.

France too were being handed a massive opportunity to end England's run of Championship wins. With no World Sevens Series commitments, their coach Christian Galonnier was able to call up all his leading players. With the return of players like Caroline Ladagnous and Marjorie Mayans, they looked even stronger than they had in the autumn. They did, however, have to navigate three away games and the French had a tradition of slipping up on the road.

Of the others, Italy had been delivering gradual improvements and their incremental successes – they had not lost to

Scotland since 2009, had beaten Wales and pushed France close – were one of the untold stories of the championship. They would not push for a title any time soon, but they could certainly make it very hard for those vying for it.

Having won the wooden spoon in 2011 and 2012, Scotland weren't looking far beyond lifting themselves off the bottom of the table while Wales were seeking to improve on fourth and were boosted by the return of some key players like Catrin Edwards, Gemma Hallett and Elinor Snowsill.

Though you could never bank on France playing away, their loss to Italy in the opening round of the championship was a shock. It was their first loss to the Italians and highlighted that this was likely to be a genuinely competitive Six Nations.

The weather was atrocious. At times it was hard to even make out who was who, such was the mud. Barely a blade of grass could be seen. Three minutes into extra time, France led 12-10 but they conceded a penalty. Veteran Italian fly-half Veronica Schiavon calmly booted it through the posts to give her side a historic win.

Head coach Andrea Di Giandomenico said after the game:

I feel like I have said before that we have grown up, and we now have. We are becoming a mature team that knows how to handle difficult moments. That has always been missing until now. Today the girls played a great game. Accurate when we had to be – combative when under pressure.

The result handed an early advantage to Ireland and England, with the latter having no problem in their opening game, hammering Scotland 76-0, though Ireland made much harder work of their opening win in Port Talbot.

Ireland took the lead early in the game against Wales when Sophie Spence crashed over in the corner and Niamh Briggs converted. Wales hit back through full-back Rosie Fletcher and the teams turned around 7-7. Wales stepped it up in the second half and were twice over the try line but were denied by handling errors. Eventually they went ahead with a penalty to lead 10-7 and it took a late try from Gill Bourke to hand Ireland a hard-fought 12-10 win. It was the best Welsh performance in years and Ireland knew they'd been lucky to come away with the points.

Round two would be pivotal, with the Irish hosting England and France desperately needing a win to stay on track.

France kicked it off on a Friday night at home, just six days after their Italian loss, and they bounced back with a comfortable 32-0 win over Wales. Jessy Trémoulière, fast becoming a star, was brilliant, scoring all 20 points in the opening half as France, led by their inspirational hooker Gaëlle Mignot, saw out the win.

All eyes were now on the game in Ashbourne. If Ireland could pull off a win, they'd be in the strongest position to contest for their first title. England named a strong pack but a backline who hadn't played much together. With the Irish media hyping up the game, a capacity crowd turned out to watch.

The home team started very well with a score in the seventh minute when Miller dived over in the corner to make it 5-0. Niamh Briggs extended the lead to eight with a well-taken penalty five minutes later. After half an hour Ireland increased their lead further, Miller proving difficult to stop again as she dived over in the opposite corner to make it 13-0. She completed her hat-trick just before the break and Briggs added the extras to make it a comfortable 20-0 lead for Ireland, who were dominating in all areas at the half-time break.

Ireland picked up where they left off and had their fourth try after 45 minutes as Briggs went over in the corner to give Ireland a 25-point advantage, the try coming from a dominant scrum and a great pass from Joy Neville. England struggled to create any momentum as Ireland continued to pin them back with some huge tackles to keep them scoreless. It was the first time since 2004 that England had failed to score a point in a Test game, with the game ending 25-0.

With Italy beating Scotland 8-0 in the other game, Ireland were now the favourites to win the title and were just 80 minutes away from a first ever triple crown. It's impossible to underestimate what a massive result it was, not just because it was a first for Ireland, but because it served a rare jolt to the pecking order in the game and would be a springboard for the Irish going into the World Cup and beyond.

With a team spearheaded by experience in the form of Lynne Cantwell, Joy Neville and Fiona Coghlan, the talent of Niamh Briggs, and Claire Molloy, the emerging star Jenny Murphy and the finishing of Alison Miller, it meant the title was theirs to lose, even if they had yet to play France.

For players like Cantwell, who had been involved in a 79-0 hammering at the hands of England a decade before, the reversal of fortunes was even more special.

Cantwell told me at the time:

> I have been reflecting a lot on that game and how far we have come. Back then we couldn't cope with England at all – players like Chris Diver were just running over us – and it's taken us a long time to come even close to matching how good they are. Hopefully the girls that come into the squad now never have to go through games like that and we can move up and up.

In the aftermath of the game, most reports did highlight the fact that England were weakened, but Irish coach Philip Doyle would hear none of it. He told the *Irish Times*:

> You could say we came up against a weakened English side but the depth of their playing pool makes that

claim laughable. They could have put out three teams last weekend against us. They had a series against New Zealand in November – three Tests in two weeks – and they put out two different teams and still won. So, I don't fall for that one.

The Irish players lingered on the field afterwards, enjoying the result with numerous past players who had been there through the hammerings at the hands of England, Fiona Steed, Patrique Kelly and Sarahjane Belton to name just some. England captain Sarah Hunter spoke beautifully to the teams after the game, congratulating Ireland on a deserved win.

France were not yet out of it. In the next round they travelled to play a deflated England team at Twickenham. England had never lost at Twickenham and never lost two games in a row but, in a Six Nations that was already breaking records, they went down 3-20 in a highly entertaining game in which French back-row Safi N'Diaye was immense.

Ireland went to Scotland and secured a 3-30 win, winning their first triple crown with a late 15-point flourish from Niamh Briggs. The result also meant that Ireland qualified for the 2014 World Cup, while Scotland would have to take part in European qualifiers. Wales managed a 15-16 win over Italy in a fine performance to continue their progression.

Ireland make history

With two rounds to go, the Irish could win the title if they beat France at home, something they'd never done, but such was their momentum that they went in favourites. The weather was poor again – a feature of this championship – and the president of Ireland Michael D. Higgins was among the crowd of over 3,000 who packed Ashbourne RFC.

Ireland had to do it the hard way, defending furiously as the wind-backed French attacked with vigour and Sandrine

Agricole nudged them ahead from a well-struck seventh-minute penalty. The heavier French pack tried to set the tone, but Ireland had done their homework and defended magnificently. French number 8 Safi N'Diaye, who had done much damage to England two weeks before, was effectively neutralised. Her attempts to break away from the scrum were snuffed out by two or three Irish players whenever she had the ball.

The French held the advantage for the opening ten minutes or so but were rocked when a fast-paced attack by Ireland saw Alison Miller break down the left. After she was tackled, the ball was quickly recycled to Joy Neville, who brilliantly released Niamh Briggs for the game's opening score. The full-back was unable to convert her own try and within minutes France swept into a 10-5 lead which they held until the interval, Agricole converting from near the touchline after a close-in effort from hooker Gaëlle Mignot.

Turning around with the wind behind them, the inspirational Fiona Coghlan and her team-mates enjoyed a better share of possession in the third quarter and they made immediate headway with prop Ailis Egan muscling over after a strong spell of rucking and carrying from the forwards. Briggs managed to add the extras as the lead changed hands again and France had to show discipline in defence as the Irish battered forward in search of more tries.

France hung in there as the crowd raised the noise level in support of Ireland. They missed a drop goal and it was left to Briggs to notch the match-winning score, firing over a late penalty after she had struck the post with a similar effort just minutes earlier.

There were ecstatic scenes on the sidelines and in the changing rooms. Ireland had broken England's stranglehold on the competition and were just one game away from a grand slam, which they could fittingly win on St Patrick's Day in Italy.

That match too was played in wretched conditions. The kindest thing to say about the game was that it was one for the purists as Ireland ground out a 3-6 win thanks to two Niamh Briggs penalties.

The players were hardly able to celebrate at the final whistle such was the weather, with Irish back-row Claire Molloy describing the experience afterwards for the *Irish Times*.

The rugby was so slow and it came down to kicks, which is unlike us, but the Italians made us grind it out. I remember seeing Siobhán Fleming warming up on the sideline as I was frozen to the side of a scrum. But I looked at Gemma Crowley, our manager, and said: 'No! Don't take me off!'

I cramped in the last ten minutes every time I jumped in the line-out, both my calves as I left the ground and then having to stretch them as I landed just to run on.

When the final whistle blew I was so relieved that I cried. A wave of exhaustion hit me. I was so cold. Ross O'Callaghan put loads of layers on me and had me running up and down the 22 so I could function enough to get my medal.

In the changing rooms the showers weren't warm so they whisked me off to the team hotel.

I don't think textbook-wise it was full-on hypothermia. I was a little bit delirious but there was no memory impairment.

As Ireland eventually warmed up to get the celebrations underway in Italy, in the remaining games England sailed close to a third loss until wing Sally Tuson scored a late try in Aberavon to deny Wales what would have been a massive victory, the hosts having taken a 16-15 lead with replacement Megan York's try in the 70th minute.

England had gone in with a 15-8 advantage at half-time, but a penalty by Elinor Snowsill cut the deficit and Wales sensed their visitors were there for the taking and were rewarded when York touched down. The victory, though, meant England finished third ahead of Wales and Italy on points differential after both won two matches in the championship. Scotland again claimed the wooden spoon having lost all their matches.

Despite the loss to England, Wales were confirmed as joining Ireland in qualifying for the 2014 World Cup in France as the top two teams across the 2012 and 2013 champions outside England and France. Italy and Scotland would have to regroup and negotiate the six-team qualifying tournament in Madrid the following month.

While the 2013 Six Nations had been one of the most dramatic in years, equally dramatic discussions were being held about its future.

Six Nations thrown into doubt

Just a week after Ireland claimed their first grand slam, I learned that discussions were underway about a new structure of the competition, with a vote expected in April to determine its future.

I reported on Scrumqueens.com that the proposals were to split the tournament into a two-tier championship with Ireland, France and England in one tier and Wales, Italy and Scotland in the other. Sides would play each other home and away in tier one, while tier two would just play two games a season, alternating home and away games every other year.

Cost and the shifting focus to sevens were understood to be behind the proposals. They were vocally opposed by France, who went on the record via their spokeswoman Nathalie Janvier:

> This is a setback. I feel angry because this choice has consequences for the 15s game. What do we say to the

young players who dream of playing in the tournament as they prepare for years to do so? What do we say to the French U20 side and their coaches? Italy fought to have a competitive team for many years and yet could be in tier two. This tournament is the source of motivation for many. The change makes no sense.

Our reporting was picked up in the Irish media, where Philip Doyle and former Irish players were quoted condemning the plans. I contacted the UK's All-Party Parliamentary Group on Women's Sport to ask them to consider intervening. The group, co-chaired by Baroness Tanni Grey-Thompson and Barbara Keeley MP, wrote an open letter to the CEOs of the English, Welsh, Scottish and Irish rugby unions asking them to reject the reported proposals. This was picked up in the media. The letter read:

> We have read with concern recent reports that the Six Nations Council will meet on the 10th April to consider proposals to disband the RBS Women's Six Nations and create a new two-tier tournament.
>
> The Women's Six Nations has been successful over recent years in raising its media profile and the level of interest it garners from the public. As a concept, both the media and the public understand the Six Nations and we feel that any move away from the current tournament structure would damage the opportunity to continue to grow the media and public profile of the tournament.
>
> This in turn, would damage its ability to act as a showcase for women's rugby and reduce its ability to inspire girls and young women to take up the sport. Everyone who takes up a sport dreams of playing for their country in the biggest competitions, it would be a shame to diminish that opportunity for women playing rugby.

The fact that women and girls participate in sport far less than men and boys is an issue that we are working to publicise and overcome. Lower participation levels have many costs in relation to the health and the personal development of girls and young women. We are concerned by proposals that would downgrade a tournament which has the potential to become a major part of the women's sporting calendar.

While we understand the concern about ensuring every side in the tournament is competitive, we do not believe that restructuring, reducing investment and reducing the number of matches played is the solution. Playing fewer games would be damaging to both weaker and stronger teams.

We would much rather see every team being supported and developed to ensure that the Women's Six Nations continues to strengthen as a tournament which has the ability to excite fans, drive commercial partnerships and inspire participation.

In the face of negative media publicity, an outcry from players and a social media campaign using the tag #backthegirls, the plans were shelved. The Six Nations organisation was forced to publicly commit to the women's championship.

That such detailed proposals and far-reaching changes were being discussed behind the scenes with no public discussion was a stark reminder of how so many of the organisations running the women's game felt about it. There was little transparency – still a huge problem today.

The proposed changes might have been dressed up as a mechanism to make the Six Nations more competitive but in reality it would have drastically reduced the number of games for teams like already-struggling Scotland. At its heart it was a cost-saving plan for the unions, most of whom still could not see the benefit of investing in the women's game even though, for many, it represented a rare area of growth.

Sevens back in the spotlight

While England had stumbled to their worst ever Six Nations finish, their sevens team was making hay, winning the second round of the World Sevens Series with a 29-12 win over the USA in the final in Houston, a result which secured them the top seed for the upcoming World Cup.

England, for whom players like Jo Watmore, Heather Fisher and Alice Richardson were key, had beaten New Zealand on the way to the title, but the Kiwis would bounce back at the third leg of the series in China. There they would face England in the final, winning 19-5 with 12 points from Kelly Brazier. The victory meant all they needed to do in the final round of the series in Amsterdam was reach the cup semi-finals to lift the inaugural World Sevens Series title.

Before then, England would host a World Cup Sevens warm-up at Twickenham with eight sides competing in the London Invitational Sevens. England were comfortable winners, beating Australia in the final at a well-run event. The world's leading sides then headed to Amsterdam for the World Sevens Series finale. The Dutch event turned out to be a superb showpiece with great crowds, entertaining rugby and an outstanding final where New Zealand toppled Canada 33-24.

The end of the first series also offered a chance to reflect on how the international sevens game was progressing. Although teams had mixed and matched their squads with the World Cup Sevens in mind, it was clear that the standard was improving.

New Zealand were now firmly the top team, with players like Kayla McAlister and Ruby Tui coming to the fore, but they were not invincible. Canada, after a quiet 18 months, were remerging as top contenders, hitting their stride at just the right time. England had strength in depth and Australia, with

Sharni Williams and Shannon Parry pivotal leaders, could beat anyone on their day.

Russia too had been a revelation. Finishing third in Amsterdam was remarkable considering a handful of the team had never played rugby a year before. Head coach Pavel Baronovsky was fast becoming one of the real characters of the women's rugby circuit. Baronovsky, who previously coached the men's national sevens side, had to resort to unusual measures to find prospective international players due to the very small number of clubs featuring women's sides. He admitted he often approached strong and athletic-looking women on the street and encouraged them to try rugby.

As the series came to an end, the IRB announced that it would increase the number of core sides involved the following year to eight. Baronovsky's team were handed a boost before the World Cup Sevens, winning the European Sevens after favourites England had sent an inexperienced team to the second leg.

The World Cup Sevens in Russia in 2013 was about to become another watershed moment for women's rugby.

New Zealand were up there as favourites. The Black Ferns had emerged champions of the first World Sevens Series and took a squad in strong form with Honey Hireme, Kayla McAlister and Portia Woodman shining. They were in the toughest pool though, with Canada and the Netherlands challenging.

Canada had Jen Kish and Mandy Marchak, two superb leaders with strong experience, and Heather Moyse, who always turned up in great form for the big competitions. The Dutch had endured a tough year but they were a creative team who, with a bit of luck on the injury front, could topple the leading teams.

Tunisia were the other team in the pool. North Africa's leading team were fully deserving of their place in the tournament but likely to find the going tough. Tunisia had hosted a week-long camp with other leading African sides before the World Cup Sevens with South Africa, Kenya, Senegal, Zimbabwe and Uganda all taking part. The game was still relatively new with women's rugby only getting off the ground in 2002. International events preceded even domestic competitions.

With some eventual government investment, eight women's clubs were established, mostly playing sevens. Captained by Ikhlas Abida, the Tunisian players faced even tougher challenges than others taking part in Moscow when temperatures soared over the two days. Many of the players played in leggings and hijabs, a testament to their dedication to playing the sport they loved.

Pool B had Australia, South Africa, Ireland and China. The Aussies had a mixed World Sevens Series, finishing no higher than fourth at any of the events and seventh at the last one in Amsterdam. They still had great talent though, with highly promising youngsters like Tiana Penitani, and they were the defending champions.

South Africa had made the final in Dubai at the start of the series but were close to the bottom in Amsterdam. They were a dangerous side with Phumeza Gadu already established as one of the best sevens players in the world, but they lacked consistency.

And then there was Ireland, switching from grand slam glory to World Cup Sevens. The Irish were targeting a place in the next World Sevens Series so they'd need to finish in the top eight. China were still developing and unlikely to challenge outside the bowl or plate.

Pool C pitted the USA, Spain, Fiji and Brazil together. The USA had finished fourth overall in the series but were now training full time as a squad in Chula Vista. In Vanesha McGee and Victoria Folayan, they had two of the top finishers in the game.

Spain were emerging as one of the most exciting teams in women's sevens but they had a small pool of players who were simultaneously preparing for the World Cup Sevens and attempting to qualify for the 2014 15-a-side World Cup. With players like Patricia García, Marina Bravo and Bárbara Plà, they were still expected to be dangerous.

Fiji were an unknown element. At least half the team had never played tournament rugby before. Brazil were the queens of South America but had found the going tougher outside of the continent.

Finally there was an exciting-looking Pool D with England, France, hosts Russia, and Japan competing. England had based their entire international year around the competition in Moscow, taking the hit at 15s to help prepare the sevens team. France were not yet prioritising sevens and Japan were unlikely to threaten, but hosts Russia were a team to watch with Baizat Khamidova a standout player.

The women's competition took place over two days, the first few rounds at the Gorodok Stadium, and later games moving to the nearby Luzhniki Stadium, an 81,000-seat ground which hosted the 1980 Olympics.

I travelled to cover the tournament and it was immediately clear that there was no real appetite or interest in the event from locals in Moscow. Few people were aware that a tournament was being played and, unsurprisingly, the stands were largely empty as the first games got underway. It was a curious location for the last showpiece sevens event before the Olympics.

The weather was also a challenge – baking hot for the pool games before an electrical storm threatened to delay the final round of games in the Luzhniki – but the players adapted well and a thoroughly entertaining event played out.

Each team's three pool games were all played on day one, with the knockouts – quarters, semis and final – on day two.

In stifling heat, New Zealand, Australia, the USA and Russia would all top their pools at the end of day one.

In Pool A, New Zealand comfortably beat Tunisia and the Netherlands before overcoming Canada 20-5 in the final game to finish top. Already it was clear that Honey Hireme, Kelly Brazier and Kayla McAlister were the stars, though Heather Moyse and Jen Kish were excellent too for Canada. The Netherlands' results meant that they would finish the tournament outside of the top eight and lose their status the following year as a core World Sevens Series team.

In Pool B, Australia's 17-year-old breakout star Tiani Penitani scored four tries in the opening win over China. Her side went on to beat Ireland and South Africa and displayed excellent form throughout. Ireland snuck a win over South Africa and ended the day with a fine win over China, with captain Claire Molloy outstanding to give her side a spot in the quarter-finals.

The USA lead the way in Pool C, just getting past Brazil and convincingly beating Fiji before a tighter match against Spain, where Victoria Folayan was in great form to help them to a 19-7 win to top the pool. Spain finished second after drawing with Fiji but beating Brazil. The Brazilians ended their day with an excellent win over the inexperienced Fijians.

In Pool D, England were beaten to top spot by a brilliant effort from the host nation. England started well enough with a win over France – Michaela Staniford scoring twice – before Russia squeezed past Japan. Russia and France then played out a brilliant 26-26 draw, in which the French came back from 19-7 down and scored in the last play with Christelle le Duff converting from the touchline.

It wasn't enough for a quarter-final slot for the French though. Russia went on to beat England by a couple of points in the final round for a sensational top spot. England would have to face the now-favourites New Zealand in the quarter-finals. The USA would play Ireland – now certain as a core team on the series the following year – Russia would take on Canada, and Australia would play Spain. The remaining sides were relegated to the bowl and plate events.

New Zealand against England promised to be the highlight of the cup quarter-finals but, as good as the Black Ferns were, England looked well off the pace. With Sarah Goss and Portia Woodman scoring early, even a 50-metre breakaway from Heather Fisher couldn't stop the Black Ferns. They won it 24-7 and comfortably qualified for the semis, pushing England into the plate competition. It was a real disappointment for the English having spent the year prioritising sevens.

Ireland pushed the USA hard, leading 5-0 at half-time before going down to a Victoria Folayen-inspired USA. A good crowd turned up for the next game as hosts Russia took on Canada. Russia led 12-10 going into the closing stages and it took a heroic effort from Ghislaine Landry to win it for Canada. Her try-saving tackle at one end led to her try at the other, sealing a 15-12 victory.

Australia v Spain was another incredible game with a dramatic finish. Australia, who lost the influential Tiani Penitani to injury early, were 10-7 up in the last play of the match only to switch off when the buzzer sounded. They conceded a soft try to Berta García, who ran 50 metres for the winning try. It was a huge result for the Spanish who sailed into the semi-finals. I was standing behind the Australian bench when García scored having prepared my questions for the Spanish captain about going into the plate. Lesson learned: take nothing for granted in sevens until the final whistle.

In the other games the result of note came between France and Fiji. The Pacific islanders showed everyone that with more experience they could be deadly, with a brilliant 12-10 win. The semi-finals followed and in the flagship event it would be a New Zealand v Canada cup final, with the Black Ferns beating the USA and Canada beating Spain.

With the weather taking a horrible turn, Australia and England first played out a thrilling plate final. The Aussies won 14-5 thanks to captain Sharni Williams's inspired form, scoring a last-gasp try to make certain of victory and making countless tackles.

In the cup final, Portia Woodman gave New Zealand the perfect start by going under the posts early and Kelly Brazier followed soon after for a 12-0 lead. Canada hit back through Arielle Dubissette-Borrice but Honey Hireme ensured New Zealand lead 17-5 at half-time. However, it was game on when the impressive Ghislaine Landry reached over and converted her own try.

Playing in their first World Cup Final of either format, Canada needed to score next. They didn't. Woodman and Kayla McAlister touched down to ensure New Zealand could celebrate come the final whistle. Woodman's double in the final meant she finished the tournament with 12 tries, easily beating the previous benchmark of nine tries set by compatriot Carla Hohepa in 2009 when New Zealand lost the final in extra time to Australia.

The experience had been an unusual one for the players. Jen Kish told me she was disappointed overall:

I had never been to Russia and was really looking forward to the experience. The 2009 World Cup had great crowds and I had this high expectation that this was going to be really big.

When we got to the final played in that huge stadium, it was almost totally empty and it was shocking to me. To run into it and see it completely empty for a World Cup Final was heart-breaking. We'd played New Zealand before the final and it was completely dry and then in the final the ball wouldn't even bounce because the weather was so bad.

We always look back at that game and almost laugh – there was so much water on the field! Overall, the lack of interest was very disappointing. This was meant to be a pinnacle event.

Lack of fans aside, the women's competition had been a success in other ways, highlighting the trajectory of the top teams with three years to go to the Olympics and the obvious improvements after just one year of the World Sevens Series.

There were some clear lessons for the next phase of the circuit. New Zealand were a class above and it was obvious they were set to dominate at the very top of the game. As for their competition, Canada were the most likely contenders, with the USA also having a great tournament.

Australia rued their mistakes but still looked a real threat with players like teenager Charlotte Caslick emerging. There would be some consolation for Australia later in the year when they would win the Oceania Sevens where the Black Ferns would be knocked out by Fiji, who continued to impress.

It was also obvious that the World Sevens Series would need to expand to ensure that improvements at the other end of the rankings could carry on. The IRB duly announced that two more legs would be added and Olympic hosts Brazil were also invited to all rounds of the series.

Race for the 15s World Cup underway

With one World Cup ending, the race for another in 2014 continued.

The European qualifiers took place over the summer in Madrid. Italy, Scotland, Spain, Sweden and the Netherlands competed for two slots alongside Samoa, who were also invited to take part. The Samoans had only played one Test game since the 2006 World Cup, an 87-0 defeat to Australia in a 2009 qualifier, and little was known about the group travelling to Spain. They were mainly expats living in New Zealand and Australia.

In the end they surprised everyone, qualifying for the World Cup alongside Spain despite being hammered by Italy in their opening match. They got their ticket to the World Cup by virtue of beating Sweden and the Netherlands, who both missed out, as did Italy and Scotland. Spain were the top side overall with three wins from three and a superb record, conceding just one try all week.

That Spain and Samoa emerged ahead of the more experienced Six Nations teams must have been something of a quiet delight for both, particularly the Spanish, who have always played with a point to prove following their Six Nations omission.

The 2014 World Cup line-up was complete when Kazakhstan and South Africa took the final two places following their victories in the Asian and African qualifiers.

As the focus now moved on to World Cup preparation, a large number of Test games would be played over the summer and autumn. France travelled to the USA to play a three-Test series. They won 2-1 although both sides were missing their sevens players, who would return to the 15s fold in the months ahead.

England's next three-Test series with New Zealand would be fascinating to see how the teams were shaping up a year out from France. With the previous two series having being held in England, this one was in New Zealand, where England hadn't won since 2001. Remarkably, the games would be New Zealand's first home Tests since 2007 when they hosted two games against Australia.

Stung by the series losses in 2011 and 2012, the hosts brought back a raft of stars. Victoria Grant brought important leadership qualities and experience while Kelly Brazier and Portia Woodman were switched in from the sevens programme. England had injuries, missied players like Maggie Alphonsi and Nolli Waterman, and travelled on the back of a disjointed season.

There was extra significance to the New Zealand and England game though. As we reported on Scrumqueens.com at the time, it would also mark the 1,000th women's rugby Test match.

It had taken the women's game just over 31 years to reach the milestone and it was a reminder of how far the game had come since the first Test game in 1982.

There were some aspects that remained far behind the men's game, apart from the obvious disparities in investment and infrastructure. There were no world rankings for the women's game, with seedings based entirely on performances at World Cups four years apart. A Scrumqueens.com project would later help tackle the issue.

New Zealand were too good in the first Test, securing a 29-10 win at Eden Park – their first win over England in seven outings – and the series was clinched with a 14-9 win in game two for the hosts. New Zealand secured a whitewash with a 29-8 win a few days later, with Kelly Brazier marshalling the team well for the hosts and England struggling despite a brilliant performance from Marlie Packer.

Next up was the Nations Cup where Canada took the win, beating an inexperienced England team 27-13 in Colorado to claim their first title. It was only their second win against England and ended a stellar year for Canada after their sevens team finished third in the World Sevens Series and second in the World Cup Sevens. USA beat South Africa to third place.

France, England and Canada would end the year with a Test series but the sevens game fittingly had the last word in 2013. Australia, now led by a new head coach, Steve Walsh, won the Dubai Sevens after a stunning comeback against New Zealand in the final.

With a 15s World Cup and an Olympic sevens on the horizon, the game was continuing to accelerate beyond recognition.

Chapter Twelve

Dare to dream

THE NEXT 24 months would be significant.

The World Cup in France simply had to build on the success of London four years earlier, while the Olympics in 2016 would be the moment to catapult women's rugby onto a global stage and reach new audiences and potential new investors.

The 2014 Six Nations was unpredictable. Ireland were defending champions but had to travel away for their toughest two games against England and France, teams that were much closer to full strength after a disappointing 2013 all round. France, with their key games at home, were confident.

France v England in front of almost 10,000 fans in Grenoble was a brilliant opening game. The French, looking forward to hosting the World Cup later in the year, were in inspired form, and won 18-6. France hadn't beaten England at home since 2004 and with a raft of players missing, including captain Marie-Alice Yahe through injury, it was a superb win in front of a raucous crowd. The home team played to their strengths and were led by the passionate Gaëlle Mignot, the hooker who crashed over for two second-half tries, with England struggling to defend a dominant French driving maul.

Ireland kicked off with a record-breaking 59-0 victory over Scotland, running in 11 tries in driving rain at their Ashbourne home. The result was their biggest margin of victory in international rugby, surpassing a 55-0 win over Japan back in November 2004. They were far superior to a Scottish side searching for a first Six Nations win in almost four years.

The opening weekend's final match brought another upset, with Italy, who had failed to qualify for the World Cup, beating Wales 12-11 in Port Talbot thanks to flanker Ilaria Arrighetti's late try. The opening-round results handed France an early favourites tag for the title, although they had a tough game against Ireland to come at home.

Both came through round two unscathed, with wins over Wales and Italy and neither conceding a try. Ireland ground out a 14-6 win over the Welsh while France were made to work hard for their 29-0 over Italy. England bounced back from the disappointment of losing their opening match with an emphatic 63-0 victory over Scotland in Aberdeen, with 11 different players crossing for tries.

France seized the advantage in the next round with a win over Wales while Ireland fell 17-10 to England at Twickenham in front of an impressive crowd of around 13,000 fans, who stayed on to watch after the men's game.

Ireland fell behind to a try from number 8 Sarah Hunter, before a Niamh Briggs penalty and a try for scrum-half Larissa Muldoon edged them into a 10-7 lead. England went back in front before half-time as player of the match Emily Scarratt sent winger Kay Wilson over in the left corner. That was enough.

Italy bounced back from their defeat to France a fortnight earlier with an emphatic 45-5 victory over Scotland. The tournament was now France's to lose.

The title came down to the final game in Pau when they hosted Ireland. Bridesmaids four years in a row, France desperately needed to win. The game began at a furious pace and France twice went close before in-form wing Marion Lievre crossed with five minutes gone after Ireland ran out of numbers. The home side wasted no time in improving their advantage at the start of the second period with tries from prop Elodie Portaries and centre Shannon Izar easing them into a 19-3 lead.

But Ireland refused to give up their title without a fight and two well-worked driving mauls brought a brace of tries for hooker Gill Bourke. It wasn't enough though and at 19-15, the final whistle sent the loud 8,500-strong crowd into raptures.

A 24-0 victory over Italy gave England second spot, with star full-back Danielle Waterman back after a 14-month injury break. Scotland were bottom again with a fourth consecutive whitewash after succumbing to a 25-0 defeat to Wales in their final game.

On and off the field, the 2014 Six Nations was a huge success and laid the ground for the World Cup to come in a few months' time. It was one of the closest on record, with three teams entering the final weekend with a chance to lift the title.

The games themselves were watched by more people than ever before, with a record ten of the 15 either live-streamed or available as live TV broadcasts. Every team, except Wales, was broadcasting or streaming some or all of their home games. Every game played by Ireland and England was available to fans in one form or another, as were three of the games played by France and Italy.

Crowds were also impressive, with all three of France's home games attracting capacity or near-capacity crowds. The game against England also established a new record for a paying attendance at a women's international outside a World Cup Final.

Ashbourne in Ireland was also packed for its games, while an estimated 6,000 paid or stayed on to watch the 2013 champions' first ever game at the Aviva Stadium and thousands took advantage of free entry at Twickenham for their game against England. Italy's home games were also played in front of full stands and interest in games in Wales and Scotland were high, despite their results.

The Six Nations had become a hugely important competition for women's rugby with an established place in the calendar – even if it would be better to have a new window – and an expectation that it would bring media profile and big crowds. It was the perfect platform to build interest and enthusiasm for the World Cup, especially as the rise of sevens was beginning to have an impact on the volume of Test 15s games being played.

The number of Test matches between 2010 and 2013 was significantly lower than for the previous four-year period, with the game's third-ranked nation – Australia – playing no Test matches at all.

At least one regional tournament, the Caribbean Championship, had disappeared from the fixture list entirely. Even in Europe, the quadrennial continental championship was competed for by only four teams, instead of up to 12 who had played in previous years.

Resources in many countries had been redirected in support of bids for medals at the 2016 Rio Olympics or the 2020 Games in Tokyo, but the Six Nations games, crowds and broadcast interest were an important reminder that enthusiasm for top-quality Test rugby remained high among the game's fanbase.

As the World Cup-qualified teams geared up for their final warm-up games before heading to France, the World Sevens Series entered its second season. Australia had taken the opening round in Dubai, the impact of Tim Walsh immediately evident, and they went tit-for-tat in the months that followed with New Zealand, who took the Atlanta title. Australia won the São Paolo event before New Zealand made a decisive play, winning both legs in China and Amsterdam to take the series.

New Zealand, Australia, Canada and England made up the top four at the end of the 2013/14 season and it was confirmed that the series would be expanded with Canada and England being awarded hosting spots for the next year and an extra round added. Australia's Emilee Cherry was named player of the year.

World Cup preparations were now in full swing. As build-up for their campaign, Kazakhstan confirmed their position as the leading Test nation in Asia with a comprehensive victory in the Asian Four Nations tournament, which took place in Hong Kong.

There would also be a series played in New Zealand, where Australia and Canada would compete in a Tri-Nations tournament. The Black Ferns would also play Samoa for the first time ever. It kickstarted an unprecedented summer of Test action.

World Cup warm-up games included matches involving all of the above plus France, Spain, Wales, South Africa and Ireland. Extra Test opposition came in the form of the Nomads, an international invitational team organised by Fiona Stockley featuring top players from around the world. The Nomads laid important foundations for the establishment of the Barbarians women's team some years later, with Stockley central to its introduction.

The preparation games seemed to confirm that New Zealand, the defending champions, would be the team to beat, despite their relative lack of game time compared to great rivals England. The Kiwis secured a clean sweep with wins over Canada, Samoa and Australia.

But the Canada victories were narrow enough (33-21 and 16-8) to suggest that the Canadians were progressing well. Players like Elissa Alarie and Magali Harvey, who would go on to have outstanding World Cups, were showing huge promise. Led by the impressive Francois Ratier, Canada had clearly been steadily building towards the World Cup and were among the frontrunners leading into the competition.

France keep a winning formula

After the success of the set-up in London, France unsurprisingly opted for a similar approach.

The pool games would be hosted on back-to-back pitches at the French National Rugby Centre in Marcoussis, a small village south of Paris, before the final knockout stages moved to the Stade Jean-Bouin in Paris, home to Stade Français. Most of the teams were able to stay on site, and the tournament retained the festival feel that had been such a hit four years earlier.

The teams were once again divided into three pools of four teams. Pool A included England, Canada, Spain and Samoa. Pool B was Ireland, USA, New Zealand and Kazakhstan. Pool C had Wales, South Africa, Australia and hosts France. The three pool winners would progress to the semi-finals along with the second-placed team with the highest points tally.

Because they continuously defied expectations at World Cups, reigning champions New Zealand were hard to bet against going into it, though England, as ever, had had much better preparation in terms of game time.

The Black Ferns' pool was no walkover, however, with Ireland a totally different team to the one that had played four years earlier and the USA one of the most physical sides in the world. New Zealand travelled with an experienced squad, bolstered by the inclusion of a handful of players with sevens experience like Kelly Brazier and with the familiar pairing of Amiria Rule and Huriana Manuel in the centre. Most expected them to dominate.

England had experience under their belt including, crucially, experience of beating the Black Ferns having played them nine times since the 2010 World Cup Final loss, winning five and drawing one. Although they'd lost all three Tests in 2013 on the road in New Zealand, England were convinced they were a better team than the Black Ferns. Given some of the mistakes they felt they'd made in 2010, this time they were leaving nothing to chance.

Led by Katy Daley-Mclean, they decided not to base themselves in Marcoussis like the bulk of the other teams, and stayed at a hotel away from the venue, which they shared with the USA. As Gary Street recalled afterwards, the management had travelled out in advance, scoped out the hotel and nabbed the best meeting rooms and spaces at the hotel. They'd also decided not to share gym facilities with the other teams at the tournament venue and had transported the entire gym from Twickenham Stadium to the local rugby club they'd be using to train in. On a rugby coaching podcast, he recalled:

> We spent thousands of pounds bringing the whole gym out there. From the equipment, the floor and the livery. It was like walking into the gym at Twickenham and the impact on the players of that was massive.

There were some external question marks over England's form though. They'd been runners-up in the Six Nations and, with the focus on sevens in previous years, had stuttered somewhat in some of their big games since the last World Cup, losing to Ireland and France, but the squad itself travelled with confidence and were mostly at full strength.

Of the other contenders, Australia were remarkably still considered in the running, such was the strength of players like Shannon Parry and Sharni Williams, but they'd played so little rugby in four years that, as ever, the knockout stages were always a stretch.

Ireland were eyeing a first ever semi-final slot, taking an experienced and successful team, but they would probably have to beat New Zealand to make the final four, something most pundits and fans considered out of reach before the competition began. Canada were building nicely under Francois Ratier and were packed with game-changing players who had built solid experience in the lead-up.

Hosts France were also in the mix. They had never reached a final, finishing third four times and fourth in 2010, but were certainly capable.

With the home crowd behind them and a favourable-looking pool, anything was possible, especially with the momentum they had from the Six Nations. They were dealt a significant blow though when their captain Marie-Alice Yahe, a superb scrum-half whose silhouette was on every poster marketing the competition, had to drop out a few weeks before because of repeated concussions.

The IRB had been promoting the importance of concussion management, hough many felt it was not a high enough priority for the game more widely at the time. Yahe had had a history of concussion, and in an interview with French media she laid bare what a serious problem it could be:

> I was practising passes during the Six Nations. My coach sent the ball my way when I wasn't looking, and I took it on the head. I did not feel well, and the more minutes passed, the worse I felt. We ended up calling the doctor, who finally arrived a few minutes after I had collapsed.
>
> He told me that the brain has a sort of reserve that could absorb a number of shocks. Me, my reserve was exhausted, and the doctor could not predict what would happen to me if I took another blow to the head. It was too risky to continue.
>
> Before I stopped, every concussion I had was more and more difficult to recover from. On the previous occasion, the headache lasted almost a month and I lost my bearings regularly.

Another New Zealand v England final was far from a foregone conclusion. With sevens attracting much limelight and investment, an unpredictable tournament with a final in front of a sold-out crowd in Paris was surely the ideal scenario for the 15-a-side game.

The opening pool games provided little shock value, though Ireland's comfortable win over the USA did set up an exciting second-round game against the Black Ferns. Ireland v USA was always likely to be the tightest of the opening round and so it proved, with the Irish edging it 23-17. Irish full-back Niamh Briggs's accuracy from the boot proved invaluable.

New Zealand demolished Kazakhstan 79-5 in the opening game of the entire event, a match played in scorching temperatures with little respite for the teams in the French afternoon sun. Huriana Manuel scored after just a minute and from there it was one-way traffic.

England opened in similar comfort, beating Samoa 65-5. The Samoans played with 14 players for most of the game after an early red card added to the mismatch. Canada beat Spain 31-7 in the same pool, with winger Magali Harvey looking a threat throughout.

In Pool C, Australia were too good for South Africa, though failed to pick up a crucial bonus point, while hosts France survived a wobbly start to defeat Wales with a bonus point in their opening game in front of a big home crowd.

The big match in round two would be Ireland against New Zealand.

World Cup turns green

The two sides had never met before but Ireland were the most improved side in the world over the four-year World Cup cycle and went into the game confident that the Black Ferns were beatable. They spoke confidently ahead of the game, a rare occurrence for any team about to play New Zealand.

Irish skipper Fiona Coghlan said in her media preview, 'We'll be watching footage of them, and we'll look at our own game. We'll be watching the videos, but they can be beaten.' With so many teams beaten mentally before even taking to the field against New Zealand, it was a brazen and refreshing approach, showing just how far the Irish had come in recent years.

The Irish of course had had a remarkable run into the World Cup. After the success of the 2013 Six Nations there had been disappointment with their finish in 2014. With a core of players with World Cup experience under their belt, the team had pulled together, got fitter and stronger and had determined their own ground rules around their behaviour, expectations and attitude in France.

They'd had warm-up games this time and had some hands-on involvement from Irish men's coaches Joe Schmidt and Les Kiss. Massive analysis work had been done, particularly on both the USA and New Zealand, by their backroom team in advance, so the team knew exactly how they'd approach both of their crucial pool matches.

They also had to deal with some quiet setbacks, including what could have been a serious injury to one of their best and most experienced players Lynne Cantwell. Three weeks before the World Cup, Cantwell had broken two bones in her back in training, landing awkwardly after a tackle by a team-mate. Nobody was made aware of the injury bar Fiona Coghlan – the team's captain and Cantwell's close friend – and the Irish coaching and medical team. She even had to keep the news quiet from her work colleagues, who happened to include the England lock Jo McGilchrist, also playing at the World Cup.

Cantwell, who with 82 caps going into the tournament was a vital player, didn't want to panic anyone or make the story about her. She was medically cleared to play in the tournament after three weeks of rest and recovery which involved sending pictures to Coghlan every day charting her improving mobility.

When Ireland led 20-10 at half-time against the USA in the opener, Cantwell was in the bathroom vomiting thanks to the combination of the painkillers she was taking and the force of the first half against a hugely physical American team. Remarkably she went back out and played every remaining minute of the game. Her inclusion in the team to play New Zealand was crucial. She said:

I knew medically it was safe to play so it was more about whether I could manage it functionally. I didn't want to freak anyone out by telling them – it wasn't important, and I didn't want people talking about it. I told the girls after the tournament, and we had a little laugh about it. Although reflecting on it now, it was a big issue; at the time I was hoping to avoid it drawing any attention.

Cantwell was as confident as any going into the game that Ireland could win:

We had no fear. We had never experienced playing New Zealand before so there was no precedent. For those of us who had been around a while, and lost so many times to various teams over the years, we or maybe I rarely went into games with winning as my goal, it was more of a focus on problem solving and being as good as possible. This helped facing playing New Zealand when having the goal solely to win may seem overwhelming. We wanted to capitalise on their weaknesses. We'd identified that in their open play kick receipts, they kicked back a huge amount, so we had a plan about how to respond to that and to have players ready to respond when those opportunities arose.

That small detail would be a vital part in the greatest upset in World Cup history.

The Black Ferns had not lost a World Cup game since defeat to the United States in the semi-finals in 1991.

The first 40 minutes were played at an astonishing pace – and almost all of it in the New Zealand half. Ireland soon made it clear that they were not remotely overawed to be taking on the world champions for the first time and put the Black Ferns under huge pressure from the first minute. New Zealand absorbed everything that came at them and a Kelly Brazier penalty and a try from Selicia Winata meant that, despite all of Ireland's pressure, they were 8-0 down.

A drinks break allowed Ireland to regather. Heather O'Brien, from my own club Highfield in Cork, was driven over to score. Niamh Briggs added the conversion before half-time. New Zealand came out of the blocks in the second half like a team reborn and quickly they extended their lead with a simple penalty for Kelly Brazier.

It was a quarter of an hour before Ireland were back in the New Zealand half, but there had been no further additions to the score. Alison Miller won a vital turnover and Ireland were on the attack. Then came the moment.

New Zealand kicked and failed to chase hard as Ireland's analysis had suggested. Niamh Briggs ghosted through the Ferns line – and there was Miller to her left. Once she had the ball in hand there was no stopping her, and she was over in the corner. Briggs nailed a vital kick from the corner.

Ireland 14, New Zealand 11. The lead did not last long. Soon a Brazier penalty had brought the teams level, 14-14, with barely a quarter of an hour left.

Crucial moments were coming thick and fast. New Zealand seemed to crack under pressure, booting two kicks straight into touch. From the second, the ball was won by Ireland, moved wide, and from the resulting ruck a penalty was awarded.

Briggs slotted it perfectly and Ireland were 17-14 ahead with just seven minutes left.

Ireland's defence was incredible, with Jenny Murphy coming off the bench and making a huge impact in that department too, as Cantwell recalled:

> Everyone was focusing on trying not to see the bigger picture and just stay engaged with what was in front of us. Jen came on at half-time and made a big impact, she made some big tackles and carries to take over from the work done by Grace Davitt. We were surprised at how little they ran the ball and how little they were putting width on their attack compared to what we'd seen. As a result, it was more manageable and with the way we were defending we felt we could contain their attack
>
> It seemed that New Zealand changed their tactics in that second half and kicked more. We also had identified they tended to tire post 60 minutes and when it got to this mark with us ahead, it gave us confidence to dig in to the end.

Most of those final minutes were in the New Zealand half and, as the clock ran down, Ireland were the team most likely to score. The final seconds counted down with Ireland right on the New Zealand line. As soon as the clock went to zero the ball was in the crowd. Ireland had won it 17-14.

The result all but guaranteed Ireland a first ever semi-final slot. It initially looked like New Zealand might end up facing England at the same stage.

There were no other dramas in the second round with the USA too good for Kazakhstan, England and Canada setting up a pool decider thanks to their respective wins over Spain and Samoa, while Australia and France beat Wales and South Africa.

Ahead of the final pool games, it was clear that Ireland's win had firmly thrown the cat among the pigeons. New Zealand were scrapping it out with two other teams for the best runner-up spot. In their favour was the scoreline they had put on Kazakhstan which gave them an advantage in points difference, but their fate was not completely in their hands.

There was a raft of permutations that would see New Zealand progress or fail. Entering the final day of pool matches, none of the seven teams left in contention could be certain of a place in the semi-finals. Four of the six games on Saturday would have a bearing on the outcome. The England v Canada game was now vital. A draw would be the worst possible outcome for the reigning champions.

It was the second game of the day and it was always likely to be tight; Canada had beaten England twice almost exactly a year before – though more recently England recorded a decisive 32-3 win at The Stoop. A draw – a rarity in the women's game – still felt unlikely, and neither side could really get a grip on the match early on.

Canada started well enough with centre Andrea Burk bursting through the middle, but Emily Scarratt gave England a 3-0 lead to continue her fine form with the boot. Karen Paquin then burrowed over the line for a try for Canada but England turned around 6-5 ahead thanks to another Scarratt penalty which ended a nervy first half.

Canada drove over the line again through Kalya Mack, but Sarah Hunter got one back for England who went 13-10 up. Eventually Magali Harvey stepped up to level things at 13-13, making for the tensest of finales. As the final whistle went, it started to become clear that New Zealand had been knocked out.

Francois Ratier told me the aftermath was far from clear:

> We really wanted to beat them and when Gary Street and myself were reading that we ensured a draw on purpose to

eliminate New Zealand, I was like wow you couldn't be more wrong – we desperately wanted to win.

It was terrible afterwards. We hadn't thought too much about a draw so for ten minutes we were in the fog of who had qualified and then England coach Graham Smith said, well done, you've qualified – and I really wasn't sure. France needed to beat Australia and so we didn't know New Zealand were out for a while. There was ten minutes of total confusion.

But New Zealand were out. Their win later in the day against the USA was scant consolation for the team that had dominated World Cups for so long.

As the final four teams to contest the semi-finals became clear, it was also clear that the World Cup was already a massive success. Tickets were selling fast for the knockout stages with hopes high that the 20,000-capacity stadium could be filled in Paris.

In the pool games, day three brought a capacity crowd on both pitches – unlike in 2010, the French sold separate tickets for each field – and fans turning up on the day were sent away.

France reaching the semi-final also kept the spotlight high on the competition. Led by Gaëlle Mignot, they were set to face Canada in the semi-finals, a match they were confident they could win. Their pack had been magnificent throughout and Mignot's accurate throwing and ability to get under the ball meant their driving line-out was almost impossible to defend. They were going into the knockout stages having not conceded a try. Safi N'Diaye had grown into the tournament after a quiet start and Sandrine Agricole had been superb at fly-half.

A massive crowd and a record TV audience was expected for their semi-final. Canada would need to be at their best, but their pack was a match for the French with Kelly Russell leading superbly and Mandy Marchak and Andrea Burk a handful in the middle.

Ireland would take on England, who had not been convincing in the draw against Canada but had all the experience and were surely favourites now New Zealand were out. England had the most talented all-round squad left in the tournament, with better strength in depth than anyone else. It was their best chance to win a World Cup since they last lifted it in 1994.

That game was first and England found their best form to win 40-7. It was their best display in some time – perhaps since beating New Zealand in 2012 – showing improvement in almost every area since their match against Canada. Their powerful scrummaging and clinical finishing had the edge over an Ireland side who never quite got to grips with them over 80 minutes.

England's scrum laid the platform for excellent performances from players like Emily Scarratt and Danielle Waterman, the former also kicking superbly to put the game beyond Ireland's reach when it mattered. Waterman was unfortunately forced off with a head injury, missing the final because of the need to go through return-to-play protocols.

England's coaches even had the luxury of rotating their bench towards the 70-minute mark. Though Ireland would have another game to battle it out for the third, or fourth-place ranking, it marked a painful end. It was a game too far for a highly talented team still lacking the depth and experience to go any further.

A massive crowd turned up to watch the hosts take on Canada next in a game that was terrifically exciting and brought with it the try of the tournament. France started well as Sandrine Agricole gave her team the lead with a penalty before Magali Harvey made it 3-3. It was 6-6 at half-time and after the break Canada raced out of the blocks. Elissa

Alarie broke through after just two minutes and raced 30 metres to finish superbly. Harvey missed the kick but Canada were 11-6 up.

It got even better a minute later. Canada were back on their own try line with a scrum but rather than kick it clear, they played it wide quickly, found Harvey and the winger raced the length of the pitch to score in the corner. It was undoubtedly the try of the tournament, made all the more remarkable by the fact that France, until a few minutes before, had not conceded a try all tournament. Harvey then coolly knocked over the touchline conversion and her side led 18-6.

France were in danger of falling apart with Canada coming at them from every angle. Though they had plenty of ball, indecision under pressure was proving costly. But, finally, they did get back into it. Going back to their strengths, a massive driving maul helped them over the line with the backing of a raucous crowd and the try was awarded. France should have had another when Caroline Ladagnous ran from one 22 to the other having called a mark, but Marjorie Mayans held on too long and, despite the overlap out wide, Canada held firm.

The clock began to tick down with France desperately seeking a levelling score. With four minutes to go their chance came. A line-out to the corner brought about a maul and they did not need to be asked twice. Agricole couldn't nail the kick though. With just two minutes left, it was too late for France to come back again. Canada won 18-16.

Harvey's try lit up social media and match reports after the game though she was modest about it afterwards, telling me in the bowels of the stadium:

My main thought when I got the ball was just to run fast! I have an amazing trainer who has worked with me on my speed, and he helped me get a lot faster so I do trust and back my speed. When I saw their full-back, I could see that her hips were turned so it was easy to just cut back in and keep on running. When I started the programme, over 40 metres I could run in 5.88 and now I can do it in 5.38 so it is a big improvement for me.

Coach Francois Ratier too said the try was vindication for the style of rugby his team were trying to play:

The try summarised what the team had been doing for two years. It came from a mistake first. We dropped the ball in front of our try line, then our loosehead MP Reid won the scrum just to save her team-mate from the position we were in! From that, Elissa Alarie decided to attack and the players around her responded and you could almost see them collectively say yes, let's do it.

It was exactly what we were trying to achieve. I was shaking our analyst and yelling and shouting at Magali to go, go, go and not to pass it! It was such a good try. At half-time we told the players that France were starting to get lazy around the breakdown and it took Alarie one second to go through a gap to score after the break.

The crowds and the drama of both games made the semi-finals a huge success.

After 20 years of near misses, England surely had to win the final.

Scarratt the star

England had an excellent record against Canada.

Twelve of their 26 players had already played in a World Cup Final, with five of them having played in two.

Canada did have big-game experience though in the form of sevens. Five of their players were in the squad who played in the World Cup Sevens Final the previous summer in Moscow, but nothing would compare to the noise and atmosphere they experienced in front of a huge crowd in Paris.

The teams ran out in front of a near-capacity 22,000 crowd on a grey evening at the Stade Jean-Bouin.

England dominated early on and Emily Scarratt, who was excellent, converted an early penalty. Canada's best threat came from their wide players with Magali Harvey in particular almost latching onto an early intercept. England had one try ruled out but when Scarratt knocked over another penalty, the pressure built and Danielle Waterman crossed for a fantastic team try just before half-time. It was a wonderful score involving a lovely dummy from lock Tamara Taylor, and an offload to Maggie Alphonsi, who put Waterman away.

Canada pulled three points back in injury time from a Harvey penalty following an England offside and they began the second half strongly, cutting the score by three following another penalty from Harvey as Canada threatened to get right back into it. Yet another penalty from Harvey cut the deficit to two points but England responded immediately with three points of their own when 20 minutes were remaining, Scarratt's boot proving accurate again.

The game needed something special to bring it to life and it came after 73 minutes through the outstanding Scarratt. She shrugged off a tackle and ran a superb line to score near the posts. It was a sucker punch for Canada. With just six minutes on the clock, they could do little as England stretched out an unassailable 21-9 lead.

After their 20-year wait to lift the World Cup, England celebrated joyously when the final whistle came. Katy Daley-Mclean eloquently dedicated the victory to all those who had missed out in the past:

It is everything that I have ever dreamed of. You start tournaments like a World Cup and you dare to dream.

The way our luck has gone in World Cups you don't hope too much. This squad of people, staff and management, have been the most special I have ever worked with and today they finally got their reward.

We've worked so hard for this, and there are so many great legends that have gone before us that haven't won in an England shirt, and that's for all of them who are here today

You come into a final and expect a real game and all credit to Canada they really showed up and put us under massive pressure. Twenty years is a long time and there has been a lot of hurt and a lot of pain for England at World Cups. It is nice to be able to change that.

With England champions, hosts France had the consolation of finishing third, beating Ireland in a superb contest 25-18, while Magali Harvey was named player of the tournament.

New Zealand were fifth, a bet that would have been given long odds before the tournament. The Black Ferns would have some home truths to consider: how prepared and supported their team was, and what would need to change to get them back into contention in three years' time. The next World Cup would be played a year earlier to ensure no clash with the World Cup Sevens so they needed to improve and fast.

The 2014 World Cup had been a success with even bigger crowds than 2010, enhanced broadcast packages and huge profile and spotlight on the game's leading players. The hosts for the next edition had not yet been announced but it was clear that the IRB would have to continue the momentum by choosing a location that could build on the success of England and France.

There was big news too for 12 of England's World Cup-winning squad. They were soon named in a squad of 20 who would be handed full-time paid contracts to represent their country at sevens. Having been one of the few leading nations not to have awarded contracts in the lead-up to the Olympics, the newly named squad included 15s captain Katy Daley-Mclean.

For the next few years, England would prioritise sevens, despite their 15s World Cup win.

The rest of the year was firmly focused on sevens too as the most important World Sevens Series – with Olympic qualification at stake – was about to swing back into action.

A number of countries announced important investments and commitments, with Ireland joining England in awarding contracts to leading players. With an eye on the future, Australia became the first side to win the sevens at the Youth Olympic Games in China.

New Zealand took out the opening round of the World Sevens Series in Dubai in December after a terrific final against Australia where they came from 17-0 down to win it 19-17. Captain Sarah Goss, who played on day two with a broken finger, dotted down in the corner with time up on the clock to steal victory from Australia, leaving Sharni Williams and her team-mates devastated.

Belated recognition for game's pioneers

Off the field, there was one last major event before the end of another momentous year in the game. Six women were named in the IRB's Hall of Fame for the first time.

The lack of women in the Hall of Fame had long been a frustration.

Earlier that year, to coincide with International Women's Day, I'd published an open letter on Scrumqueens.com to CEO of the IRB Brett Gosper, asking for the situation to be addressed. I wrote:

Since the IRB Hall of Fame was established in 2006, 79 players, teams, clubs and other institutions involved in the game from the 19th century to the present day have been inducted.

None have yet been women.

When the IRB opened the Hall of Fame the stated aim was 'to recognise the proud history and traditions of the Game, including its origins', and in addition since 2012 to 'celebrate rugby's expansion to become a global sport played by millions of men and women worldwide'.

I am sure you would not only acknowledge the hugely important role women have played as players, officials, coaches and administrators to our great sport, but also the often hidden history of the struggle women had in the previous century to be allowed to play the game at all.

Scrumqueens.com believes their absence within this accolade is out of step with the enormously positive changes and growth in the women's game itself, and indeed the influence of women across the wider game.

When we asked our readers to suggest women who they would love to see inducted into the Hall of Fame, the responses highlighted that the IRB would not be short of options.

This weekend it's International Women's Day and what better time to shine a spotlight on some of the legendary women in our sport.

We are hopeful that in this World Cup year the current status quo will indeed change but also feel strongly that honouring the achievement of women in rugby should not require a once-in-four-years World Cup – this should happen anyway and should have happened long ago.

The letter concluded with a shortlist of 12 worthy candidates put forward by Scrumqueens.com writers and readers. Our suggested list included Emily Valentine, Maria Eley, Carol

Isherwood, Kathy Flores, Gill Burns, Dr Farah Palmer, Donna Kennedy and Anna Richards. We also put forward teams like the Wiverns, who had played such an instrumental role in developing the standards of the game.

We received no reply from Gosper or the IRB but, coincidence or not, it was gratifying to see the situation remedied when the first list was announced just months later and when it included four of our recommendations with Burns, Isherwood, Richards and Palmer all named while Patty Jervey and Nathalie Amiel were also named.

Since then several more inspirational women have been added to the list with surely many more to come.

Chapter Thirteen

The Olympic stage at last

AS AFTER every World Cup, the following year was one of transition. The 2015 Six Nations returned with a raft of new faces.

Ireland coach Philip Doyle stepped down after the French event and wasn't replaced until a few weeks out by Tom Tierney. The Irish had also seen several key players like Lynne Cantwell, Fiona Coghlan and Grace Davitt retire.

A bigger surprise was announced at the turn of the year: the departure of Gary Street from England.

England and Street had been feted for their World Cup win with individual and team accolades, including Team of the Year at the BBC's prestigious Sports Personality of the Year awards.

Street's departure was, therefore, a surprise. It was also announced that his assistant Graham Smith would leave after the Six Nations. Given the proximity of that competition, Nicky Ponsford, the RFU head of performance for women and a former World Cup winner, would lead the coaching team on an interim basis.

With the competition dovetailing alongside the World Sevens Series that was crucial for qualification for the Olympics, it also meant that numerous star 15s players would be missing from the Six Nations. England, for example, would be without at least 14 players from their World Cup squad when you added in retirements. The title was up for grabs.

World Cup qualification for 2017 was also on the minds of Scotland, Wales and Italy. This Six Nations would be key to their chances.

Wales had finished eighth at the World Cup but benefited from some of their younger players building experience. Led by Rachel Taylor, they had the ability to cause headaches for teams, especially at home.

No one seriously expected them to turn England over on day one. But Taylor was magnificent as Wales pulled off a shock win in Swansea with the score 13-0 and, in doing so, became the first team since Ireland two years earlier to shut out England. It was only Wales's second ever win against England in their history and it came thanks to second-half tries from tight-head prop Catrin Edwards and winger Laurie Harries, who had earlier kicked the home side into a 3-0 interval lead.

France opened with a 42-0 win over Scotland with Julie Billes grabbing a hat-trick and the result made it 241 minutes since Scotland had scored a point in the championship.

Tom Tierney began his reign in charge of Ireland with a comfortable 30-5 win against Italy in Florence. Their game against France in round two already had the look of a title decider.

In round two, Wales continued their good form to beat Scotland 39-3, a result that meant back-to-back opening wins for the Welsh in the Six Nations for the first time since 2009. They were top of the table at the end of the weekend after France went to Ireland.

It had been a scoreless opening 40 minutes, although France had dominated in front of a few thousand people at Ireland's home venue of Ashbourne. The game then descended into something of a farce at the start of the second half when a series of floodlight failures due to a generator stalling put the remainder of the game in doubt. After an hour off the field, the problem was resolved and the teams remerged to play the rest of the game in biting cold air with the match restarting at 9.15pm, almost two hours after it had kicked off.

Prop Ailis Egan grabbed a try for Ireland a few minutes later but, just when another memorable result was in sight for the hosts, winger Caroline Boujard intercepted a pass and raced away to score. Jessy Trémoulière added the conversion and then a penalty to secure the 10-5 win for France. Much of the media coverage focused afterwards on the floodlight failure, with the *Irish Times* damning the IRFU's inability to host women's games at Test-quality venues.

Long-time women's rugby writer Gavin Cumisky wrote:

Has the penny dropped yet? The arrival of women's rugby is for keeps. Despite this agonising 10-5 loss to Six Nations champions France, Ireland's status as sporting heroines remains intact and surely, after Friday night's farcical events, they have earned a modern stage to show their worth.

The good folk of Ashbourne RFC are not entirely to blame for the blackout, having made their basic facilities such a cosy home with so many happy memories over the years. But the 2013 grand slam and reaching the World Cup semi-final last year has not been enough to convince the IRFU that their senior women deserve an arena befitting their soaring stature.

Maybe they will see the light when investigating this floodlight failure that took an hour of far too much confusion to fix. The RDS and Donnybrook were empty tonight. So too Thomond Park. A healthy crowd of about 2,100 crammed into the Meath venue. Lots of French visitors, sniggering at Ireland's inability to play a Test match in a proper stadium.

Against that backdrop, England bounced back from their opening-day defeat to Wales with a six-try 39-7 victory against Italy at The Stoop. Katy Daley-Mclean kicked the first points of the afternoon after returning to the side from sevens action in Brazil, but the first try fell to Italy, who had never beaten England in 14 previous attempts, when Flavia Severin barged her way over. England responded well and replied with a try from Alex Matthews after a period of sustained pressure. From then on, it was largely one-way traffic.

France remained on course to successfully defend their title with a 28-7 victory over Wales in front of a near-capacity crowd at the Stade de Sapiac in Montauban. Gaëlle Mignot's early try was backed up by two Julie Billes efforts and a penalty try, as well as eight points from the boot of Jessy Trémoulière.

Ireland were the story of the weekend again as they beat England 11-8 on a freezing cold evening once more in Ashbourne. England led 8-3 at half-time but Ireland picked up the pace in the second half, and eight minutes in scrum-half Larissa Muldoon's decision to tap and go from a penalty was rewarded with five points.

Ireland's defence held firm to secure just their second win in 21 matches against England.

Meanwhile Italy beat Scotland 31-8. The Scots at least bagged a try, only their third in three seasons.

The next round was even more dramatic. France suffered a shock loss to Italy and, with England and Ireland winning, five of the six teams in the competition would go into the final round of matches with a mathematical chance of winning the title.

Unbeaten for their last nine matches in the Six Nations, France went to Italy having made several changes – some enforced through suspension and sevens commitments – to the side that defeated Wales in round three. Italy looked the more assured of the two teams from the start and were rewarded for a bright opening when they crossed at the corner with just five minutes on the clock. Veronica Schiavon turned the five points into seven with a brilliant touchline conversion.

France hit back almost immediately when Julie Billes touched down for her sixth try of the championship and Jessy Trémoulière levelled the scores with the conversion. There were no further scores until the 37th minute when Italy struck for a second time through Sofia Stefan. But back came France again, Safi N'Diaye setting up Caroline Boujard for a try as the sides entered the break locked at 12-12.

A great rearguard action from Italy and two penalty misses from Trémoulière kept France scoreless in the second half, and it was left to Maria Magatti to seal a famous win when she squeezed over in the corner for her second try of the match – and her fourth of the championship – in the dying seconds.

Ireland, meanwhile, kept their title hopes alive with a 20-0 win over Wales in Swansea while a hat-trick from Ruth Laybourn on her home pitch ensured England got their campaign back on track against a dogged Scotland side in Darlington.

The results meant that France and Ireland were joint top of the table with one round of fixtures left. France were in front on scoring difference with a tally of +63 compared to Ireland's +43 but had the more difficult fixture against England at Twickenham to contend with next. In contrast, the Irish had an away assignment against Scotland.

France kicked off the final weekend by setting Ireland a 27-point target after chalking up a 21-15 win over England at Twickenham. Jessy Trémoulière finished second to Briggs as the tournament's top points-scorer after scoring a try and kicking 11 points to boost her overall tally to 43.

The other French try was scored by captain and hooker Gaëlle Mignot.

The result meant England finished a disappointing fourth just months after winning the World Cup. Though the tournament finish was poor by their standards, it did spark a review of the strength in depth of the English women's game, out of which would later emerge a new elite league which significantly improved the quality of the country's top-level club game.

Italy finished strongly after an impressive 22-5 win over Wales at the Stadio Plebiscito in Padua. Their three victories put them in pole position for World Cup 2017 qualification, with the best two teams outside of England, Ireland and France across the 2015 and 2016 Six Nations booking their tickets to Ireland in 2017, where the next World Cup would be held.

The title was Ireland's again after a 73-3 win over Scotland. Tom Tierney's side racked up 11 tries to record their biggest score in an international and a tenth straight win over the Scots. Winger Alison Miller ran in a hat-trick of tries and full-back Niamh Briggs celebrated reaching her 50th cap with a 23-point haul through a try, six conversions and two penalties.

Though Briggs was injured in the first half, she recalled in the book *Six Nations, Two Stories*, written about Ireland's men's and women's Six Nations wins that season, that it was one of the best days of her rugby life:

> I loved the fact that we went to another level – it was the most satisfying thing that we became absolutely ruthless. We have never been able to do that in all the years I have been playing for Ireland.
>
> We had always been considered too nice, so to keep turning the screw like we did was amazing. It was surreal after about 60 minutes to look up at the clock and know that you have won a Championship, you are playing

on this artificial soccer pitch, the stand is full of Irish people, and you know your mother is at home watching it. It was unreal ...

The final whistle goes, and you don't know whether to laugh or cry.

Then it all hits you – you look across at the scoreboard ... You look at the 70-odd points and you look across at the Scottish girls and you can't help but feel a bit sorry for them. I ran straight over to my dad and I celebrated with the girls. I did something I didn't think I would ever do – to lift the trophy after such an amazing performance, to be a 50-cap captain. It was probably the best day of my life in terms of my rugby career.

NZ and Australia out in front

As the Six Nations title headed back to Ireland, the World Sevens Series was in full flight. It was a vital year for those with hopes of going to Rio with the top four at the end of the season going on to qualify for the Olympics and teams outside those places needing to qualify through their regional tournaments.

New Zealand and Australia were by now looking unassailable as the two top teams in the world. New Zealand won again in the second leg of the series in Brazil, beating Australia in the final and making it almost a year since they'd last lost a game. Only the Aussies looked like keeping pace with them at a time when standards had been developing at a remarkable pace.

It was the seventh tournament in succession that the trans-Tasman rivals had met in the final. Portia Woodman was established as one of the best players the game had ever produced. Canada were not far away but always seemed destined to finish just outside the top placings.

Atlanta was the next stop and New Zealand won again, though this time it was more competitive overall. The Black

Ferns beat the hosts USA in the final with a 50-12 hammering and Kayla McAlister the overall star. The USA had taken strength from being in front of home fans to shock Australia on the final day with a 10-5 win. Canada had also come close to toppling New Zealand, losing 24-22 despite being without their talismanic captain Jen Kish.

At the next leg in Langford, New Zealand were too good again, winning their fourth tournament of the season, their sixth consecutive victory if results from the previous season were included. This time there was another different final opponent as they saw off Russia, who continued to improve.

Finally, a few weeks later in London, New Zealand were beaten, not by any of the sides who had run them so close in the season so far, but by an inspired Spanish team in the knockouts. When Shiray Tane scored twice early on for New Zealand, it looked like the start of another regulation win for the Ferns, but Spain had other ideas.

First Patricia García pulled a try back after some great work from Irene Schiavon. Then, early in the second half, namesake Berta García put her team ahead, 14-10. With time running out, Katarina Simkins looked like she had pulled the game around, but a poor restart gave Spain the advantage. From the long final play, Patricia García finally got over the line to give Spain a historic first win and end New Zealand's 37-match unbeaten run.

The result shook up the tournament. This time the title would be Australia's as they beat Canada to win their first event of the season, having chased New Zealand so hard since Dubai.

Amsterdam, the final leg of the 2015 series, had the potential to be thrilling, not least because teams were competing for four places at the Olympics and a new World Sevens Series champion would be confirmed. New Zealand were 20 points clear at the top so likely to complete the latter. They were also on track to take an Olympic spot alongside Canada and Australia.

The battle for the final place would be tense. The final games of the event were therefore exciting as it boiled down to England, the USA and France battling for the one remaining spot. England thrilled with a brilliant win over the USA to secure qualification for Team GB. Canada were crowned the event winners overall, with New Zealand winning the plate. The remaining teams would now have to try to qualify through regional competition routes.

As the race for Rio came to a temporary halt, a Super Series for some of the world's best 15s teams was about to be played in Canada. With Ireland having just been confirmed as World Cup hosts for 2017, the shorter turnaround between World Cups was sharpening minds on preparation. The Super Series featured New Zealand, England, Canada and the USA and was played over a condensed schedule.

England welcomed back some of their sevens players, including Emily Scarratt, who would play her first 15s game of the year. New Zealand, with a new coach in Greg Smith who ended up being replaced by Glenn Moore before even a ball was kicked, named 12 uncapped players and included sevens faces like Honey Hireme. Canada too were in transition with 14 new faces, while USA coach Pete Steinberg chose just five players who had been at the World Cup in his squad.

Despite hosting the event and finishing second at the World Cup the year before, the Canadian players were forced to pay to play in the series as their governing body, Rugby Canada, admitted it could not cover all of the costs. Each member of the squad had to come up with CA$1,200 to take part, a stark reminder of the major challenges facing players at the top end of the game, despite the game's rapid progress. The fees were originally set higher but were dropped a little and players took part in personal fundraising drives online to meet the costs.

There had been long-standing issues between Rugby Canada and its leading women's 15s players over costs, with players often struggling to come up with regular fees to represent their country. In 2011, numerous leading players boycotted a Test series for the same reason.

With World Rugby covering costs for teams at the World Cup, the players were spared having to contribute to travel to France in 2014, but paid fees for every tour leading up to it and were continuously frustrated by a lack of investment from its union in simple areas like kit. Remarkably, the Canadian women's team wore the same shirts in every single game at the 2014 World Cup, including the final.

Former 15s player and now sevens star Jen Kish admitted she'd got into debt when forced to pay to represent the national team:

> I have done the pay-to-play model, spent thousands and thousands of dollars to play for Canada and when sevens became fully funded it was a huge relief. At one point I was in debt because of having to play for Canada. If you have to go into debt to play for your country then there is something wrong with your sport's organisation. Someone is not doing their job if that is happening. When the girls won a silver medal at the World Cup, they were still paying to go on tours.

The Black Ferns were the stars of the Super Series, winning all their games, including a morale-boosting 26-7 win over England with new face Victoria Subritzky-Nafatali shining.

Summer of sevens

There was a raft of summer sevens action in 2015. Fiji won the Pacific Games, beating a young Australian team in the final. Canada won the Pan-Am Games, beating the USA in front of a remarkable 18,000 people. And Hong Kong won the Asian Sevens for the first time.

Olympic qualifiers were also underway. France grabbed a European spot thanks to their win in Rugby Europe's Grand Prix Series. They'd gone into the second leg trailing Russia but pulled off some superb performances to grab the all-important spot.

France's victory was followed by some remarkable accusations by their team manager, Jean-Jacques Gourdy, who accused the Russian organisers of the first leg of the series in Kazan of 'clearly not complying with the rules of the game'.

In a frank interview with local newspaper *Le Populaire*, Gourdy set out a number of ways in which France and the other visiting teams were disadvantaged compared to the Russian team:

> We can clearly say that the Russians have done all they could to help their team win. Do not be afraid to say it. The organisation, reception, playing conditions, were all unfit for a tournament of this standard.
>
> The teams were not housed in the same location. The specification of the IRB says all teams staying at the same place. But in Kazan, this was not the case. We were in a university city with all that that entails. In Kazan, the sun rises at 2:00 am and it shines at 3:30. Strangely, none of the rooms of our players had any shutters or blackout curtains.
>
> At the stadium, there were three teams per changing room while the Russians benefited from a quiet and air-conditioned environment. And so on …

Whatever the reality, France were through. Russia would have to wait a year to know their fate. They and three other European sides – Spain, Ireland and Portugal – went through to the world repechage the following summer.

The French would soon be joined by the USA and South Africa, the USA qualifying through the NACRA Championships and South Africa through the African Sevens. With ten teams taking part, that was the biggest ever rugby event in Africa, though the build-up for the teams was often shambolic due to lack of funding. Kenya had to leave their journey to South Africa to the last minute to reduce costs.

Somewhat farcically, despite the win, a few weeks later South Africa were told they would not compete at the Olympics and Kenya would take their place. The decision was taken by the South African Sports Confederation and Olympic Committee who applied their policy of not accepting Olympic places for teams if they only qualified via African continental routes, because in most sports they considered the competition to be too weak.

President Oregan Hoskins expressed the frustration of the South Africa Rugby Union.

> We are extremely disappointed for our Springbok Women. We placed our top players on a full-time programme two years ago and they are trailblazers for professional women's sport and rugby in South Africa. Their appearance at such a showcase sporting occasion would have been inspirational for many young female athletes but it was not to be.

There were a handful of autumn Tests at the end of 2015 in Europe, with France, England, Ireland, Spain and Scotland in action. Scotland, under new coach Shade Munro, bagged an impressive win over Spain with a hat-trick from Rhona Lloyd in a 34-10 win, while England lost to France and snuck past Ireland.

Australia rounded off the year with victory in the opening round of the World Sevens Series, beating Russia 33-12 in what was probably the most exciting, unpredictable and memorable leg ever. Russia had swept the floor with New Zealand on the opening day sending the Kiwis to the plate, before Australia, led brilliantly by Shannon Parry, proved too good.

With the Olympic season now upon teams, New Zealand's dip in form must have been something of a concern, but the series had now at least become highly competitive. The Black Ferns' dominance was broken and Australia looked like the team to beat.

Rankings emerge at last

A significant announcement was then made by the IRB – now rebranded as World Rugby – regarding women's Test rankings.

Test rankings had been introduced for the men's game in 2003, but there was nothing official developed for the women's game. Rankings for major tournaments were based on results in the World Cup, which, given a four-year cycle between competitions, quickly became out of date and only ranked those teams who made the finals. Rankings should have been vital in deciding seedings at international tournaments and could also play a big role in promoting the game more widely, generating interesting narratives for the media.

John Birch and I found this frustrating. How could you compare a team from one part of the world with one from another when sides like, say, Australia, barely played at all between World Cups? For us, rankings were also hugely important to record historical moments in the game.

Several followers of the game had started to produce unofficial rankings for women's Test rugby and on Scrumqueens. com we started to publish a version which had been attempted by statistician Serge Piques in 2009. By 2013, fed up with waiting for something official, John had a go himself and we launched the Scrumqueens.com World Cup rankings in advance of the 1,000th women's Test game which would be played that year.

With Piques's kind permission, we adopted his ranking list choosing to use a methodology close to that of the IRB. It considered the relative ranking of teams for each match, as well as venues, competitions and how recently each match was played.

Publishing updated rankings monthly, the feature quickly became one of the most popular items on the website and was widely featured in articles and TV commentaries, following which World Rugby committed to producing an official version. That promise was made good in 2016, although the list contained some frustrating oddities. It only included results from what they called 'first official women's international matches dating back to 1987'.

As previously described, the first Test match has been widely accepted as that between Netherlands and France in 1983. As a game organised and formally recognised by both the French and Dutch unions at the time, it was as official as it was possible to be, and had been recognised as such by World Rugby in the past.

The rationale was technical. Although World Rugby do not control what is and is not a Test match – essentially if the unions involved say a given game is a Test then that is what it is – for the purpose of World Rugby's records and rankings they only include games where both teams were members of the IRB/World Rugby at the time.

Between 1983 and 1986 there were 12 Test matches involving France, Netherlands, Sweden, Italy, Belgium and Great Britain. However, before 1987, only France were members of the IRB. Italy joined in 1987, Belgium, Netherlands and Sweden joined in 1988 and the unified Great Britain has never been a member. As a result, although all of these early games were Tests and caps were awarded, none of them are recognised as Tests by World Rugby and none are included in the rankings.

France back on top

Though 2016 would all be about how the women's game could make a splash at the Olympics, an exciting Six Nations was also about to play out. There was just 18 months to the next 15-a-side World Cup and for Italy, Wales and Scotland, there were places up for grabs. Two of those three would qualify by virtue of their results over two years in the Six Nations. Going into the event, Italy were leading the way, with Wales second.

England were still playing with the balance between sevens and 15s. France, with the most favourable fixture schedule, were slight favourites starting, at least on paper.

The opening round of the Six Nations went to form. England beat Scotland, Ireland beating Wales and France beating Italy. France were especially strong with their pack dominating. Their clash at home with Ireland in the second round was set to be special. A crowd of just under 12,000 turned out to cheer on a France team who beat Ireland 18-6, something of a redemption for the hosts, who had lost the title to the Irish on points difference the year before.

Wales beat Scotland while Italy, somewhat surprisingly, put England under significant pressure in their match. England escaped the try-fest with a 33-24 win in Ivrea. The Italians had started the game at blistering pace with a try after just 52 seconds for Manuela Furlan, but England, led by Sarah Hunter, dug deep for the win.

Though England had yet to hit their straps, they were efficient in the next game again, beating Ireland at Twickenham thanks to tries in each half from Emma Croker and Abbie Scott, plus an early penalty from Amber Reed. With Italy beating Scotland, it looked briefly like the title shoot-out was now between England and France. But Wales had other ideas.

They pulled off a shock 10-8 win over the French in Neath on the Sunday.

It was the first Welsh win over the French since 2008 and it was well deserved in front of around 3,000 fans. Dyddgu Hywel sped past her marker on an arcing run from the 22 to score in the corner after the game had barely kicked off, but Safi N'Diaye levelled after 15 minutes. Wales defended heroically as France attacked in waves but the visitors had to settle for a penalty instead. Wales had time to conjure up a brilliant move when wing Bethan Dainton saw a gap and raced forward with the ball to send out to Elen Evans on the left. She put through Megan York, who sped down the touchline for a memorable score.

With England up next, Wales would have to be heroic again if they were to keep winning. England just edged it at The Stoop to keep their grand slam ambitions intact. It was an entertaining game with Elinor Snowsill prominent for Wales, but England, with Amber Reed excelling, did enough to win it 20-13. Scotland beat France and Ireland beat Italy.

Ireland ended on a high when a hat-trick from Alison Miller helped them to a 45-12 win over Scotland and they finished third in the table. Italy beat Wales and ended fourth, but all eyes were on the other match.

With France hosting England in the final round, the title came down to a winner-takes-all game in Vannes. It was a terrific climax to the competition and it would be broadcast live on Sky Sports in the UK and on French TV.

There had only been one finale like this before, back in 2004 when both teams came into the final game unbeaten and France took the honours 13-12. This time France could not win the grand slam, but a far better points difference meant that if they won the game they would still take the title. For England, not only the title was up for contention, but also their first grand slam since 2012 – also the last time they beat France in France.

The largely French crowd was magnificent again with over 10,000 there to watch a fantastic game.

France began brightly but their only reward was a penalty attempt which Camille Cabalou pulled wide. Having survived the opening ten minutes unscathed, England began their best period of the game which resulted in a try from Lydia Thompson, after which Amber Reed sent over a brilliant touchline conversion. France responded quickly, however, with Gaëlle Mignot getting the touch as the pack drove over from close range. The conversion was missed, so England led 5-7 at half-time.

The hosts, with the advantage of the slight sea breeze at their backs in the second half, began with some quick passing moves down the narrow side, led by the example of young scrum-half Pauline Bourdon who was having a superb first game in the Six Nations. A penalty opportunity was missed, but soon a driving maul took Audrey Forlani over the line and Camille Cabalou this time nailed the conversion. England pulled level almost immediately after Tamara Taylor powered over but Reed's conversion hit the post to leave the score tied, a result which would still be enough to give England the title.

Then, with ten minutes left, shortly after a French maul was ruled to have been held up, another French line-out led to a maul which drove over the English line, giving Mignot her second try and a 17-12 lead. England desperately fought back, dominating possession for the final few minutes, but the French defence held firm to take out the title after a terrific finale in front of a superb crowd.

Though all eyes would soon turn to Rio, the following months heralded some massive announcements and investments. Scotland confirmed that powerhouse number 8 Jade Konkel was to become their first full-time women's player when she was handed a contract as part of the Scottish Rugby Academy.

Then came a game-changing announcement from England where the RFU confirmed that at least 16 players from their 15s squad would be given full-time contracts to prepare for the 2017 World Cup. England had first awarded contracts to 20 sevens players in October 2014 to prepare for the Olympics but this was a significant expansion, allowing players to attend residential camps ahead of major tournaments, including the Six Nations and the World Cup.

At the other end of the scale, after seven years of absence, Germany came back with force to secure a dominant 36-0 win over their rivals Switzerland over the summer. German captain Dana Klein-Grefe put on a particularly outstanding display, with excellent kicking and ingenuity which led to several tries.

Germany had a long history of women's rugby with a first Test match as far back as 1989, only eight months after England took the field for the first time and a year before New Zealand's first Test. They had once belonged in the top 12 teams of European rugby and their return was very welcome, despite the challenges they faced in growing numbers in a country that had no significant rugby pedigree.

Road to Rio

Although a year earlier New Zealand had been everyone's favourite for Olympic gold, there were signs in the months leading into the event that things were not entirely going to plan in the Black Fern camp and Australia were the coming team.

They were beaten by Canada at the World Sevens Series in São Paulo in February before Australia went on to lift the title. England lifted the cup in Langford, beating the Black Ferns comfortably in the final. Australia, having claimed the top prizes in Dubai, São Paulo and Atlanta, could claim the series title at the next round in Clermont-Ferrand. Their party was somewhat spoiled by Canada, who turned in a magnificent final day to beat them in the final thanks to some brilliance from Ghislaine Landry.

Landry, who had once been told she was too small to make it in international rugby, was a remarkable talent, retiring in 2021 as the all-time leading scorer in the World Sevens Series with 1,356 points and sitting third in the all-time tries (143) and in the all-time matches played (208).

The remaining spot in Rio was still to be determined, as 16 sides headed to Dublin to battle it out at the final repechage. The event had double significance for Ireland, who were using it to test out the venue that would also host the World Cup at the UCD Bowl.

Russia were the top seeds and favourites, not just because of their superior experience at the highest level of the game, but because of their excellent form heading into the event. However, the pressure on them was enormous. If they failed to qualify for Rio the future of their programme would be thrown into doubt. It is the Olympics that excites Russian sports bodies and it is Olympic potential that generates funds.

Spain were also confident, not least having seen their men's team unexpectedly win qualification the weekend before in Monaco. They had proven a match for Russia in most meetings in the World Sevens Series and there was a now-or-never sense for the Spanish squad who had a core of impressive experience in Dublin.

Ireland, at home, were hopeful too, but they were placed in the toughest pool and qualification ahead of either Russia or Spain would require their best performances over the weekend.

At the end of an entertaining day one, eight sides still had a chance of winning the last spot in Rio. Russia, Argentina, Ireland, Tunisia, Kazakhstan, Samoa, Spain and China all secured a spot in day two but there was heartache for Hong Kong, the Cook Islands, Trinidad and Tobago, Mexico,

Venezuela, Zimbabwe, Madagascar and Portugal, who failed to get out of the pool stages.

The semi-finals saw Ireland face Russia and Spain face Kazakhstan. I sat in the stand to see the Irish team draw loud support as a tense match played out.

Russia scored first through Iulia Guzeva but a brilliant finish and fend from Aoife Doyle saw Ireland level it. Ekaterina Kazakova then raced over to help Russia lead 12-5 at the break. Elena Zdrokova pushed it out to 19-5 and, though Alison Miller grabbed a try back in the left corner, it was too late as Russia marched on to the final. The cruelty of sevens had been laid bare as Ireland's hopes on home soil were over in a flash.

Russia would face Spain in the final, who had been brilliant throughout and who had scored a 28-0 win over the Kazakhs in the semis.

The final was a belter. Spain did exactly what their men had done the week before and secured passage to Rio thanks to a quite superb performance. Patricia García was the star with her two tries doing early damage. Her conversions too played a crucial role in an all-round virtuoso display. For Russia it was back to the drawing board.

With the Olympic teams now finalised, the pools were also confirmed. The pools for the first ever appearance of Olympic women's rugby would be Australia, the USA, Fiji and Colombia in Pool A. Pool B had New Zealand, France, Spain and Kenya. Pool C comprised Canada, Great Britain, Brazil and Japan.

Australia were favourites in Pool A. The World Sevens Series champions had timed their build-up almost perfectly. In just over a year from May 2015 to the end of the World Sevens Series, Australia finished in a podium position in seven consecutive rounds, reached the final in six and won four. Coach Tim Walsh, who uniquely saw the Australian men through their qualification process too, had built his team from the ground up, looking for the sort of players he wanted to meet his vision.

Remarkably, 11 of the 12 players in his Rio team did not come directly from a rugby union background. Six were from touch rugby – very much a separate sport down under – two were from rugby league, while others were originally from sports as diverse as basketball, hockey and athletics. Only Shannon Parry was primarily a rugby union player. Nicole Beck was also playing union when Walsh signed her up, but originally she too was a touch player. Sharni Williams originally came from hockey. Walsh and his squad saw the diversity as a real advantage and it certainly allowed Australia to develop a style of play perfect for sevens without having to 'unlearn' 15s, a problem faced by most of their key rivals.

Walsh had prepared his team for almost every eventuality. They had taken part in a number of three-day tournaments which replicated what they would expect at the Olympics. He had his players stay in an apartment-style hotel similar to the Olympic village and the team travelled a similar distance to what would face them in Rio.

He also threw in some curveballs:

We had another camp with Japan after the World Series. We had some fire alarms go off in the night, and I asked Charlotte Caslick to pretend to pull up injured in the warm-up. She should win an award for her performance – she was screaming, and she cried and everyone was really upset because they thought her Olympics were over. She was so convincing I thought she had actually been injured. She was still standing there in a sling after I'd told the girls! They were pretty annoyed with me but the point I was making was that we had to be prepared for anything.

Apart from the months before a World Cup, Australia had no real 15s programme, allowing them to concentrate entirely on sevens. It was hard to imagine Australia coming home without medals around their necks. The only question was what colour it would be.

In the same pool the US had had a disjointed lead-up to the Games. Richie Walker was their third coach in a year, although after a disastrous 11th place in Dubai, the Americans had still reached the quarter-finals in all of the remaining rounds of the World Sevens Series.

Fiji had huge potential, and were capable of beating anyone on their day, but they were staggeringly unpredictable. That they were still considered an outside bet for a podium spot was testament to their ability. They had been part of the World Sevens Series for just two seasons and the socially conservative nature of the islands was still a barrier to women's rugby achieving its full potential.

Several players in the Fiji squad, including Lavenia Tinai and captain Ana Maria Roqica, took up rugby despite parental opposition and coach Chris Cracknell's first impressions were that the 'opinion of women's rugby was very low'. As he said in an interview with *Sport*:

When I took on the role, a squad of 18 or 19 girls were staying in a two-bedroom flat. That wasn't healthy. They had no financial support, no equipment. What was obvious was that they were supremely talented. They could offload as well as the boys. Their decision making and raw power were unbelievable. But they weren't fit. We brought them out of Suva to Pacific Harbour, where the men were based. When the girls got fitter, their game became more fluid. The main thing was helping the girls realise how good they could be if they were professional 24/7.

Colombia started the tournament as the bottom seeds and did not expect to compete in the pool matches but had hopes of doing well in the lower tier. A late decision to select former US

Eagle Nathalie Marchino, comfortably the most experienced player available to them, was a boost however tough their pool.

New Zealand led Pool B. A year before there was really only one team heading for gold in Rio. Six back-to-back tournament wins in the World Sevens Series. Eleven successive finals. Three overall series wins. And, to crown it all, the 2013 World Cup Sevens winners. Sean Horan's team seemed unstoppable.

But then it did stop. A semi-final loss in London meant the Ferns missed out on a final, something that had only happened once before to an official New Zealand women's sevens team. And, perhaps significantly, that defeat was to Australia.

New Zealand had not won a World Sevens Series round since. Their two subsequent finals saw defeats to Australia and England. Since May 2015 there had also been losses to Spain, Canada, the United States (twice) and Russia. Something was clearly amiss.

One of their challenges was internal. Sarah Hirini (then Goss), still relatively young in the game, had taken over from the injured Huriana Manuel as captain. There was some disquiet in the camp when Manuel returned but was not reinstated as skipper.

The disruption off the field contributed to a poor run by their own standards. Although in time they would come together brilliantly and go on to become the most successful sevens team of all time – with Hirini considered an inspirational leader in the game – the build-up to Rio was far from ideal.

France would be tough pool opponents despite how late they had converted to the sevens cause. Back in 2013 in Amsterdam, while the rest of the world was watching the exciting climax to the first World Sevens Series, coach David Courteix and his team could be found on the back pitches playing invitational competitions.

Their growth since had been outstanding. To begin with, 15s had priority, but once the 2014 World Cup was out of the way sevens became all that mattered. A quarter-final was almost a certainty and from there anything was possible.

Spain were riding the crest of a wave after their Dublin heroics, while Kenya were lucky to even be there having been handed South Africa's place; however if they did manage to pull off two or three wins, Kenyan and east African women's rugby would be transformed.

Finally there was Pool C, where it was likely Canada and Great Britain would be battling it out for top spot. Canada, so close on so many occasions, had an impressive record with a remarkable eight podium finishes in the 14 tournaments prior to Amsterdam the year before. Too often they found themselves trailing New Zealand and Australia on the scoreboard and in the rankings. They finished third again behind the big two in the current season once the World Sevens Series points had been added up.

But they had won two of the last six World Sevens Series tournaments and were finalists in the World Cup Sevens in 2013. They were one of the first nations to benefit from new investment in sevens, with their centralisation and funding programme bringing them early success once the sevens game went global.

For many years they were second to their great rivals, the USA, but over the past few years they had overtaken them at both forms of the game. While others had since been catching up, Canada remained consistent as one of the world's top three sides. Their major challenge in Rio was taking the next step to titles and trophies. They were capable of winning gold, but Pool C gave them a trickier path to a final than their Antipodean rivals.

With just one non-English player in their squad – Wales's Jasmine Joyce – the Great Britain squad was analysed in the context of England's recent form and finishes. After a forgettable World Sevens Series in Sao Paulo where they finished only seventh, England impressively turned things around with three semi-finals in the remaining three tournaments, including a series win in Langford and third place in Atlanta. A fourth-place finish overall in the World Sevens Series was a reminder that alongside Canada, Australia and New Zealand, England were part of the elite quartet driving the standards and moving ahead of the chasing pack.

Japan, Asia's premier team, may have struggled on the global stage but had shown glimpses of real potential. Japan's hopes at the Olympics did not lie with winning a medal but rather in the final rankings, which would determine if they earned a place in the World Sevens Series in 2017. For that, they were up against Brazil, Kenya and Colombia, with whoever ranked highest of the four in Rio qualifying for the 11th core place.

Finally there were the hosts Brazil, South America's leading team, but they were likely to find the going tough in their own backyard. Chris Neill's team had been building their experience in a squad which still remained centred around the talents of Edna Santini and Paula Ishibashi. The centralisation of the squad had been a huge asset for Brazil with players coming from all over the country including Rio Grande do Sul, Santa Catarina, Paraná, São Paulo, Rio de Janeiro and Pernambuco.

The shock value on day one was relatively limited. France's Camille Grassineau had the honour of entering the history books as the first try-scorer at the Olympics for 92 years in her team's win over Spain. The favoured teams breezed through their opening pool games. New Zealand, Canada and Australia comfortably got past Kenya, Japan and Colombia while Great Britain beat Brazil. If there was any upset, it was Fiji's 12-7 win over the USA. The favoured teams were then again too strong for their second-round pool opponents.

Day two was much tenser, ultimately bringing the expected semi-finals but with some scares along the way for most of the top teams. On a far breezier afternoon than day one, an understandably nervy Spain – with future funding at stake if they could not get out of their pool – faced Kenya in the opening game, winning 19-10. Though Spain's win meant the quarter-finalists were confirmed (Australia, Spain, Canada, France, Great Britain, Fiji, New Zealand and the USA were all through) the excitement was far from over.

France worried New Zealand, despite the 26-5 scoreline, and the form teams from day one were brought down to earth. Canada were not only beaten by Great Britain, but well beaten, 22-0. England's head-to-head form in the World Sevens Series was a great guide to the game. Then the round finished with a dramatic tied game between USA and Australia.

Again, World Sevens Series history should have been a guide. The USA had won the majority of the team's previous meetings but, based on day-one performance, an Australian win seemed a given. Yet after holding them to just 5-0 in the first half, the USA had a great second half. Australia lost Ellia Green early on and Charlotte Caslick was rested at the break. The USA took advantage with the pace of Jessica Javalet proving too much with two tries. In the last play, Emma Tonegato levelled the scores to end a great pool match.

Australia went into the quarter-finals with confidence regardless and powered to a largely untroubled win over Spain, who defended well but rarely threatened, losing 24-0. The France v Canada game was far more exciting. France took an early lead and looked the better team for much of the game but a missed opportunity right at the end of the first half proved costly. Canada hung on and scored two tries in the final couple of minutes to win 15-5.

Great Britain then won a bruiser against Fiji. A first-minute score from Abbie Brown set them on the way but Fiji recovered well to draw level from Lita Naiqato. Two scores just before the break gave Team GB a lead that was never seriously threatened in the second half. Finally, the United States dominated most of their game with New Zealand but it was the Ferns, with Portia Woodman seizing the Eagles' one real error, who got the only score of the game and it ended 5-0.

The semi-finals were now set. New Zealand would take on Great Britain and Australia would face Canada.

Canada began brightly against Australia but after a tight opening couple of minutes it was Australia who set the scoreboard in motion with Emilee Cherry benefiting from a huge overlap to score. An error from the restart then put Australia straight back on the front foot. The Canadian defence fought hard, but in the end an opportunity came for Emma Tonegato. She was hauled down short but Cherry was on her shoulder and it was 12-0 to Australia at half-time.

The second half began like the first, with Canada looking strong, but an over-hit kick ahead gave away possession and within a minute Australia were extending their lead with Chloe Dalton touching down in the corner. Australia, now three scores ahead, used their bench and were happy to run down the clock. Charity Williams finally found a gap but with less than 45 seconds to go there was no time for the third seeds to pull back the score. Australia were in the final.

The second semi-final had a similar start. Great Britain began strongly but a high-risk kick failed to be taken cleanly, a referee's decision went New Zealand's way, and moments later Portia Woodman's pace saw her in for the Ferns' first score. That was soon cancelled out by a well-taken try by Alice Richardson, set up by some great work from Emily Scarratt, which gave Great Britain a 7-5 lead. But it did not last long, and Ruby Tui put the number two seeds back ahead 10-7.

Now came a crucial few seconds of play. First Katy Daley-McLean grabbed the shirt of Woodman as she chased a kick ahead, resulting in a yellow card. From that penalty, Amy Wilson-Hardy mistimed her challenge, tackled the New Zealander in the air, and a second yellow card was the result.

Down to just five players, Great Britain did remarkably well to only concede two tries to the unstoppable Portia Woodman either side of the break, but by the time they were back to full strength the score was 20-7.

Great Britain needed a quick score but New Zealand regained possession and patiently held onto the ball before Gayle Broughton finally found space to extend the lead to 25-7. Great Britain battled to the last, but that was the final score.

It was the final many had predicted; the top two seeds who had dominated women's sevens, winning both World Cup Sevens and all four of the World Sevens Series between them. The teams ran out to a good, though not full, crowd in a historic first Olympic women's rugby final.

New Zealand created the best of the early opportunities when Huriana Manuel, on her 30th birthday, was hauled into touch two metres out by Shannon Parry. Charlotte Caslick's line-out throw was not straight and the Kiwis worked the ball wide for Kayla McAlister to touch down for a fifth-minute lead.

Australia then came into their own. Emma Tonegato looked set to score a try until Tyla Nathan-Wong hauled her down metres short. Sarah Hirini turned over the ball but was penalised for holding on and Tonegato managed to squeeze over in the corner to tie the scores after eight minutes.

A defining moment came when Portia Woodman, hat-trick hero in the semi-finals and the competition's top scorer, was sin-binned for a deliberate knock-on with time up in the first half. Australia made their advantage count as Alicia Quirk held the defence before releasing Evania Pelite. With Woodman cutting a frustrated figure on the touchline, Australia scored again after the break as Caslick made a break, finding Emilee Cherry who had speedster Ellia Green outside to run in a third try to stretch their lead to 17-5.

A fourth followed for Caslick, one of the standout players in the competition, who tapped a penalty and made the most of having two forwards in front of her, running straight and hard to crash over the line and put Australia within sight of the gold medal they craved.

The lead was 24-5, but with four minutes to go, there was still time for New Zealand to mount a remarkable comeback as they had done many times in the World Sevens Series. There was still little more than a minute remaining when Kayla McAlister darted through the defence for her second.

Woodman grabbed a try with time up on the clock – her tenth of the competition – but was inconsolable after touching down, knowing that it was too little too late. The Australian celebrations could begin.

Canada claimed the bronze medal after a confident 33-10 win over Great Britain. Devastated after the loss to Australia in the semis, Ghislaine Landry told me that the team had had to almost literally pick themselves up off the floor to win a medal:

> The whole thing was a rollercoaster. Your gold medal hopes are gone once you lose that semi and our changing room was dark. Half the team was crying, the other half was silent and then we had two hours until the bronze-medal game. Looking back that was a pivotal moment. No one was talking and I can remember turning to people and saying take the time you need now because this will feel a lot worse if we finish fourth. We gave ourselves a bit of time to grieve that gold medal loss and we came out and played really well. It spoke to the resilience in the group. We hadn't won all the tournaments leading into the Olympics but we had believed we could win. That final win felt like gold given how we had come back and performed. We were on cloud nine after that.

The 2016 Olympics had been a huge moment for rugby, giving the game a window on the global sports stage and platforming stars of the women's game like Charlotte Caslick, Portia Woodman, Emilee Cherry and Ghislaine Landry at a level never seen before.

As one massive event ended, they were moving quickly to another. The World Cup was now just over a year away and the autumn of 2016 would bring a record number of Test games, with 14 international teams playing in 18 matches (16 of them full Tests) across seven countries. Games took place every weekend between October and Christmas.

The highlights included an entertaining game at Twickenham where New Zealand beat England 25-20 and a historic game in Suva where Fiji created history by winning the first official Oceania Test Championship when they beat Papua New Guinea 37-10 at the ANZ Stadium in Laucala Bay.

Despite the flurry of end-of-year Tests though, 2016 would be remembered for one thing only – the debut of women's rugby at the Olympics.

Chapter Fourteen

Fallouts and world firsts

WITH THE World Cup cycle shortened to three years to avoid a clash with the World Cup Sevens, the success of Rio quickly moved on to the major event taking place in Ireland in 2017.

Although no other countries had bid to host it – in part a sign of how difficult it was to make a return on the investment – Ireland was a solid choice to help build momentum from the events in England in 2010 and France in 2014. The Irish national team was still riding the crest of a wave following their Six Nations wins in 2013 and 2015 and their historic victory over New Zealand.

Given their plans to bid to host the men's 2023 World Cup, the IRFU were keen to show World Rugby that they were good partners who could deliver high-profile events. As part of their preparation they'd agreed to host sevens events in the preceding years to pilot the venue they were planning to use in Dublin.

The Six Nations would prove an important testbed for the five teams from the competition who were to be part of the World Cup – Scotland hadn't qualified – with France, who had won two of the last three titles, just about favourites. Led by Gaëlle Mignot once again, the French had a settled-looking squad while Ireland headed into the championship with their first full-blown November series behind them, where they had lost to England, Canada and New Zealand.

England started the competition with a full squad being paid to train full time, with 15 of their World Cup squad from 2014 involved. Wales would start under Rowland Phillips after four wins in a row, confident that they could build on their good form, and Italy were heading into their tenth season of Six Nations rugby. Having suffered the disappointment of failing to qualify for the World Cup, Scotland, led by Lisa Martin, also had something to prove.

Off the field there was excitement about the volume of TV coverage the women's game was attracting. The year 2016 was the first time every game in the women's Six Nations was available on TV or live stream. Admittedly, to see all the games required some under-the-radar work with VPNs, a UK Sky subscription and putting up with feeds of variable quality, but it was all just about possible.

A series of announcements meant that this would be a thing of the past in 2017, when games would be streamed live via official channels or shown live on television. A highlights programme would also be shown on the BBC.

The opening weekend brought together defending champions France and England at Twickenham, where an entertaining game saw England prevail 26-13 despite trailing 13-0 at half-time, thereby overcoming the biggest half-time deficit in women's Six Nations history.

Ireland topped the table after the end of their game with Scotland. They won 22-15 but only secured victory in the dying seconds when Jenny Murphy crashed over after the sides went into the final stages level. Jade Konkel, Scotland's first full-time professional women's player, scored twice in the first half. Having lost 73-3 to Ireland at the same venue two years before, the result could definitely be seen as something of a turning point for Shade Munro's team, who looked organised and very well coached.

Wales defeated Italy 20-8. That good result plus England's first-half wobble the week before meant a crowd of over 4,000 turned out to see them play England in the next round. The game was expected to be close but England scored 11 unanswered tries to win 63-0. It was Wales's third-largest defeat ever, and a match where Tamara Taylor made her 100th appearance in white.

Backed by a big crowd at La Rochelle, France were too strong for Scotland and won 55-0, while it took 82 minutes for Ireland to secure a try-scoring bonus point against Italy, their 27-3 win meaning they sat top of the table after two rounds.

The first two rounds of the championship had seen impressive crowds and broadcast interest. There was even better to come when the second-largest paying women's Six Nations crowd was present to cheer France on against Scotland at La Rochelle. Some 10,058 filled the stands.

The 4,500 crowd who attended the Stadio Tommaso Fattori in L'Aquila for Italy v Ireland also made it the largest recorded crowd for a women's Six Nations game in Italy, surpassing the 3,500 for Italy v Wales in Padua in 2015. Even Scotland's 1,200 for their opening game against Ireland was the biggest published attendance at a Six Nations game since Scotland moved their home games to Broadwood.

TV audiences were solid too. France 4 recorded 615,000 for France v Scotland, the highest audience for the channel on the day and a 2.8% audience share at peak time on a Saturday evening. England v France achieved a similar audience the week before.

But, with the World Cup on the horizon, it was the audience on RTÉ2 in Ireland that stood out. In the opening week, Scotland v Ireland achieved a remarkable 12.6% share of the audience on a Friday evening. At 159,000 it was very nearly the highest ever Irish TV audience for the women's Six Nations. They also recorded an 11.6% share for the game against Italy. These were significant numbers and suggested the World Cup later that year would be a huge hit with the Irish public.

The pick of the next round was Ireland v France, but Scotland against Wales was also a huge game, particularly for the Scots who would have been targeting the match from the outset for a much-needed and long-awaited win. It had been seven years and two weeks since Scotland had last tasted a Six Nations victory – and nearly 12 years since they had last beaten Wales – but all that changed in Cumbernauld in the third round in 2017.

It had been coming. Since Shade Munro arrived, Scotland had been improving game by game. In the first round of games against Ireland they had the lead but fell just short.

To begin with, the artificial pitch at Cumbernauld came into its own, the snowy effects of Storm Doris being swept to the touchlines before play began. Scotland dominated possession and territory in the first half with little reward until the final play of the half, while Wales made two visits to the Scotland end and came away with converted tries on both occasions. It was 7-14 at the break but still all to play for.

Rhona Lloyd got Scotland to within two points with a well-taken early try. Then, with just a few minutes left, Sarah Law knocked over a penalty for a Scottish lead. They clung to it until the final whistle, signalling raucous celebrations from the entire winning squad.

Elsewhere, Italy put in their best ever performance against England, losing 29-15 but playing a full part in an exciting and quite dramatic game. There was a hat-trick for Victoria Fleetwood – the first by a front-row player in the women's Six Nations – and a narrow as-you-like second half which Italy actually won 10-5. There were two yellow cards, one per team, and a red card for former England captain Katy Daley-Mclean, who had just come off the bench.

The Ireland v France game attracted some pre-match publicity after the IRFU decided to send three key players to Vegas to play in a leg of the World Sevens Series. Sene Naoupu, Alison Miller and Hannah Tyrell, all contracted sevens players, were removed from Ireland's back division in a decision that sparked criticism given Ireland were pushing for the title and in the middle of a home World Cup year.

In recent years Ireland v France had been the standout game of almost every Six Nations. In 2017 it was no different. Ireland won it 13-10, despite their missing players, but it was far more enjoyable than the scoreline suggests with an open game generating limited finishes but plenty of opportunity.

Ireland played Wales next. The Welsh set-up had just been rocked by the tragic death of Elli Norkett in a car crash. She had been the youngest player in the 2014 World Cup squad and had also represented Wales at sevens.

Wales rose to the occasion and, despite losing 7-12, put in a fine performance in a game that could have gone either way. The result meant Ireland would go into a grand slam decider against England, who hammered Scotland 64-0, on the final weekend in Dublin. To make it even better, the game would be played on St Patrick's weekend ensuring plenty of media attention and a decent crowd.

England were clear favourites. When they had been good, they had been devastating while Ireland had been grinding out their results. While all eyes were on that game in the final round, there was also a memorable last result for Scotland, who beat Italy to cap their best Six Nations for over a decade. The wooden spoon was handed to the Italians.

Scottish players Jade Konkel, Chloe Rollie, Lana Skelton and Lisa Thompson were just some of the players who had come into their own over the five games, laying down real hope that, under Shade Munro, their fortunes could rapidly change.

In Dublin, England were comfortably too strong, winning the grand slam for the first time since 2012 with a 7-34 win. Amy Wilson-Hardy grabbed the first of England's five tries in the only score of the first half but it was all England after that, with further scores from Laura Keates, Amy Cokayne, Emily Scarratt and Lydia Thompson, with Scarratt adding nine points from the kicking tee.

France bowed out on a high note with a 39-19 win over Wales in Brive to finish third in the final standings.

Momentum building

The 2017 Six Nations had been a massive success and could go down in history as something of a turning point. It marked the beginning of the year that women's rugby went mainstream.

It also served a reminder of just how important the competition had become to the profile of the sport. It was launched on a wave of unprecedented support. Every game was available in broadcast-quality feeds. Every France, Italy, Ireland and almost every England game was broadcast live on domestic TV alongside weekend summary programmes on mainstream channels. TV audiences responded, with both RTÉ in Ireland and France 4 reportedly very pleased with viewing figures and audience share.

The crowds were impressive too. Record paying attendances for home women's Six Nations games were broken in England, Ireland, Italy, Scotland and Wales, while France recorded their second-biggest crowd ever. Given that it was not so long since the top teams were playing at small club grounds with capacities of under 2,000 and even then not selling out, this was meteoric progress. I'd watched multiple England games at Esher in front of tiny crowds, barely hitting the hundreds, just a few years before.

Hosting women's Six Nations games became close to a commercial proposition, not just in France, but also in Italy,

Wales and Ireland. And, on top of the positives, the competition lived up to expectations, with attractive tense rugby, shock results and a winner-takes-all game in front of an excellent crowd in Dublin.

Nevertheless, there remained significant challenges to the structure of the competition. The scheduling had always been difficult, with broadcasters reluctant to show women's games if there was a clash with men's matches. At times the women's schedule seemed self-defeating with games pitted up against each other in the same slot. It was fast becoming impossible to follow or report on every women's game over a weekend live, hardly conducive to building a fanbase or improved media coverage.

While the sevens game was taking a backseat in terms of priorities in 2017, its own World Cup was just a year away and the World Sevens Series was an important benchmark to assess progress. New Zealand had won the opening round in Dubai in December but there was a gap of almost two months before the next leg, which clashed with the Six Nations and meant lots of absent European players.

Australia hosted the event in Sydney and the title went to Canada, who knocked out the hosts in the semi-final and beat the USA in the final, who in turn had overturned New Zealand in their semi-final. That itself was a remarkable result. The USA went from 11th place in Dubai to winning their pool on day one in Sydney, squeezing through their quarter-final against Ireland, before coming up against the Black Ferns in the semi-finals and, inspired by Naya Tapper, beating them 19-0. The all-North American final finished 17-21 to Canada.

The Kiwis bounced right back in the next leg, winning in Las Vegas and looking back to their best. The pace and power of Portia Woodman, Michaela Blyde, Niall Williams and player of the final Ruby Tui were just far too much for any team to handle.

In the bronze final, Canada beat USA 31-7, much to the disappointment of around 30,000 home fans packed into Sam Boyd Stadium. Captain Ghislaine Landry, who became the all-time series leading points-scorer over the same weekend, was also the first to pass the 700-point mark, overtaking Woodman in the process.

European teams had been deeply disappointing in the series so far and their woes continued. The three surviving teams in the cup failed to win any games against teams from outside the continent and England and Spain languished around the bottom of the table.

There was a World Sevens Series qualifier before the next round, with Japan winning their place for the next season thanks to a 100% record over the likes of South Africa, Italy and China. The next round was fittingly in Kitakyushu but, though there was a new venue, the outcome was familiar. New Zealand won their third title in four in the season's series, giving them a vice-like grip on the title going ten points clear.

There were now just two legs left, one in Canada and one in France. Since its introduction in 2015 the Canadian leg of the series in Langford had been the best-supported event with near sell-out crowds, and a great atmosphere guaranteed. While New Zealand seemed to have the series sewn up, there would be a fight to avoid relegation that looked like going down to the wire.

The final saw hosts Canada and New Zealand battle it out in a brilliant game which the Black Ferns edged 17-14 thanks to a last-ditch score from Michaela Blyde. Relegation was still far from decided by the final whistle, with Spain marginally increasing their lead over Brazil going into the final round.

Heading to France, New Zealand just needed to reach the quarter-final to secure the overall series win, but there was much on the line elsewhere. World Cup Sevens qualification for the following year had not yet been determined, with England

and France in contention, while there would also be a battle for the sides to take silver and bronze in the series.

Sarah Goss, Kelly Brazier and Portia Woodman were all absent for New Zealand, with all three switching their attention to the 15s World Cup. As it was they were still too good, winning both the title and the World Sevens Series, beating Australia in the final. The two bottom teams – Spain and Brazil – came together in the challenge semi-finals. Spain won 12-5, securing their place on the series for the next year and relegating Brazil.

A series that had come in the shadow of the Olympics and ahead of a World Cup year meant it was challenging to take a long-term view about where teams might really stand, given the number of new faces, but New Zealand had highlighted their astonishing depth over the rounds.

Only Australia and Canada seriously challenged them. Both reached three finals but only Canada lifted a title – in Sydney, as Australia fell to the curse of the host team, something that Canada only shook off at the third attempt.

Just weeks after the series ended, the 2017 European Grand Prix, also heavily overshadowed by the upcoming World Cup, saw Russia come out on top. Wales finished fifth – impressing enough to suggest that if they had been allowed to go to the promotion play-off in Hong Kong earlier in the year they would surely be a World Sevens Series team already. Unfortunately, as they played as Great Britain in 2016, they did not qualify for that tournament.

All attention now swung back to 15s as a frantic period of World Cup warm-up games kicked off. Canada beat the USA twice in a row to claim the CanAm Series with a 76-15 aggregate score in San Diego before heading to New Zealand to take part in an exciting Super Series where four of the world's top-six teams would come together to compete in June.

The Black Ferns, Australia, Canada and England were using the event to fine-tune preparations for the World Cup and the round-robin tournament saw matches take place in Wellington, Christchurch and Rotorua to mirror the turnaround between matches in the pool stages.

With just 90 days to go to the main event, these were important confidence-building games. England and New Zealand got off to the perfect start. The Black Ferns gained an early psychological boost over their World Cup pool opponents Canada with a 28-16 win first off – a two-try display from former World Rugby Women's Player of the Year Kendra Cocksedge proving the difference.

England recorded an emphatic 53-10 win over Australia at Porirua Park, with Sarah McKenna helping herself to a hat-trick.

New Zealand then downed Australia with brilliant displays from Portia Woodman and Selicia Winata helping them to a 44-17 win. The England v Canada game was much closer with England edging it 27-20. Lydia Thompson scored two tries while Abbie Scott and Kay Wilson also went over. Seven points came from the boot of Emily Scarratt as the world champions battled to a hard-fought victory.

The series concluded with England facing New Zealand at Rotorua International Stadium as part of a double-header with the men's Maori All Blacks against the British and Irish Lions. It was an exciting finale and a preview of what everyone expected to be the next World Cup final.

The weather was poor and England smartly reverted to a tight game up front to secure a morale-boosting win. Using their driving maul to perfection, they scored three tries from a tactic that New Zealand simply had no answer to in a 29-21 result. Canada ended the series on a high note with a 45-5 victory over Australia, their first victory in the series, sending Australia home winless.

Exciting news followed for the English women's game with the RFU confirming that ten clubs had been offered places in a new domestic competition from September 2017. The competition, initially called Women's Super Rugby, would receive a multi-million-pound investment over the first three years to help deliver the minimum standards expected and provide high-quality coaching, facilities, training environments and community-engagement plans.

The women's game in England, with a World Cup looming in neighbouring Ireland, should have been on a high, but instead a mess was made of the communication around the future plans for their contracted players. Over the course of 2017, the English players had been fully professional but, surprisingly, the union confirmed just weeks before the World Cup that the focus of contracted investment would switch back to sevens the following year since the World Cup Sevens, the Commonwealth Games and the Olympics were on the horizon.

Though there was logic to the decision given finite resources and the back-and-forth nature of priorities in England, the timing of the announcement was change astonishing to a surprise. A wave of negative coverage highlighted that if England won the World Cup, their players would be out of a job almost as soon as they landed back at Heathrow.

The RFU was bullish in its defence, that the players 'fully understood the position and are focused on the World Cup in Ireland next month'. Yet the decision, which came to light on a weekend when the England women's cricket team won the World Cup at Lord's, left a sour taste. MP Barbara Keeley called it 'shameful' and the now-retired Maggie Alphonsi called it 'very disappointing'.

On that off-note, the World Cup loomed for the reigning champions as the opening round in Dublin grew ever closer.

Dublin and Belfast the focus

Though billed as the most competitive World Cup ever, with standards improving and professionalism entering the game since the Paris edition, England and New Zealand were once again overwhelming favourites to contest the final.

England were professional (for now), well resourced and the bookies' favourites with huge expectation on their shoulders to defend their title. They brought enormous strengths with a squad that oozed experience and talent and an exceptional driving line-out. They went to Dublin on the back of a nine-Test winning streak which included wins over the world's other top-four sides. Though the switching back and forth between 15s and sevens had had an impact, it had also boosted England's forward pack, who had carried extra pressure in the preceding years with many of England's backs off playing on the World Series.

Then there was New Zealand. 'If they don't make the final there's something wrong,' said former Black Fern Melodie Robinson in her preview, neatly summing up the expectation that always comes alongside wearing the black shirt at a World Cup.

The shock of being knocked out in the pool stages at the last World Cup had long passed and New Zealand travelled to Ireland in better shape, physically and mentally, than in 2014. Captain Fiao'o Fa'amausili led the team, playing in her fifth and last World Cup, while there was also transferable sevens talent with Sarah Hirini and Portia Woodman included.

Woodman was fast becoming the most marketable player in the game. She was an all-rounder with searing pace – as a child she'd dreamed of becoming an Olympic sprinter – and she had unbeatable footwork, combined with a tough work ethic and excellent defensive abilities. She'd already lit up the global sevens stage and she arrived in Ireland with a huge profile.

Named in the same pool as New Zealand, 2014 finalists Canada also brought a strong squad. Coach Francois Ratier had spent the past three years trying to get his squad together more often and building on the experience of the core squad he took to France with such success three years before. He was boosted by the arrivals of Kelly Russell, Elissa Alarie, Karen Paquin and Magali Harvey from the sevens programme, all huge talents who brought vital experience.

Ranked fourth in the world, France too were dangerous and they'd put in some strong performances in the previous couple of years. The loss of the talented Jessy Trémoulière was a definite blow. The full-back had been France's best and most reliable kicker for some years, a role that had otherwise been a weak spot for Les Bleus for most of the past ten years. They had also not quite nailed down their number 10 shirt since the retirement of Sandrine Agricole and their pool game with Ireland was billed early on as one of the initial-round highlights.

Though Irish fans had been rocked by the news that captain Niamh Briggs had been ruled out of the event through injury at the last minute, the news was rather less of a surprise to the players, who knew how she was struggling, but still it was an inauspicious start to Ireland's home tournament. It's a mark of how far Ireland had come that they would begin their campaign knowing that anything but a semi-final appearance would represent under-achievement. But Australia and France in their pool presented serious challenges and Japan were improving out of sight. If Ireland were going to go one further than 2014, they were going to have to do it the hard way.

With sevens success having become the dominant story within women's rugby in Australia, the national 15s programme had been pushed even further down the pecking order. Although some of their Olympic gold medallists would be in Ireland for the World Cup, with just five Test matches under their belts in three years, it was hard to see them progressing too far. However, though they were light on recent Test experience, the Australians were nothing if not resilient. Mollie Gray was a case in point. The forward suffered a horrific knee injury in February with damage to her ACL, PCL and MCL, a dislocated kneecap and cartilage damage, but had battled her way back to fitness in time for the World Cup.

The USA had slipped to seventh in the rankings after a tough three years that saw them win just one Test, in 2015 v Canada, and lose nine. It was the worst record for any team in Ireland apart from Australia. This may have been partly because the USA management used the games to try out 34 new players, 18 of whom made the grade to travel to Ireland, but it was difficult to see how the Americans could build momentum on such poor results. However, with the experienced Pete Steinberg in charge of an athletic squad, improving on sixth from four years earlier was certainly possible.

Spain were likely to be highly competitive in their pool, at least against the teams who weren't England. Coach José Antonio Barrio named a highly experienced squad including top sevens players.

Italy were returning to the World Cup after a gap of 15 years, dating back to before they joined the Six Nations. However, after putting such an effort into qualifying the year before, they had played no Tests outside of the Six Nations – no autumn internationals, no summer tours, no warm-up fixtures – and the 2017 Six Nations saw them lose all of their games, picking up their first wooden spoon since 2009.

This apparent lack of interest from the Italian Federation resulted in such a build-up of confusion and frustration that it was even rumoured in Italy that they would not take part in the World Cup, which forced Cristina Tonna, head of women's rugby at the union, to explain and defend their policy. In an interview on Scrumqueens.com she said that the lack of games was due to personal challenges for Italy's amateur players and some bad luck organising games with teams like Hong Kong, which had fallen through.

Wales, with a relatively new head coach in Rowland Phillips, frankly were in a terrible pool with New Zealand and Canada, though the squad had played a number of warm-up games to help prepare following a Six Nations which had brought just one win.

No Asian team had ever finished higher than eighth at a World Cup but Japan were on the up. A recent tour of Ireland and Wales, where they narrowly lost two games against strong Irish selections before comfortably beating a young Welsh team, kickstarted success at home in the Asian Championship, where they beat Hong Kong twice. They also had a star player in Mateitoga Bogidraumainadave, who brought speed and power to a team that was improving game by game.

Finally there was Hong Kong, the lowest-ranked team to ever play in a World Cup. They were in Ireland after World Rugby's planned Asia/Africa/Oceania World Cup qualifier suffered the withdrawal of the three strongest and most experienced World Cup teams (South Africa, Samoa and Kazakhstan) leaving just three teams with little recent World Cup experience – Japan, Hong Kong and Fiji – competing for two places. As Fiji had only played one Test in the ten years prior to the qualifier, it was no surprise that the two Asian teams beat them easily.

It was hard to see Hong Kong making a significant impact on the World Cup, but perhaps that was not the point. As coach Jo Hull said after the squad was announced, 'Our objectives transcend wins and losses in terms of creating our legacy. We want to inspire more girls to take up rugby after our appearance.'

The IRFU wanted the competition to be an all-island affair and decided to host the pool games in Dublin and the semis and finals in Belfast. University College Dublin (UCD) was the chosen first venue, boosted by the fact that it could accommodate all the teams staying on campus for the duration, though extra infrastructure had to be built, including stands, terracing and TV gantries.

The World Cup had come a long way since England had first trialled a one-venue back-to-back pitch set-up in 2010. Ireland continued the format with 18 pool games taking place at UCD over three pool days, with games split between the UCD Bowl and Billings Park. The pool games sold out quickly. Extra capacity was added to take the number of seats at the Bowl and Billings Park to 3,500 and 2,000 respectively before the teams even arrived.

On the opening day, there were strong performances from all the leading teams, though Ireland looked shaky.

In the opening match of the World Cup, England were too strong for Spain, winning 56-5 with four tries for Kay Wilson. New Zealand beat Wales 44-12.

Canada came just short of 100 points against Hong Kong, putting 98 on the board, with five tries in all for Magali Harvey. The USA and Italy played out a fantastic and high-paced match with the Americans winning it 24-12. It took France just 12 seconds to score against Japan, with Romane Menager powering over, and though the Japanese were determined, they leaked 72 points and scored 14.

The opening day ended in front of a massive crowd to see Ireland take on Australia. Fittingly it was the best game of the day. Ireland had to be patient to unlock the Australian defence until scrum-half Larissa Muldoon sneaked over for the opening score and Nora Stapleton's conversion gave them a seven-point advantage. Australia hit back with Mahalia Miller reducing the deficit to two points at the interval.

When Wallaroos captain Shannon Parry crossed the line early in the second half Ireland were facing potential embarrassment. They reached the hour mark trailing by three. Ciara Griffin went over to restore the hosts' lead and another Stapleton conversion gave Ireland a four-point cushion. Replacement Sophie Spence then went over to make it 19-10 with ten minutes to go and the game looked wrapped up.

But Australia were not done and bulldozed their way back to the Irish 22 thanks to a powerful burst from Hana Ngaha off the bench freeing up Hilisha Samoa to crash over. When Ashleigh Hewson slotted the extras it was 19-17 with just seven minutes to go and it made for a tense final few minutes, but Ireland used all their experience to see the game out – just.

On paper, France v Australia should have been the pick of the second round, but Ireland's nervy start meant their game against Japan would face more scrutiny and interest than expected.

New Zealand kicked on from their Welsh win with a massive result against Hong Kong. The game ended 121-0. Pool rivals Canada had a tougher outing against Wales, coming through just 15-0, the low score thanks to heroic Welsh defence throughout a game that the Canadians dominated.

Wins for England and USA in their pool effectively set up a winner-takes-all between the two teams the following week. England were comfortable over Italy, winning 56-13, while the USA were highly impressive against Spain, scoring 43 and conceding none.

In the final pool, France turned on the style against Australia with an exhibition of wonderful handling and support play backed up with a solid physicality that the internationally inexperienced Australian team had no answer to. They won 48-0 with Romane Menager again in brilliant form and France looking ominously good before their showdown with Ireland on the final day of the pools.

Ireland beat Japan 24-12 but it was not a performance to set the world on fire. The home side had to come from 14-0 down at half-time in front of a shocked home crowd. Japan had Ireland under pressure from the off with a stunning scrum performance from Makoto Ebuchi forcing the Irish coaches into changes just 30 minutes into the game. The hosts recovered but there were serious questions asked about their ability to get out of their pool and whispers that all was not well in the Irish camp.

With no bonus point picked up yet, Ireland simply had to beat France to make a semi-final. Off the field there was grumbling too about the swathes of empty seats visible at games, due mostly to how tickets were sold for the game with spectators unable to move between venues yet the tickets being valid for all games on a day.

Although there were no quarter-finals, day three was unofficially the start of the knockout rounds. Seven teams – New Zealand, England, Canada, France, Ireland, the USA and Canada – were vying for the four semi-final slots.

New Zealand made it through easily, beating Canada 48-5, the Canadians' worst World Cup defeat since 2006. The Black Ferns looked scintillating with Portia Woodman, Kelly Brazier and Victoria Subritzky-Nafatali in superb form. England and the USA both went through, though the Americans went down to a heavy 47-26 defeat to an English team for whom Emily Scarratt was impressive.

There was one semi-final slot left for Ireland and France to fight for. All the pressure was on the hosts after two patchy performances while France had been building momentum brilliantly. Ireland were on the back foot almost immediately after the kick-off and France scored after just two minutes when the unstoppable Romane Menager crashed over. Centre Caroline Ladagnous then grabbed a brace as France rocked Ireland's defence with Safi N'Diaye, Julie Duval and Menager all involved in a brilliant blur of pace and power.

With Shannon Izar and Montserrat Amédée slotting the kicks, France went into a 21-0 lead with Ireland struggling everywhere, despite a heroic effort in midfield from Jenny

Murphy. The second half was better for the hosts, but their try was far too little too late. They were left standing on the pitch shocked at the final whistle having failed to get out of their pool. Their departure would also prove a real headache for those tasked with selling tickets for the knockout games in Belfast.

It would be an England v France and New Zealand v USA semi-final line-up. New Zealand started as clear favourites in their match despite the USA's resurgence. Players who had stood out included lock Stacey Bridges, back-row Sara Parsons and centre Alev Kelter, but they would have to be at their absolute best to beat a New Zealand team full of astonishing talent.

Relative newcomer Kelter was a particular talent for the Americans. An underage star in both ice hockey and football in her native Alaska, she had just missed the cut to be in the US Olympic ice hockey team for Sochi in 2014 and decided to transition to rugby after an invite to trial for the sevens programme from Ric Suggit, who was exploring transferable talent. She excelled and quickly became a core player for both the US sevens and 15s programmes.

The England v France match was undoubtedly the more anticipated semi-final. France had dazzled throughout the competition with their passing, offloading and high-tempo rugby and were rewarded with record viewing figures on French TV. The form of Romane Menager, Julie Duval and Safi N'Diaye up front, allied with the wizardry and footwork of Shannon Izar, Elodie Poublan and Montserrat Amédée, meant if France played well, England's defence would have to be at its absolute best. However, they were hit with a massive blow with the late injury withdrawal of Menager, who had been their star.

England had also been outstanding so far. Fly-half Katy Daley-Mclean was in brilliant form with her outstanding field kicking and wonderful range of passing.

There were classification games played before the main events. Ireland suffered more misery in losing 24-36 to Australia. Canada hammered Wales and Italy just got past Japan. Hong Kong improved to stay within range of Spain but lost 31-7.

In the first semi-final, England took on France.

A crowd of around 10,000 were at the Kingspan Stadium to watch a game that was in the balance for long stretches. In the end, England's superb, well-organised and patient defence paid off and France's shambolic line-out cost them dear, as time and time again they wasted great territory by handing the ball straight back to willing white shirts.

France started the better, throwing everything at England in the opening 20 minutes. With Safi N'Diaye and Elodie Poublan prominent, the French attack came hard and straight at England, with the Red Roses forced to defend deep in their own 22 for much of the period. England's rearguard was superb, staying patient in slippery conditions. With the France line-out desperately wobbly, England had just enough possession to stay in touch.

An excellent strike from Emily Scarratt put England 3-0 up as the rain started to pour down, but in between some strong shows of defence from both sides, Shannon Izar returned the favour to level it up. The rain had a real impact as the half wore on with handling errors abounding.

There was nothing else to separate the sides at the break but England looked far more organised afterwards. Although loose passes stymied their efforts, the ball carrying of the brilliant 20-year-old Sarah Bern and Alex Matthews started to cause more and more problems for France. Scarratt added a penalty and finally their efforts up front were rewarded when Sarah Bern's brilliant power running saw her barrel over the line to stretch the lead out to 13, thanks to Scarratt's conversion.

It was desperate stuff for France as they tried everything to get back into the match. Their best effort came from a brilliant Jade Le Pesq break but she was hauled into touch by Amber Reed. In the end, England added the icing on the cake when Meg Jones, who had a positive impact off the bench, pounced on a loose pass to add another score at the death and help her team win it 20-3.

In the other game, it was comprehensive for New Zealand, but the USA gave their all in an excellent game full of running rugby and great tries in a game that ended 45-12. Portia Woodman's four tries were the highlight as New Zealand had too much speed and accuracy for their opponents, scoring seven tries to two. The result was even more impressive given New Zealand only led 15-7 at the break after an enthralling first 40 minutes.

The four-time world champions took a third-minute lead when fly-half Victoria Subritzky-Nafatali touched down. After their opponents briefly led through an excellent Kris Thomas try, a Kendra Cocksedge penalty edged New Zealand back in front before she converted Woodman's opener to secure a 15-7 interval advantage. A second Woodman score and Cocksedge penalty opened up a 16-point gap, then New Zealand underlined their quality during a blistering final quarter that saw them claim four tries in 15 minutes.

Woodman added two more, replacement hooker Te Kura Ngata-Aerengamate claimed another touchdown and Kelly Brazier completed an emphatic second-half display with a try which Cocksedge converted.

The final would likely be something of a contrast in styles. England's defence had been superb all tournament and their kicking game and organisation up front made them difficult to break down. New Zealand, on the other hand, relied on their ability to create space for players like Woodman, Winata and Wickliffe with the distribution skills of Brazier vital.

The final was awarded to referee Joy Neville, a deserved reward for the former Irish player who had excelled since taking up the whistle and was part of an impressive cohort of women who were climbing the ranks in officiating.

With our first child having arrived just a few weeks before, I had to settle to watch the final from home. What played out on screen was easily the best game of women's rugby I had ever seen – certainly the best World Cup Final.

The opening ten minutes of the game were played at a frantic pace. Sarah Bern and Toka Natua both had eye-catching runs and England almost scored after five minutes, but the flick pass from Emily Scarratt didn't work out and New Zealand could breathe again. It was Selicia Winata who broke the exciting deadlock when a fine kick from Victoria Subritzky-Nafatali headed her way. With the bounce falling unkindly for the covering Emily Scarratt, Winata broke away to finish and take the early lead.

Scarratt had taken a knock in the move but was soon to her feet and making impacts all over the park. It was her penalty kick on the 15-minute mark which registered England's first score. As England started to dominate up front, a harsh yellow card for Sarah Goss handed them even more momentum.

When Katy Daley-Mclean kicked for the corner, it set up a great passage of drives from a confident England pack. Alex Matthews drove over but was held up, but there was no such luck for the Ferns at the next scrum, as Joy Neville awarded an early penalty try with England marching forward.

It was all England now and Rachael Burford's lovely break through the middle set up Lydia Thompson for a try she couldn't fail to finish. Scarratt's touchline conversion was typical of a player who thrives on the big occasions and, at 17-5, New Zealand were already staring down a barrel.

They needed something, and they got it just before the break.

The brilliant running prop Natua got on the end of the ball after patient charges, well organised by Kendra Cocksedge, and despite being on the back foot for most of the first half, New Zealand turned round just seven down.

The Ferns started the second half strongly with Aldora Ituni, Natua and Fiao'o Fa'amausili carrying hard in the tight exchanges. It was Natua again who profited when a series of crashes close to the England line saw the prop dive over and finish, with Subritzky-Nafatali vital in the lead-up.

Scarratt's penalty restored England's lead before a brilliant break from Stacey Waaka put England under huge pressure back in their 22. With Aroha Savage carrying through the middle, Charmaine Smith did brilliantly to touch the ball off the bottom of the post and score the try.

It was hard to keep up as momentum swung both ways. When Subritzky-Nafatali kicked loosely, Thompson showed a clean pair of heels to break down the wing and score again and put England back in front. But, seconds later, New Zealand were back ahead with the unstoppable Natua barrelling over once again. Her try made her the only prop, male or female, to score a hat-trick in a World Cup Final.

England's coaching team then made a surprising decision making a raft of substitutions all in one go. The entire front row was replaced before Marlie Packer and Mo Hunt were taken off. It was a surprise and it seemed to lift New Zealand.

Portia Woodman found herself on the ball for a rare occasion in the game and her break led to some space for Cocksedge who snuck over around the fringes to push New Zealand 11 points ahead. When Winata grabbed her second, thanks to a Subritzky-Nafatali kick, it was game up. Izzy Noel-Smith's late try was only a consolation for England.

If the final was superb, the World Cup had also highlighted that some key action needed to be taken to improve the competitiveness of the pinnacle event.

It was clear that the length of the competition needed to be expanded, with four-day turnarounds putting huge demands on players and making it difficult for organisers to manage crowds. It didn't help the quality of the game on the field and it was simply unfair to ask players to put their bodies through the wringer as the games got progressively tougher.

Pete Steinberg, the USA coach, was particularly vocal about the format, describing the four-day gap between games as 'discrimination' by World Rugby.

> I see this as a slap in the face for the women's game. I see it that World Rugby doesn't treat the women with the same respect as they do the men. I am not saying 'equal' because I recognise the men's World Cup, and I recognise that there is a cost issue, but I think World Rugby could throw an extra £500,000 into this event and actually treat the women in a way that demonstrates respect.
>
> I think the Irish Rugby Football Union have done a really good job hosting the tournament but I think it is really disappointing that World Rugby treats the women the way they treat the boys' under-20s.
>
> I think it is wrong. I think it comes from a lack of investment in the women's game. I think World Rugby needs to step up and do what is right.

For their part, World Rugby strongly refuted his comments saying that there was no evidence to suggest that there was an increase in injuries owing to four-day turnaround versus longer periods.

However, despite their vehement statement, less than a year later they confirmed that the turnaround times between games for the next World Cup would indeed be expanded to guarantee longer rest periods – five or six days during the knockout rounds – to 'greatly benefit player welfare by aiding recovery and preparation'. It was a welcome U-turn.

The structure of the competition also clearly needed a change. The growth in the event's popularity meant simultaneous games surely had to be ditched, while in order to expand from 12 to 16 teams, more competition was needed regionally.

The 2017 World Cup was also a potent reminder of the power of the 15s game to draw audiences. Three and a half million viewers in France, over two and a half million in the UK, an audience share of nearly 20% in Ireland – never had more people watched women's rugby before. These were astonishing audiences that built over the tournament and persuaded ITV to transfer the climax of the tournament from ITV4 to ITV1, with French TV also taking a similar decision.

Backed by the comprehensive streaming of games that were not broadcast, the audiences dwarfed anything recorded for any sevens tournament up to that point and were proof that well-promoted 15s rugby with the top teams and players could attract an impressive audience.

Ireland's story unravels

Ireland's disastrous home World Cup on the field was not the end of their woes. The Irish media sought to understand where and how things had gone so badly wrong and the IRFU, having been excellent hosts, jumped headfirst into another PR debacle of their own making.

Just a few weeks after the tournament, Irish prop Ruth O'Reilly – a former team-mate of mine at UCC – gave a remarkable interview to the *Irish Times*, in which she laid bare her own views of the failings of the IRFU and an insight into the struggles of the Irish camp behind the scenes.

She detailed how she'd been dropped from an Irish camp by head coach Tom Tierney for airing concerns with his approach over email and was frank on her views about how much the union really cared about the women's game:

> How much of a shit do they give?
> That goes down to club level. I am highly involved with Galwegians. I've been highly involved in the committee structures of Connacht rugby. You are looking to get things done, to grow the game and the attitude is 'Of course, we are really supportive of our women's team, sure we have one.'
> Well done lads. To be honest, I prefer them staying out of our business because we run our side of the club, our team our way.

Tierney stepped down after the World Cup but there was another wave of negativity when the IRFU, who seemed quite unable to help themselves, advertised his full-time role months later as a part-time position.

The news was enough to prompt Irish centre Jenny Murphy to break ranks and describe it as 'a kick in the teeth' while former Test player Fiona Steed, who was a regular pundit for the game in Ireland, added further criticism. 'This decision shows a lack of respect and vision and diminishes all of the progress that took years to achieve,' she told me at the time for Scrumqueens.com.

The IRFU publicly apologised and tried to explain the decision as a temporary one that would be reviewed after the Six Nations but the damage was done. What should have been a glorious era for the women's game in Ireland instead became the start of a slide that ended with the team failing to qualify for the next World Cup.

The 2017 World Cup year ended with further history being made when the Barbarians played their first ever women's game at Thomond Park against Munster.

Driven forward by Fiona Stockley, who had run the Nomads team for years, the first women's Barbarians team included star Test players Emma Jensen (New Zealand), Kelly Russell (Canada), Christelle Le Duff (France) and Fiona Coghlan (Ireland) and was coached by an England World Cup winner Giselle Mather, who was fast becoming one of the most highly rated female coaches in the game.

They won the game 19-0 and went on to organise and play further fixtures against full Test sides.

As England's new top-flight competition got underway – then called the Tyrrells Premier 15s – there was a new agreement between the players and the RFU in the wake of the furore around the ending of player contracts.

England's national 15s players would receive match fees for games played and an annual squad fee was agreed ahead of an end-of-year three-Test series against Canada. Players involved in all of the games would receive a payment of around £4,000. Some 17 players were additionally handed full-time sevens contracts.

The three Tests included a game played in front of 12,000 at Twickenham, with both sides using the games as a chance to blood new faces after the World Cup. England won all three while introducing new faces like Jess Breach, who scored a remarkable six tries on her debut.

France beat Spain and Italy in their autumn games while, after a gap of three years, Test rugby returned to the Nordic countries when the recently revived Finnish and Swedish teams met in a friendly. The Swedes won 39-10.

December also brought the start of the sixth season of the World Sevens Series with just five rounds ahead of the World Cup Sevens in San Francisco. Numerous teams would also be bidding for a Commonwealth Games medal in 2018.

Australia took the World Sevens Series opener, beating the USA in the final with Emma Tonegato the star over the weekend. But 2017 had firmly been New Zealand's year, as they won the previous World Sevens Series and stopped the rot in their 15s programme. Their momentum in sevens at least would prove almost impossible to stop in the years ahead.

Chapter Fifteen

A whole new world

GIVEN ITS largely amateur status, there had never been a serious discussion about pay in the women's game. However, it was fast becoming obvious to some unions that in the sevens game excuses for top teams to be earning less than their male counterparts were running out.

Recognising that it would not be acceptable for the Olympic champions to be paid less than a men's team that achieved far less on the international stage, Rugby Australia announced a new collective bargaining agreement in early 2018 including full pay equality for men's and women's sevens teams with the same entry-level full-time minimum salaries. The deal also included a pregnancy policy for female athletes and an agreement that players representing the Wallaroos would receive Test match payments for the first time.

Pregnancy policies had been given scant debate in the women's game but it was also an integral part of an announcement in the same year from the New Zealand Rugby Union, who confirmed that 30 Black Ferns would be given contracts worth around $40,000 to $45,000. These would initially pay the players to be part of national camps, as well as for more local training within the high-performance men's provincial programmes.

Speaking to me at the time for the magazine *Rugby World*, Kendra Cocksedge made it clear that although the deal wouldn't be life-altering, it was a significant move from a union that had for so long been reticent about investing in women's rugby:

> The way it's being modelled means for a lot of us it's about being rewarded for what we were doing anyway. The commitment is something like training ten to 14 hours per week in our hubs and individually. I was certainly doing that, but for some players the contracts mean extra support in areas they might not have had, like medical, insurance and so on.

Cocksedge, who had been part of the negotiating team involved in agreeing the deal, also suggested, somewhat prophetically, that handling contracts was something that women's players were ill-equipped to deal with at such an early stage of the game's development.

> That is something that we're going to have to work on. The more the game goes down this route, the more players are signing on with agents and so on, the better that will be. It is a new world.

Later in the year, that concern would prove absolutely true when the English women's team reached a standoff with the RFU, who had U-turned on their decision to divert full-time contracts solely to their sevens programme and now wanted to contract its 15s players fully from 2019.

That would be a historic move – England would become the first and only full-time professional 15s programme – but the communication between the union and the players was poor, resulting in a bumpy introduction to something that should have been hailed as revolutionary.

Having gone from full time in 2017 in the lead-up to the World Cup back to part time, the players had been under the impression that their next contracts would again be part time, for now anyway, only to read in the media that the union was planning to reintroduce permanent deals.

As the players grew ever more frustrated at the lack of information, with many having given up careers or turned down promotions to play for England, critical coverage started to surface in the media. Owen Slot in *The Times* wrote that the players had been locked in a room at a training camp when they'd been given their most recent part-time contracts and were not allowed to leave until they had signed them.

The coverage overshadowed the official announcement a few weeks later though it was recognised as a huge moment in the game.

Writing about it in *The Guardian* in the aftermath, I suggested that it had the potential to change the women's game forever. England had certainly significantly moved the goalposts for everyone else.

There were already contracts in the game, but they were largely restricted to sevens, where the security of funding from Olympic federations meant that most of the top players were professional. This was different and a huge leap from the RFU. Several top 15s players from other countries beseeched their own unions to follow suit.

Although unlikely that many would do so immediately, it fed a fear about how far the full-time England and part-time French and New Zealand teams could streak ahead.

Receiving less attention but still significant was Scotland's novel contract agreement. Eight players were handed '2021' contracts, indicating the importance of qualifying for the next World Cup. In hindsight it was a smart strategy, with Scotland reaching the final qualifiers in 2021 and knocking a heavily favoured Ireland out of the running.

Despite more certainty of funding for the world's top sevens teams, there were significant pay battles still being fought.

Having become one of the first teams in the world to centralise their programme in 2012, Canada had stolen a march on everyone in getting to grips with professionalism early on. On paper their model looked exemplary. The players were all based in Victoria, they had some of the world's best athletes in their ranks and they were consistently among the top-four teams in the World Sevens Series. Their results meant that funding from their Olympic agency Own the Podium was relatively secure, but a different story was playing out with Rugby Canada, their national governing body.

In 2013, the women's players found out that Rugby Canada was paying tour fees to the men's international sevens team. No such offer was available to them. After privately calling out the disparity, the team were eventually offered fees, starting out at $150 a tour before both sets of players were earning the same amount.

In 2018, it then emerged that the men's team also had performance bonuses written into their Rugby Canada contracts. If they won a tournament, they would receive around $3,500 each, with a sliding scale to around $500 for finishing in the top eight. The women's team, who would stand to benefit enormously from such a deal, were getting nothing. They had never been made aware of the difference between what they were being offered and what the men's team, who were nowhere near top-four contenders, had written into their deals.

The players were incensed. They understood immediately that the offer was an easy one for the union to make because they never had to pay it out, but were angry about the unequal terms the teams were working off.

They went to the leadership team at Rugby Canada and embarked on a painful two years of negotiations, sapping energy from players supposed to be focusing on performing for their country. One of the players at the forefront of the talks described the stress of it:

When we took it to the top, right away the response was we agree and we support you but from there it still took two years of meetings and negotiations. Two years of saying that they support us but no action being taken. Our side gig when we were meant to be playing and training was dealing with meetings and having to fight for something that was so ridiculous but if you stopped doing it you just felt that they would quietly back away so you couldn't.

In 2020 we were eventually offered the same deal and then Covid hit and Rugby Canada scrapped all bonus payments. We were at the point finally that if we were performing we were earning a good living wage and now we are back to where we were in 2012.

That there were challenges surrounding the introduction of contracts was hardly a surprise. Paying women's players was still in its infancy and there was a significant lack of knowledge among the players themselves about what represented fair terms.

Only in recent years have the game's top athletes signed with agents who can help them to access legal support and develop a profile that might lead to increased investment. The attitude among some unions was to pay the minimum possible. Recent contracts offered to Welsh players were reportedly worth just £19,000 a year.

On the field, there were major titles to be decided in 2018. A Six Nations plus a revived European 15s Championship were on the cards for leading European sides, while there was another massive sevens programme with a Commonwealth Games and a World Cup in the offing.

England should have been favourites going into the Six Nations despite their disappointment in the World Cup. The development of the new Premier 15s league had started to bring through exciting players like Shaunagh Brown and Lagi

Tuima, but England faced a tricky away game with France, who had a new captain – a young and talented flanker called Gaëlle Hermet.

Ireland had a new coach in Adam Griggs following their disastrous 2017 and welcomed Niamh Briggs back into the squad, while Scotland were finally starting to look upwards. Wales had enjoyed a decent World Cup and ended on a high, while Italy were blooding a raft of new faces.

The opening weekend went to form, with England beating Italy 42-7, Scotland falling by just a point against Wales and France recording their 13th home win in a row over Ireland in a 24-0 result. It was the first time Ireland had failed to score against France since 2006.

Ireland picked it up in round two with captain Ciara Griffin grabbing two tries against Italy in a 21-8 win, while England went past the 50-point mark against Wales at The Stoop as Poppy Cleall and Ellie Kildunne starred. Scotland made France work for their 26-3 win but crucially did grab a bonus point thanks to a late Jade Le Pesq score.

Ireland built on the win with a comfortable 35-12 win over Wales in round three while another big England win over Scotland and a victory for France meant that the tournament's top two sides were on course for a showdown in Grenoble. The coverage and interest in the match was massive with more than 15,000 tickets sold in advance, making it easily the most anticipated women's Test game outside a World Cup. England went into it on top of the table on points difference, but with France running out to what in the end was a record 17,400-strong crowd – the biggest ever crowd for any women's Test game including World Cup Finals – it was going to take a heroic effort to come home with a win.

England scored first when Danielle Waterman put up-and-coming winger Abby Dow away in the corner. France looked nervy in front of so many fans roaring them on but hit back when Jessy Trémoulière skipped over out wide and Caroline Drouin powered over to give them the half-time lead.

England went ahead again on 51 minutes with a simple score as France foolishly held back at a line-out, allowing Amy Cokayne to power through at the back of a maul. For England, Katy Daley-Mclean was outstanding. On the other side, Hermet was superb, showing just why she'd been chosen as captain, with inspirational plays all over the field.

Daley-Mclean made it a four-point lead on 70 minutes but the best was yet to come for France. In the last minute of the match, the ball was spun wide and Trémoulière was again on hand to expose England's wide defence and power through for the score, winning it 17-18 and sending the fans into raptures.

With just one game to play, France would surely win the grand slam, especially given the other results on the penultimate weekend. Isabella Locatelli, Maria Magatti and Beatrice Rigoni scored tries for Italy in a brilliant 22-15 away win in Wales while Scotland also secured an impressive victory in Dublin. In a game of few chances, Chloe Rollie's second-half breakaway try proved decisive as Scotland achieved their first win in Ireland in a dozen years winning 15-12.

The title and grand slam did indeed go back to France as they beat Wales 38-3 in Colwyn Bay. England were runners-up as they compounded Ireland's misery with a 33-11 win, while Italy ended well with a win over Scotland.

With several new faces emerging – Giada Franco, Cyrelle Banet and Ellie Kildunne among them – and record-breaking crowds, the 2018 Six Nations should have been another exercise in building momentum for those in charge. Instead the tournament's maddening scheduling became a talking point. Women's Six Nations games had long bumped up against each other and, despite clear growing interest, games continued to run simultaneously, denying fans and media a chance to see and cover all the games live.

While the Six Nations had been underway, Spain had won the revived European Championship with comfortable wins over Germany and the Netherlands. Run as a single event for four teams over five days, the 2018 championship was played at two different venues in Belgium, the fourth nation taking part. The snowbound Stade du Pachy in Waterloo hosted the semi-finals and third-place play-off while the final was played on artificial turf at the Nelson Mandela Centre in Brussels as part of a double-header with the men's Rugby Europe Championship match between Belgium and Germany.

The quality of play over the course of the tournament highlighted the talent and potential available in European rugby outside the Six Nations, but was also a stark reminder that it was talent unlikely to develop given a lack of playing opportunities.

While much of this comes down to money, the absence of Six Nations teams from the fixture lists of the second tier of continental women's rugby continues to be significant. A glance through the rugby history of these countries shows how teams from England, France and Italy used to be regular opponents, but no longer.

Although British Forces teams such as the Army and Royal Air Force have to an extent stepped into the breach, it was becoming hard to see how the Netherlands or Germany could develop without the chance to play and learn against the higher-quality teams that used to enter the European Championship.

Gold on the Coast

Attention turned back to sevens as the Commonwealth Games approached in April. Rugby had been part of the programme at the event since 1998 but a women's tournament was not included as the original purpose for adopting sevens was to provide a men's sport to balance women's netball. However, the success of the Australian women's team resulted in pressure to include a women's rugby event at their home Commonwealth Games.

With the Games being played on the Gold Coast, Tim Walsh's team went in as favourites. There had already been two rounds of the World Sevens Series, with Australia winning in both Dubai and Sydney. The latter was a spectacular win on home soil in which the Australians became the first team ever to complete a tournament conceding no tries. The fact that this would also be Walsh's last tournament before taking over the men's team added just a little extra motivation.

The Australians were one of three World Series teams in Pool A alongside England and Fiji in what appeared to be the toughest pool, although there were no weak teams at the event. South Africa had proven their ability to beat the best in the world and Kenya too had recent World Sevens Series experience. Only Wales had not previously competed at this level.

New Zealand had a disrupted build-up with Ruby Tui going down with the mumps which required the entire team to be quarantined, missing out on the opening ceremony. Stacey Waaka explained the situation at the time.

> It was isolation, literally inside for a whole day and a half. We weren't allowed any contact with anyone else, so that was weird, but we did have a lot of entertainment indoors.

Her comments about the hardship of 36 hours' isolation would be looked back on with a certain wry irony within a year or two.

Tui missed the entire tournament and New Zealand were forced to stay in a set of apartments rather than the athletes' village as a further precaution. Canada were strong contenders despite the injury-enforced absence of Jen Kish, with Ghislaine Landry and Julia Greenshields in top form.

New Zealand ultimately became the party poopers in a dramatic final played against the hosts in front of 27,000 fans. The Kiwis dominated the first half of the final. Portia Woodman opened the scoring early on and, after Australia's attempt to counter from the restart was lost through an uncharacteristic handling error, the Ferns maintained possession throughout the rest of the half, ending it with a second try from Michaela Blyde.

But Australia came back. A near certain Emma Tonegato try was snuffed out by some great tracking back but the resulting line-out led to a score under the posts by Emilee Cherry. The speed and power of Ellia Green then levelled the scores, but despite her running around to near the posts, the kick was crucially missed.

The rest of the half could have gone either way but, as the buzzer went, Australia regained possession. They moved the ball right only for Cassie Staples to sensationally kick the ball into the crowd, a decision later explained as a miscommunication with the Australian bench who had been shouting 'have a crack' which on the field sounded like they were encouraging the players to kick it out.

The 27,000-capacity crowd went near silent. It was an error that resulted in six minutes of extra time.

The rest of the game became a test of physical fitness with both sides having chances against tiring defenders. The buzzer for the end of the first period of extra time went with Australia looking like they might steal it, but the Ferns defended brilliantly. Suddenly Kelly Brazier saw a gap and sprinted for the corner. With two Australians in pursuit, she just held on to score to win gold for New Zealand.

It was the first time Australia had not won sevens gold in a multi-sport games after triumphs at the Olympics, Youth Olympics and Youth Commonwealth Games.

The final followed a bronze-medal match that also saw a reversal of a Rio result. Aided by an early yellow card, England swept to a 19-0 lead in the first half against Canada, with scores from Lydia Thompson, Deborah Fleming and Claire Allan, trapping Canada inside their 22 for most of the seven minutes.

Canada pulled a try back to end the half just two scores down but Jess Breach restored England's three-try lead at the start of the second half. After that it was all about England holding on, with Canada eating into the England lead. With well over two minutes left – an age in sevens – they had pulled the score back to 24-19, but England held on to win bronze and their first visit to a podium in a multi-sport games.

Fiji blitzed Kenya to take fifth place with a 40-5 win and Wales ended the tournament well with possibly their biggest sevens scalp since winning the European Championship a decade before, beating World Sevens Series qualifier-finalists South Africa 19-14 to finish seventh. Wales had come within a minute of beating Kenya earlier in the day, leading for most of the match before losing 14-12 right at the end.

South Africa had the most disappointing weekend, finishing with five defeats over the three days and eighth place. Their substandard haul included a second pool defeat to Kenya in two weeks, having lost to them at the same stage in the World Sevens Series qualifier.

A week later, the World Sevens Series headed to Japan and New Zealand continued their Commonwealth momentum with a blistering two-day performance, beating France – playing in their first series final – to win the title and close the gap at the top of the standings to just six points. As the series headed to Canada, the Black Ferns completed a golden month with a brilliant final display against Australia, winning 46-0 and setting up an exciting finale in the final round in Paris for the overall series title.

Going into the final round, Australia were four points and two places ahead, meaning that if they just reached the final, they would win the series. With the World Cup Sevens looming, several squads showed significant levels of experimentation. In the end Australia did just enough to take the series but New Zealand won the round. New Zealand were now clear favourites for the World Cup Sevens as the form team and the defending champions.

It was the third time women had featured in the World Cup Sevens and in the five-year gap since Moscow the game had moved on significantly. The World Sevens Series was now well established, the top teams knew each other very well, the next Olympics were around the corner, and professionalism among the top teams was now the norm. It was most unlikely that a team making their debut in San Francisco would repeat Ireland's success in Moscow.

The 16-team event featured an innovative knockout format so teams would have to win every match to be crowned World Cup winners. Moreover, they only knew their first opponent as the tournament kicked off.

The Marmite format attracted both excitement and scepticism. Could a tournament at this level provide a true and fair representation of the quality of all sides if a poor opening game resulted in elimination from the competition? And if so, could it make up for that via the excitement it would surely generate? Would it offer, as a World Cup should, a chance to celebrate the lower-ranked teams, or would it more equitably siphon the teams off into the right levels earlier than how regular pool play might?

New Zealand were favourites with four World Sevens Series titles in six years, a Commonwealth Games gold medal from earlier in the year and a 23-match unbeaten run going into the event in San Francisco. They were captained by the impressive Sarah Hirini while Portia Woodman and Michaela Blyde had proven their deadly finishing abilities. It would be up to everyone else to try to match the standards they set.

The 16-team format provided for teams right at the outset of their development, such was the infancy of the world sevens game in women's rugby. Little was expected results-wise of teams like Mexico and Papua New Guinea, but much was expected of how partaking in the event would help to develop the players involved.

The opening day was brutal. Teams were thrust straight into knockout play where a win in the opening game meant progression to a quarter-final. The games were played at AT&T Park, home of the San Francisco Giants of Major League Baseball. The women's event kicked off with Spain battling to a 19-12 win over Fiji to set up a championship quarter-final with Australia, who saw off Papua New Guinea with Charlotte Caslick scoring two of their six tries in a 34-5 victory. Australia were too strong against the Spanish with a hat-trick from Evania Pelite securing a 34-0 win. Spain were out of contention before they really got going.

New Zealand had no trouble on the opening day in their two games. Captain Sarah Hirini scored the tournament's first hat-trick in a 57-0 win over Mexico before her team powered past Ireland in the championship quarter-finals. Michaela Blyde also crossed for three tries in that 45-0 win. Ireland had earlier sprung a surprise and killed off England's chances, with Amee-Leigh Murphy Crowe's second try proving the difference as her side held on to triumph 19-14. It condemned their rivals to a finish of no higher than ninth place for the second World Cup Sevens running.

That was the only game to go against the seedings in the round of 16 with 2013 runners-up Canada, hosts USA, Russia and France all keeping themselves in the race to lift the World Cup.

If the first two quarter-finals were straightforward affairs for New Zealand and Australia, the third between Canada and France was a nail-biting game that swung one way and then the other. France raced out of the blocks with tries by Marjorie Mayans and Lina Guerin, only for Canada captain Ghislaine Landry to touch down on the stroke of half-time.

A great solo try by Charity Williams edged Canada ahead for the first time before Guerin and Bianca Farella traded scores to leave the sides locked at 19-19. Extra time seemed on the cards until Coralie Bertrand, rookie of the year in the 2018 World Sevens Series, managed to reach out for the winning try to spark wild celebrations among her teammates given it secured a first World Cup Sevens semi-final for France.

Then two first-half tries by Naya Tapper looked to have crowd favourites USA on their way to victory over Russia with a 21-5 half-time lead, but the Europeans battled back to within a score before quick-fire tries by Ilona Maher and Cheta Emba made certain of a semi-final showdown with defending champions New Zealand.

New Zealand though were far too good for everyone on day two and produced some outstanding rugby to beat surprise finalists France in the final, winning 29-0 to secure back-to-back World Cup Sevens titles. The Kiwis had knocked out the USA in the semi-finals and were brilliant against the French, with Michaela Blyde scoring a brace.

France's run to the final was well deserved though. They had long had the potential but never managed to discover the magic formula until 2018, when they reached their first World Sevens Series Final in Kitakyushu only to also fall to New Zealand. The David Courteix-coached team showed that that was no flash in the pan by reaching the semi-finals in Langford and Paris to claim the series bronze medal for the first time, a big improvement on seventh the previous year. With captain Fanny Horta leading by example alongside another stalwart in Marjorie Mayans, and Camille Grassineau, anything seemed possible for the now silver medallists.

Australia claimed bronze, bouncing back from a semi-final defeat to France by beating the USA. Spain claimed fifth place with a narrow 12-7 win over Ireland, who had beaten Russia earlier in the day, with 2013 runners-up Canada having to settle for a disappointing seventh.

Brutal it may have been for teams, but the event was also exciting and dramatic and the best team won. For a version of the sport for which the Olympics would continue to be its pinnacle event, the innovative format worked very well.

It was not the only change of format in women's rugby. World Rugby announced soon after that the next 15-a-side World Cup would introduce quarter-finals, increase squad sizes and an expanded tournament from 23 to 35 days. It was also confirmed that New Zealand and Australia were the final two host bidders. New Zealand would eventually be named hosts.

There were some notable 15s Tests to end the year. New Zealand headed on tour to the USA to play at Soldiers Field in Chicago, part of a unique triple-header where Italy's men also played Ireland and the New Zealand Maori played the USA first. The Black Ferns then headed to France for a two-Test series, while the Oceania Championships gave valuable and rare Test time to Fiji, Samoa, Tonga and Papua New Guinea.

South Africa were also making a return to the international game with their first match in four years, against the UK Armed Forces in London. The autumn was a struggle for the USA, who were hammered by the Black Ferns and England, but the New Zealand trip to France produced two outstanding matches and a fitting end to a packed year.

New Zealand had already beaten Australia twice over the summer in the Laurie O'Reilly Memorial Trophy, with their Test in Sydney played in front of 28,842 fans thanks to a double-header scheduling. They headed to France with momentum and won the first Test in Toulon, a cagey 0-14 result with Renee Wickliffe and Eloise Blackwell on the scoresheet.

Where the first game had been cautious, the second game was spectacular. A crowd of 17,102 – just a few hundred short of what would have been a world record – saw France lead from start to finish and beat New Zealand 30-27 in a classic. We hailed it on Scrumqueens.com as one of the best Tests ever. France were dazzling through Romane Menager, who scored early, and New Zealand matched what the hosts were throwing at them with Kendra Cocksedge playing a vital role.

The result sparked huge French celebrations as it was technically their first ever win against New Zealand, although France did beat New Zealand 3-0 in a hastily arranged and very unofficial third-place match at the 1991 World Cup. The game appeared in French records and caps were awarded but New Zealand rugby history ignores the game completely.

A disrespectful afterthought

What should have been a celebratory end to a successful year for the women's game at the World Rugby annual end-of-year awards ended in frustration, at least for me.

The federation announced its eight-person panel to decide who would win the Women's Player of the Year award, alongside the men's gong. Maggie Alphonsi joined Fabien Galthié, George Gregan, Richie McCaw, Brian O'Driscoll, Agustín Pichot, John Smit and Clive Woodward in making the call on who the best women's player in the world had been in 2018.

The makeup of the group was laughable. There was not even a pretence of gender balance on the panel, but that in itself was no shock. The greater problem was that, Alphonsi apart, none of the others had any involvement in the women's game and were unlikely to have seen a single full Test that entire year. Now we were expected to accept that they had enough knowledge between them to determine the best women's player on the planet.

World Rugby's history with women's rugby awards was patchy. The official awards didn't even start out with a Women's Player of the Year. There was a Women's Personality award split between players and administrators, meaning many well-deserving athletes missed out over the years. Fantastic administrators ought to have been considered in other categories designed to celebrate long and distinguished service as per the men's game. Panellists were forced to choose just one name while the men's game mopped up numerous other awards across a variety of categories.

Finally, in 2012, a Women's Player of the Year award was introduced, although it was again just one award with no distinction between sevens and 15s players. By 2014 there was an individual award for both and women were also now finally being named in the Hall of Fame for the first time and things have to be fair improved out of sight since.

But the panels choosing the shortlists had always been questionable. This one was even more so at a time when the women's game was riding high. The problem was fixed in 2019 and a far more representative panel was chosen, but that it had to be pointed out was another frustrating reminder of how the women's game had to continue to be treated fairly and respectfully.

England's history makers

History was made before a match was played in 2019 when 28 England players started the year as the game's first full-time professional 15s team. It was now full-time England, part-time France and semi-part-time New Zealand leading the way with resourcing their players.

Although the full impact of all that time together would take a while to show itself, England still started the 2019 Six Nations as favourites despite a brilliant French showing the year before due to the massive pressure on teams to secure Olympic qualification.

France decided to prioritise qualifying through the World Sevens Series and it was reflected in their opening Six Nations squads, which excluded Jessy Trémoulière and Caroline Drouin, who would at least be absent against Wales. England benefited the other way around. Key players like Emily Scarratt, Jess Breach and Mo Hunt swapped one contract for another and now were fully focused on 15s.

Ireland welcomed back Alison Miller, a world-class winger, and had started to introduce some exciting young talent including teenager Beibhinn Parsons, who would soon make herself known on the Test stage. Scotland and Wales were dealing with the loss of talismanic players through injury. Jade Konkel and Sioned Harries were both ruled out.

Italy were arguably the team to watch. They came into the championship quietly confident, with two big autumn wins against Scotland and South Africa boosting them to the position of the third-ranked team in Europe. Manuela Furlan led an experienced team with Sara Barattin at scrum-half, Michela Sillari in the centre, and Lucia Gai and Melissa Bettoni up front. The fixture list had been kind, giving them three very winnable matches before taking on England and France in the final two rounds.

Italy started well away from home with a 28-7 win over Scotland. The Scots were impressive defensively for large spells but Italy were too strong with Sillari on immaculate kicking form. France brushed away any concerns about who they were missing with a thumping 52-3 win over Wales at home, their biggest ever result against the Welsh, with scrum-half Pauline Bourdon in brilliant form.

England recorded their biggest win against Ireland for 17 years with a 51-7 result in Dublin. It was scant consolation for Ireland that they played in front of their biggest crowd in a standalone fixture with almost 5,000 in the stands despite the farcical kick-off time of 5pm on a Friday. The challenges of scheduling a men's, women's and U20 competition on the same weekend and with competing broadcast demands were starting to become untenable.

Though just one round had been played, it was already clear that France and England were playing on a different level to everyone else. With seven of their nine conversions missed, the French result actually flattered Wales while England were so clinical that Ireland never got in the game at all. Already it was clear that whoever won the round-two game between England and France would likely win the Six Nations. It was a headache for those tasked with finding investment for a competition when this one would in effect be over after just two weekends.

England on the day were too good, storming to a 24-0 half-time lead and ending up with a 41-26 win. Jess Breach's double, one from Kelly Smith and the first of two tries from Poppy Cleall did the damage before the break as England dominated. France were better in the second half, with Safi N'Diaye and Romane Menager scoring either side of a brace from Pauline Bourdon, but it was too late as England all but won the title in front of almost 5,000 people at Doncaster's Castle Park. Ireland beat Scotland in Glasgow while Italy and Wales slogged it out for a 3-3 draw.

England proceeded to storm though the championship, beating Wales 51-21, Italy 55-9 and Scotland 80-0 to end a one-way-traffic few months. The sheer volume of the scorelines prompted immediate concerns that a professional England team could make the Six Nations even more uncompetitive.

There were other storylines, though. The Italians were a success story, finishing runners-up with a fine 31-12 win over France in the final round. It was a remarkable result. The team had only finished third once previously.

Despite England's dominance, record crowds throughout the Six Nations in 2019 were once again the huge plus point. England's win over Italy was played in front of a 10,545 crowd in Exeter, more than any other international women's rugby match in England outside of the 2010 World Cup Final. Ireland drew another record home crowd when just over 6,000 people turned out to see them play France. Outside France, who have long excelled in drawing crowds, the figures for Ireland and England would have been scarcely believable a few years before as Katy Daley-Mclean reminded everyone when she noted that for her debut there were just 300 people in the crowd, mostly family and friends of the players.

England's crowds at Doncaster and Exeter were also a potent reminder that the women's game should continue to do what is right for the women's game. The RFU took a punt in taking the game out of the capital twice and it paid off handsomely. The rotation has continued successfully.

Better media coverage was also bringing welcome critical scrutiny to the game. Ireland's fall from World Cup semi-finalists and Six Nations winners to fifth-place Six Nations finishers was scrutinised in a manner not seen before. Former players Lynne Cantwell, Fiona Steed and Jenny Murphy ran over the ruins of the campaign on national television in Ireland.

The Times in the UK reported that despite winning a grand slam, England women received no bonuses. The men could have received a handsome sum for the same achievement. I appeared on *Today* – a flagship radio political news programme in the UK – and was asked why Wales, a successful men's rugby nation, invested so little in its national women's team.

Seeing these debates playing out across national media was a new world for women's rugby. Pressure was starting, finally, to come on those running the game to offer more transparency and answer tough questions about their women's rugby strategies.

While England were dominating the Six Nations, Spain were winning the European Championship with a comfortable 54-0 over the Netherlands in Madrid with the brilliant Patricia

García scoring a hat-trick. Even the story of that win was about the crowd with a remarkable 9,000 people turning out to watch.

The sevens season was well underway having kicked the year off with a four-team event in Hamilton, a warm-up event but one which attracted a profile and significance far beyond that for one important reason. Over 20 years after they first took the field, the Black Ferns sevens team were remarkably only just making their debut at home.

New Zealand went on to win the Sydney Sevens. In Japan it was Canada's turn on the podium, beating England in the final in a weekend where the form book was overturned. New Zealand regathered their momentum on the Series when they were crowned champions in Canada and secured their spot at the Olympics at the same time with a hard-fought 21-17 victory over Australia in the cup final.

The Sarah Hirini-led Black Ferns were already the series winners by the time the final round in France came around but the story of the weekend was the USA, who won the round with Alev Kelter in sensational form.

While teams scrambled to secure their tickets to Rio, there was a sad end to the Olympic dream for the Netherlands. The Dutch had made unlikely history eight years earlier when they had become the world's first professional women's team.

They became one of the six core teams in the first World Sevens Series and finished seventh in the first event which, in any other year, would have been enough to qualify for the following season, but the IRB decided that qualification for the second series would be decided by the 2013 World Cup Sevens. The quarter-finalists would be the eight core teams for 2014. The Dutch were drawn in the toughest pool with New Zealand and Canada and missed out.

Outside the World Series, any advantage the Dutch may have had was quickly lost. The 2014 series was the Olympic qualifier which meant the Dutch had to win a place at the qualifier in Hong Kong in September 2014, but they lost in the quarter-finals to South Africa.

The 2015 European Championship was their next hope, but the Dutch lost in the quarter-finals to Spain. The last chance was the repechage. To make that, the Dutch needed to finish third in a qualifier tournament in Lisbon, but they lost in the third-place play-off to Portugal, who they had never lost to before.

The Rio dream was over. Funding was cut, most of the leading players retired and, in 2017, the Dutch slipped into the second tier of European sevens.

Not so super in San Diego

Another 15-a-side Super Series was slated for that summer, returning after three years off. This time it would feature the world's top five sides: England, New Zealand, Canada, France and the USA. It was previewed enthusiastically, with the games being hosted in San Diego at the USA's Elite Athlete Training Centre in partnership with World Rugby.

Hardly a ball was kicked before the series descended into controversy with poor facilities attracting criticism from media and fans. The opening games were played on a terrible surface and players were forced to change in poor-quality, temporary changing facilities.

New Zealand sports broadcaster Scotty Stevenson, who has regularly covered the progress of the Black Ferns, used social media to set out a series of criticisms highlighting that players were changing in a tent with portable toilets, that the quality of the field was no better than a training ground and that fans were asked to bring their own seats.

USA Rugby was forced to defend the ground saying that it was 'proud' to host the series at the venue but conceded that 'pop up facilities were needed close to the pitch and the practical setup was discussed with all the teams ahead of the tournament'.

The issue of substandard facilities had long dogged the women's game, but this was a competition involving the world's five leading Test teams at an event run in partnership with the game's global governing body. It reinforced the narrative that international women's players should simply be happy to be playing at all.

A similar issue occurred when the final games of Ireland's Interprovincial Championship between the country's top four representative sides attracted horror in 2021. Images emerged of the teams forced to change beside bins where rats could be seen running around. The IRFU were forced into two public apologies.

At least the action on the field was better in San Diego. New Zealand won the title following an exciting final day's action. England began the day top of the table but, despite taking an early 10-3 lead and playing against 14 players for a quarter of the match, they were unable to get the better of a Renee Wickliffe-inspired Black Ferns side, who scored three tries.

New Zealand's summer carried on with a two-Test series win over Australia, who themselves had beaten Japan a few months earlier. It constituted something of a packed few months for the Aussies, who were still barely playing Test games between World Cups. There had, however, been some positive developments in the Australian domestic game with the start of a new club competition, the Super W, which would add much-needed competitive fixtures to their schedule.

With an avalanche of Test games slated over the final few months of the year, 2019 was fast becoming the busiest 12 months in a non-World Cup year ever for the international 15s game. Even more positively, some 35 different nations fielded Test games before the year was out, including two debutantes, a record for any year.

The launch of official Test championships in Africa and South America had pulled nations back into the Test fold. As a result, in addition to Madagascar and Colombia playing their first ever Tests, nations such as Brazil, China, Sweden, Zimbabwe and Zambia returned to Test rugby after, in some cases, a decade away.

The winter also saw the return of the Elgon Cup, the two-Test series between Kenya and Uganda that had not been played in four years. Neither side had played any Test rugby at all since 2015, when World Rugby's decision to bar the two nations from the qualification process for the 2017 World Cup resulted in the abandonment of the fixture and a focus on sevens. A change of policy for the 2021 World Cup, which included a competitive African qualifier, saw the games revived.

The Barbarians also brought some fun to the end-of-season calendar, beating the USA in a thriller. Welsh star Jasmine Joyce scored four tries. The Barbarians then lost to England.

Scotland also had something to celebrate, winning two Tests in South Africa under new head coach Philip Doyle – their first back-to-back wins in a decade.

An expanded 2019/20 World Sevens Series started earlier than ever, with the eight-round competition beginning in Glendale in the USA in October. Though the series was expected to be overshadowed by the Olympics, its expansion and the fact that six rounds were combined with men's events aimed to create an atmosphere that had so far eluded the women's series. Hosts USA were the early leaders, taking a home-leg win, before New Zealand retained their Dubai crown and took the new leg in Cape Town.

As 2020 dawned, women's rugby looked forward to a year that promised to be spectacular with the Olympics and a World Cup. It ultimately proved to be the sport's most challenging ever.

Chapter Sixteen

Hard lines and Covid chaos

THERE WAS a business-as-usual start to 2020 as New Zealand won their third consecutive round of the World Series in January in Hamilton, opening up a 12-point gap as the expanded competition reached its halfway point. Though Covid-19 was in the news, there was little sign of the massive impact it would soon have and rugby carried on relatively normally in the first couple of months of the year.

As New Zealand then became the first team to successfully defend the Sydney Sevens in February, beating Canada in the title decider, preparations for the Six Nations also carried on. England were the team to beat, a year into professionalism and on the back of a strong 2019 with 11 wins in 13 games.

Their opening game of the championship though was away in France and the winner was likely to go on and take the whole thing. The scheduling first of the match between the two best teams was a shame, designed as ever to mirror the men's competition, and did little to increase the appeal of the entire tournament to current or new women's rugby fans.

England had beaten France a record four times the year before but, with France playing at home with a relatively new and electric half-back partnership of Laure Sansus and Pauline Bourdon, nothing was a given and the opener was highly anticipated.

It was clear that there were problems in Wales. Coach Rowland Phillips took some time away from his role and two of their most experienced players, Carys Phillips and Sioned Harries with over 50 caps each, failed to make their squad. Italy had ended the year disappointingly despite their incredible Six Nations finish 12 months earlier.

Scotland had one eye on the World Cup qualifiers later in the year but their clash against Ireland on the opening weekend was well profiled in advance. Head coach Philip Doyle was lined up to coach against the team he'd helped reach the World Cup semi-final.

As it was, the competition was over before it ever began. A brilliant try from Emily Scarratt helped England to secure a 19-13 win over France on the opening weekend. It was England's first win in France in the Six Nations since 2012, but with it came an anti-climactic feel. No one else would get close to the Red Roses, as England's women's team were now branded.

The victory made the calls for a total rethink of the tournament structure even more potent. The aping of the men's schedule meant no scope for tinkering with the format even though it was glaringly obvious that it was not working for the women's game.

In the other opening games, Italy managed to withstand a fightback late on to beat Wales 19-10 while Ireland did just about enough to beat Scotland 18-14 in their opening matches. There was, at least, after those results a decent narrative playing out among the minor placings. No one gained a try-scoring bonus point and every losing team claimed a bonus point.

With Italy, Scotland and Ireland competing with Spain for a place in the World Cup and the qualifying repechage, those opening results suggested that there was nothing to choose between them, as would be evident a year later when the final qualifiers were finally held.

As the second round of games loomed, both Covid-19 and stormy weather were throwing sport into question across Europe. Just two games were played on schedule in round two before the fixtures descended into chaos.

Ireland backed up their first-round win with a defeat of Wales with emerging star Beibhinn Parsons scoring. France were comfortable 45-10 winners over Italy, the highlight being a length-of-the-field score from the brilliant wing Cyrielle Banet. Scotland's match against England was postponed until the Monday because of adverse weather conditions in Glasgow. In the event, England made light of the snow to win 53-0 at Murrayfield and backed it up with a win in Doncaster over the Irish the following weekend, with France also cruising past Wales with a 50-0 result.

Covid-19 was by now tearing through Italy and it was no surprise when the Italians called off their game against Scotland given rising infections in the Milan area. It seemed a matter of when and not if the schedule would have to be ripped up.

Ireland called their game off with Italy the following weekend. The France and Scotland game was also off after a Scottish player tested positive after travelling to Italy for the game that never happened. The England and Wales game managed to go ahead, though the Welsh might have wished it hadn't, shipping over 60 points in Twickenham.

Confirmation soon followed that none of the three fixtures would be played the following weekend. Soon fixtures and competitions all over the world started to drop, including the World Series, Asia Championship and European qualifiers.

When it was announced in March that the Olympics would be postponed, the pressure came off World Rugby somewhat to cram in its qualifier events, something that looked impossible anyway, but the delay also presented a pile-up for the following year, 2021, when there was also due to be a 15s World Cup.

Not until August did the Six Nations announce a restart, with the remaining six games to be played from October through to December. Even that was a mess. The first round went ahead, bringing a brilliant draw for Scotland against France, but the other games were called off again as the European winter brought worsening infection rates and increased restrictions. England were finally crowned title and grand slam winners after beating Italy 54-0 in November.

Elsewhere, New Zealand were declared winners of the World Series after the final three events were called off. It was a well-deserved title despite it being awarded in the boardroom. By the time the pandemic closed down the tournament they had already opened up a 16-point lead at the top of the series, meaning that they would have needed little more than three semi-final appearances in the final three rounds to confirm the title. More likely they would probably have won the title before the final round had taken place.

France ended the series as Europe's top team by far. With four semi-finals in five events they were the continent's best team in every tournament and finished in fourth place, four points clear of the United States. The French form suggested that they could well be a massive threat in the Olympics – if they ever took place.

Rugby returns

Though the pandemic wiped out fixtures all over the world, careful planning and Covid-specific resources meant that some important Tests did get played at the end of 2020.

England and France agreed a two-Test series to be shown live on French television and the free-to-air BBC after the culmination of the Six Nations. England won 10-33 in Grenoble in round one and came from 10-23 down with 14 minutes left to win again in Twickenham in what was easily the game of the year.

It was my first time attending a live game since the pandemic began. I watched in surprise as England coach Simon Middleton took the unusual step of bringing his entire bench on in one go with 20 minutes left. But it worked. Poppy Cleall – fast becoming one of the best players in the world – crashed over almost immediately and Ellie Kildunne showed her brilliance to score a few minutes later. Emily Scarratt knocked over the winning penalty and France, who had been unplayable at times, were left to stare at the scoreboard, stunned.

Though 2020 would not be remembered fondly, there had been some significant moments in the game.

The changes to the World Cup were welcome and would boost the development of a wider range of Test nations. The expansion from 12 to 16 teams from 2025 onwards would mean a sharper focus on developing the standards outside of the top teams, while the 2021 World Cup launch in New Zealand featured the prime minister and was the most high-profile affair yet in the women's game, generating real excitement for the event despite the world's state of flux.

Eventually, that too would be delayed due to Covid-19, but the excitement and profile the launch helped to generate demonstrated what a crown jewel the World Cup had become.

The year 2020 was also one in which women's rugby started to find its voice. Prominent names in the game used their public profiles to discuss and raise serious issues across the sport. That had been a rarity in the women's game for too long. Current players feared selection reprisals if they spoke out and ex-players were unwilling to expose themselves to the possibility of negative publicity. They were understandable fears perhaps, though it made the job of holding those in power to account even more difficult for people constantly advocating for progress.

But in 2020 there was significant progress. Concussion was one topic of public debate with ex-Test players like Kat

England captain Katy Daley-Mclean lifts the World Cup at the Stade Jean Bouin in Paris in 2014 having beaten Canada in the final. (Credit: World Rugby)

Nathalie Amiel (France), Gill Burns (England), Patty Jervey (USA) and Anna Richards (New Zealand) were among the first women inducted into World Rugby's Hall of Fame in 2014. (Credit: World Rugby)

New Zealand's Portia Woodman evades Emily Scarratt's tackle at the Rio Olympics in 2016. (Credit: Wang Peng/Xinhua/Alamy Live News)

New Zealand celebrate after scoring a try against England in the brilliant World Cup Final in Belfast in 2017 (Credit: World Rugby)

South Africa celebrate qualifying for the 2021 World Cup thanks to a win over Kenya at the Bosman Stadium in Brakpan in 2019. (Credit: World Rugby)

Australia co-captain Sharni Williams and Japan co-captain Mayu Shimizu show their respect before kick off at the Tokyo Olympic Games in 2021. (Credit: World Rugby)

New Zealand's Ruby Tui and Portia Woodman celebrate the final win over France at the Tokyo Olympic Games in 2021. (Credit: World Rugby)

Fiji players celebrate with their bronze medals at the Tokyo Olympic Games in 2021 (Credit: World Rugby)

French star Lenaig Corson celebrates after scoring a try at Twickenham for the Barbarians against South Africa in 2021 in front of a world-record crowd. (Credit: INPHO/Craig Mercer)

Russia's Baizat Khamidova in action against Japan in the World Series. Khamidova has been one of the most consistent stars in the world sevens game. (Credit: World Rugby)

Irish referee Joy Neville has been paving the way for female referees at the highest level. She is pictured in action here in a game between Ulster and the Southern Kings in 2018. (Credit: INPHO/Morgan Treacy)

The USA sevens team gathers together during the 2021 World Series. (Credit: World Rugby)

France's Anne-Cecile Ciofani is one of the new stars of the sevens game and was named World Sevens Player of the Year in 2021. (Credit: World Rugby)

Ireland's Erin King is one of an increasing number of sevens stars also making waves in the 15s game. (Credit: Europa Press via AP)

A new Women's Rugby World Cup Trophy was launched ahead of the 2025 event – on show here in Brighton, one of the host cities. (Credit: Elsie Kibue/Alamy Live News)

Crowds are growing in the women's game, as evidenced by this turnout in Exeter in England's PWR league game between the Chiefs and Bristol Bears at Sandy Park in 2025(Credit: nidpor/ Alamy Live News)

New Zealand celebrate during the victory ceremony at the Olympic Games in Paris in 2024. (Credit: Lui Siu Wai/Xinhua/ Alamy Live News)

Ilona Maher in action for the USA in Paris during the Olympic Games. Maher has been recognised as a gamechanger in women's sport, growing fans and driving visibility. (Photo by Maya Vidon-White/UPI Credit: UPI/Alamy Live News)

Merchant and Nic Evans speaking publicly about their fears and concerns, while outlets like the BBC and *Telegraph* ran in-depth analysis about the lack of research in sports science for women.

There was also a campaign launched by Wasps and Wales player Florence Williams regarding brands using models instead of real women's players to launch kit, which garnered vocal support from a wide range of women's rugby players. England captain Sarah Hunter used her profile to campaign to support the challenge of food poverty in the UK.

Social justice issues dominated the public discourse like no other in 2020, with Black Lives Matter protests becoming enormously prominent after the murder of George Floyd in the US. Racial diversity had rarely been discussed in a women's game that had been far more preoccupied by gender inequalities but powerful discussions began to emerge, in the USA, Canada and England in particular, about experiences of racial inequalities in the game.

This was not something that we had ever explored on the Scrumqueens.com website and I emailed Maggie Alphonsi to ask if she would talk me through her experiences. It resulted in one of the most powerful conversations I've had in my time in the game and undoubtedly the most important interview we have ever run. It was picked up by a range of national media outlets.

Alphonsi told me that she was deeply upset by what had happened and that, as a pregnant mother-to-be, it had made her step back and think about the future for her child.

Alphonsi was England's only Black player through the majority of an outstanding playing career that featured 74 caps, a World Cup win and seven Six Nations titles, though when she joined the set-up in 2003, the picture was much more diverse. Paula George, who is mixed-race, captained the team and Maxine Edwards, who would take on the captaincy, was a leading Black player from Alphonsi's club Saracens:

> To be honest, when I was starting out in rugby when I looked at the team and when I saw Paula was the captain it was just huge. There were other sports I was interested in at the time but that was a really big draw to rugby. I saw myself reflected there and it made everything possible for me.
>
> But after they left, it was mostly just me and even now there are very few players in the squad representing BAME communities – Shaunagh Brown has probably been the most prominent. When I was coming to the end of my career, I felt like I needed to keep playing so that there was at least one person that young Black girls could see in the team who looked like them. It's the same with broadcasting – I keep in there because there are so few Black women out in front of a camera and because visibility is so massively important.

Among other roles, Alphonsi now sits on England Rugby's powerful council, and one of a handful of women among its 61-strong membership, and she told me her goal was to become president. Her ambition was widely reported once our interview ran, and one I hope will soon come true.

She acknowledged that because she was a standout player, people often looked past her skin colour, but she spoke movingly about the whiteness of women's rugby and how that made her feel:

> When we would go to certain countries and I would be the only Black person in the entire travelling squad including all the coaches and support staff, I would be very conscious of my skin colour and conscious I stood out.

There are some places – like when I went to Moscow to watch the World Cup Sevens – when I felt very uncomfortable and other times, I would just be acutely aware that I was often the only Black person in an entire ground at some games when I played for England. I never really talked about that, so I doubt my team-mates even considered it was an issue for me.

The country I felt most comfortable in was France – it always felt that their team reflected their communities a bit more and at times I felt more comfortable playing in France than in some parts of England.

Since Alphonsi's powerful intervention, women's players and the game have been much more vocal on issues around race and ethnicity and wider social justice topics. A year later, the Canadian women's team held a press conference wearing black T-shirts with the words 'BIPOC Lives Matter' and orange masks reading 'Every Child Matters'. Players around the world have continued to take the knee before games.

Women's rugby is a long way off the progress of leagues like the USA's WNBA when it comes to having a powerful collective voice on such issues, but it is at least starting to find its way and starting to call out wider inequalities across our sport.

Despite the challenges of the year, there was real evidence of the positive revival of Test rugby in 2020 too. World Rugby's renewed emphasis on 15s, thanks in part to the leadership of Katie Sadleir, was starting to bear fruit. The final Test before the worldwide shutdown was Guatemala v El Salvador, the first Test match ever played in Central America.

Had Covid-19 not hit, it would have been even better. Tunisia were due to play Algeria just a couple of weeks later and the Africa Gold Cup had promised to take Test rugby to new places, with the first Test scheduled for Madagascar.

The worldwide shutdown of international rugby also inadvertently demonstrated how widely women's rugby was now played. If asked to name two locations that would bookend the halt in rugby, it is unlikely anyone would come up with Guatemala City and Budapest. But it was Budapest that saw international rugby return, in August, when Hungary, Slovakia and Poland met in a two-day sevens tournament. It was a somewhat low-key event but it was the first light at the end of a depressingly long and dark tunnel. The page was finally turned on a terrible year, though plenty of challenges were yet to come.

Although vaccines brought hope that life and sport could start to get back to normal, 2021 got off to a rocky start with confirmation that the women's Six Nations was postponed due to cross-border travel restrictions still being in place. New Zealand had not yet confirmed the World Cup would be moved but it was clear that it would almost certainly have to. The delays to qualifiers involving European teams meant they would struggle to be played in time and the New Zealand border was still closed to international visitors.

The delay handed Six Nations organisers a golden opportunity to try a new format in a new window later in the year. When confirmation came that the competition would happen in April over four weekends – with teams playing two games fewer, there was both excitement and scepticism. Nobody truly trusted that the shortened format wouldn't become permanent – which would have been a disaster for the game – but everyone wanted to see what better scheduling and lack of competition from a packed weekend of games would bring.

Spain finally wrapped up the European Championships at the fourth attempt to get it played, beating Russia and the Netherlands and thereby winning a chance to compete for a place at the World Cup against Ireland, Scotland and Italy later in the year. Those qualifiers would be one of three high-profile events to play out in 2021 with the Tokyo Olympics and the new-look Six Nations on the horizon. Off the field there were significant announcements around the future of the Test 15s game and a smattering of new nations emerging.

The former included the long-awaited W15 competition from World Rugby, driven forward by Sadleir, the general manager of the women's game at the organisation, who did a terrific job in accelerating important innovation and governance changes. W15 is the governing body's attempt at aligning the international game around a fixed global calendar, something the men's game has consistently failed to agree.

It would feature 16 teams and be hosted in a September and October window, with teams qualifying via finishing positions within the existing annual regional competitions such as the women's Six Nations. These regional competitions would happen earlier in the year and would mean the introduction of a raft of other new competitions including a cross-region league involving Australia, the USA, Canada and New Zealand.

More importantly for the wider development of the game was the introduction of a second and third tier of the competition, opening up opportunities for developing countries, who ultimately could compete in an enlarged World Cup. The announcement had been years in the making, with painstaking efforts to align the countries involved, and it came with a £6m commitment for its first two years.

For certain teams it was also a huge step up on what they had. Australia having six Test games a year was a vast improvement on their usual programme. There would be real incentive for all nations to play more Tests, given that Test rankings help determine access to the competition at the lowest level.

A new-look Six Nations

Though there would be no crowds, the return of the women's Six Nations in April did mark the return to some sort of normality in the game. For the first time in years there were no fixture clashes, games took place at peak viewing times on Saturdays and there was free-to-air coverage of the new tournament final across most of the nations involved.

England, with two wins over France in the autumn, were the favourites again, though they were having to cope with the retirement of Katy Daley-Mclean, who had hung up her boots after a remarkable career which brought 116 caps and a World Cup win.

France had been focused on Olympic preparation with a raft of crossover players. None of the players involved in sevens tournaments over the same period would play in the Six Nations, ruling out Romane Menager and Iän Jason for example.

The other side story was that Ireland, Scotland and Italy were all playing with one eye on the World Cup qualifiers later in the year. As was becoming the norm, there was tumult in Wales. The appointment of Warren Abrahams as head coach was overshadowed by the resignation of skills coach and former national captain Rachel Taylor, the latest in a long line of major off-field disruptions hitting the Welsh women's programme.

Speaking about her exit to the *Back the Girls* podcast some months later, Taylor suggested that the programme needed far more support and was not professional enough:

I probably can't emphasise enough how stressful and I guess traumatising, to a certain degree, how it was for me.

Obviously getting that job was massive for me. I always had an ambition and still have an ambition to coach Wales. Everything sounded like a dream, I can't lie to you, it was probably the perfect scenario for me.

Everything started really well, but I had concerns quite early on with where the programme was going.

I reported my concerns, tried to do everything the right way, I'm not a HR guru but tried to do everything the right way.

Taylor suggested she did not see any support or change:

> It was really difficult because it didn't agree with my values of rugby, I felt like it was going against my own integrity. I found it really difficult to put my name to it. Rightly or wrongly a lot of people will look at me and be like 'if Tayls thinks it's alright, then obviously it's okay', but I didn't feel like it was right and okay. I couldn't justify staying in it.
>
> Ultimately, I want the best for the women that play in Wales, and I want the best for those that represent the national jersey and I didn't feel like they were getting it.

A disastrous Six Nations would throw the Welsh programme back into the spotlight. It started badly enough with a 53-0 loss to France. The Welsh players were blown away by a brilliant French performance which included a magnificent debut from full-back Émilie Boulard, who had a hat-trick inside 15 minutes.

They then shipped 45 points and scored none in Cardiff against Ireland and rounded it off with a 27-20 loss to Scotland. Wales finished bottom of the table and the alarm bells were sounded – again – about the support and interest from the WRU in developing its women's game.

England and France were on course to meet in the first ever Six Nations Final. The new format brought the competition to an exciting crescendo. France had continued their good form by sweeping Ireland aside 56-15. It was their second-largest win over the Irish and something of a reality check for Ireland. England had thrashed Italy.

The final was anyone's. England were the full-time professionals; France called on a full squad, including their sevens players, and coach Annick Hayraud named her strongest possible team. After so many one-sided matches, the tournament badly needed the game to be tight and exciting.

Neither side had been tested as yet. The result was a tense game, mostly a battle of the packs, played out at The Stoop in London.

Though France had the upper hand in the set pieces, England's big carriers, Poppy Cleall, Marlie Packer and Cath O'Donnell, got more and more into it as the game wore on and began to dominate. France conceded too many penalties to get ahead and lost 10-6. The game was most memorable for a thumping tackle that young prop Rose Bernadou made on Poppy Cleall, one that all of us in the crowd felt.

Though it had not been the hoped-for thriller, it did at least bring a tight game and suggested that England, despite their professional status, would not have everything their own way.

Attention switched back to sevens and the Olympics. Just a couple of months out, there were still places up for grabs. Russia were the final qualifiers, winning the repechage in Monaco in July, a whole two years after they had missed out on automatic qualifying. Europe would have three teams in Tokyo (Great Britain, France and Russia), as would Oceania (Australia, New Zealand and Fiji), Asia and North America would have two each (China, Japan, the USA and Canada). South Africa and Brazil completed the 12 for Africa and South America.

Tokyo time

The women's event at the Olympics was due to run over three days, starting on Thursday, 29 July, with two pool games on the opening day, the first round of knockouts on the Friday and the medal games on Saturday.

Pool A pitted New Zealand, Russia, Great Britain and Kenya together. Pool B had France, Fiji, Canada and Brazil. The USA, Australia, China and Japan made up Pool C.

New Zealand were not just simple favourites this time. They were overwhelmingly expected to go one better than Rio and take gold. Even in tight games they seemed to be able to go to another level and they travelled to Tokyo with eight players who had lost out four years earlier: captain Sarah Hirini, Kelly Brazier, Gayle Broughton, Theresa Fitzpatrick, Tyla Nathan-Wong, Ruby Tui, Portia Woodman and Michaela Blyde. Three of them – Tui, Woodman and Blyde – were former Women's Sevens Player of the Year award winners. Since Rio the team had won 16 of 22 World Sevens Series tournaments, the World Cup Sevens and Commonwealth Games gold.

Russia, having only just qualified, were captained by Alena Tiron, who could have gone to the Olympics as an athlete. She was one of Russia's leading sprinters before she switched to rugby in 2013, and she led a team full of experience including former captain Nadezhda Sozonova (formerly Kudinova), Elena Zdrokova and the brilliant Baizat Khamidova – at 30 the oldest member of the squad.

Khamidova was arguably one of the game's most interesting players with a fascinating backstory. Originally from Ibragimotar, an isolated village in Dagestan, a mile from the border with Chechnya, Khamidova grew up around the horrors of the Chechen war. She told Russian sports magazine *Sport Express* what it was like:

My sister and I did not realise then how dangerous it was or how real it was. Ibragimotar is next to the Terek River – you could go through the forest and easily cross the river and border into Chechnya. We did not understand who was fighting, or why, but we went out into the street to watch fighter aircraft fly over and drop bombs. We counted the seconds, closed their ears – and everything began to shake! It was great fun for us. Realisation came later.

That realisation came in 1999 when the Chechen rebels started to take the war into Dagestan.

I remember 1999 very well when the second Chechen war began. The village was woken up and everyone was taken to a field and told to sit in silence for the day in the grass. They said that an attack was being prepared from across the Terek. We sat so as not to move because if they came, they would go to the village itself, and the field was some distance away. We sat there for almost all day, and many showed real fear on their faces and many children cried. I was most afraid for my little brother, not for myself. As soon as we heard a small rustle, everyone went quiet and listened. The next day we were all evacuated to Makhachkala.

Thank God they didn't come to our village. We spent a month with my aunt in Makhachkala but I remember that before leaving, Navrat and I walked around our house, and there was a loaded automatic machine gun behind the chair. The men were going to defend the village. Every day after work, they gathered on the bridge at the entrance and learned to shoot.

My father stayed in the village and waited. My grandma also. Because come what may, we had no choice. But people were preparing for a real war. Thank God [the rebels] didn't touch us. Only in the mountains was there actions.

When Khamidova's athletic talent was noticed, she and her sister Navrat began to play rugby. It would take them all the way to the Olympics, a remarkable rise for the most unlikely of rugby families.

Of the other possible contenders, Great Britain had the potential to pressure New Zealand. They had narrowly missed out on a medal in 2016, finishing fourth, but their preparation for Tokyo had been calamitous. The pandemic triggered a financial crisis in the RFU, who were funding their preparations – uniquely they received no financial support from the Olympic federation, UK Sport. Although sponsorship by the National Lottery closed some of the gap, it was less than ideal and they had not had the build-up they would have liked. It was hard to see Kenya threatening the more experienced trio in the pool, though in Janet Okello they had one of the true emerging stars of the game and she was a constant threat over the three days.

Canada headed Pool B but they had also had a shocking build-up. Coaching turmoil resulted in the departure of long-time head coach John Tait, and the players had limited playing opportunities. They had a vastly experienced squad, though, with six survivors from Rio including captain Ghislaine Landry, easily one of the best players Canada had ever produced.

Their pool clash with France promised excitement. The French came into it with more preparation than any other team, having played in 27 games already that year. Fanny Horta, France's captain at Rio 2016, was one of four players returning to the Games. Anne-Cécile Ciofani would follow in the footsteps of her parents, who were both former Olympians.

Fiji had played just six games since the Sydney Sevens in 2020, all in the Oceania Sevens in June where they beat Australia – a result that illustrated they could never be discounted. As ever, the story of Fiji was that they had talent but had never been able to match it with consistency. They too had had a difficult build-up. Simply getting to Tokyo at all had been a challenge, with some players being forced to take unscheduled cargo flights.

Reigning South American champions Brazil would struggle in the pool, having failed to break through after their debut in Rio four years earlier.

Australia led Pool C. On paper they were one of the favoured teams, but in reality they had never recaptured the heights of 2016. Since they lost the Commonwealth Games Final to New

Zealand in 2018 the rest of the world had started to catch up, while the Ferns had simply accelerated away. The squad did not include Ella Green – the most prolific try-scorer in Australian women's sevens history – who was left out by coach John Manenti. He admitted it was the hardest call he'd ever made.

The USA had a powerful but inexperienced team. Only Lauren Doyle and Alev Kelter were playing in their second Olympic Games. China had not played any international events since January. Their all-Asian clash with Japan promised a mini-derby in the middle of the competition.

Pandemic restrictions meant a very different feel to the village-style set-up the players had experienced four years earlier in Rio. This time, teams were housed in apartment buildings with limited interactions with other teams and events, leaving only for training and dining. Conditions were strict. Even acknowledging players from other countries was frowned upon as interaction could lead to a Covid case that might wipe out not just a specific player or team, but many others from the same country inside their bubble.

Pulsating start

Fiji were the story of day one of the competition and their win over a disjointed Canada and narrow loss to France the picks of the opening day's results. Others largely went to form, though Great Britain gave New Zealand a huge scare. The Black Ferns had to come from 21-0 to win that game in a thrilling encounter.

Four teams in all remained unbeaten at the end of day one with Australia, France, the USA and top seeds New Zealand all getting off to a perfect start winning consecutive matches.

Great Britain had gone into the game against New Zealand on the back of a 14-12 win against the Russian Olympic Committee (ROC), the name under which Russia competed at the Olympics due to the country's ban for doping. They then started brilliantly against New Zealand and looked on course for a shock win against the favourites, racing into a three-score lead in the first half as Helena Rowland, Meg Jones and Jasmine Joyce scored tries in the opening five minutes.

However, the New Zealand comeback started before half-time as Michaela Blyde scored twice, before Tyla Nathan-Wong scored a sensational solo try midway through the second half. Great Britain led until the final minute, but Blyde found space again to score for a third time and secure an incredible comeback win.

The aftermath of the game was also notable for Ruby Tui's brilliant pitch-side interview with the BBC, giving the sporting world a glimpse into one of the game's most charismatic players who had an incredible backstory and rise to the top.

Before becoming a professional player, Tui came through a difficult childhood that included coping with an alcoholic father, constantly moving house and ending up in a women's refuge, something she speaks publicly about in an effort to help others facing similar challenges.

Long recognised as one of the most energetic and brilliant personalities in women's rugby, the interview with Jill Douglas quickly became a sensation. Tui managed to combine humility, humour and ambition, making her quickly one of the stars of the Games.

Starting off with a thank you in Samoan to her family and supporters, Tui credited the Russian team they'd earlier beaten comfortably with giving them a tough workout, revealed that the New Zealand team had contributed to Team GB's fundraising efforts and ended with a great answer about the impact of the poor weather conditions.

What rain? Bring on the thunder, we're at the Olympics, let's be happy, let's compete safely and peacefully, peace and love, love you guys.

If that was superb, so too was Fiji's win over Canada. First Reapi Ulunisau ran in the fastest try of the competition, after just 14 seconds, and Fiji kept up the pressure for the rest of the first half, touching down twice again. Ulunisau scored Fiji's fourth try within a minute of the restart and, though Canada hit back with late tries from Ghislaine Landry and Kayla Moleschi, they looked off-form throughout and would go on to struggle.

The final pool round brought plenty of drama. Canada, so lacklustre on day one, suffered their heaviest ever defeat to France with a 31-0 loss to start the day. The result meant that Canada had to rely on Russia v New Zealand to determine if they would make the quarter-finals or be playing for ninth.

In the same pool Fiji were also dominant in a 41-5 win over Brazil. Reapi Ulunisau became the first player, male or female, to score four tries in an Olympic match. The USA, who had been full of power on day one, came back from a 12-0 deficit against Australia to win it 14-0 and secure top spot in their pool.

China knew they had to beat Japan by at least 19 points to join Australia and the USA in the last eight and they did just that, running in five tries to win 29-0. Jasmine Joyce scored two of Great Britain's five tries as they confirmed their place in the medal quarter-finals with a 31-0 defeat of Kenya.

Finally, New Zealand beat Russia 33-0 in a lightning-delayed final match of the pool stage. The match was dramatic because Russia needed to keep the score under 34 points to ensure they went into the last eight and not Canada but they seemed unaware, playing on late in the game despite the score being at 33-0.

Fiji again provided the headlines in the quarter-finals, this time knocking out Australia thanks to a superb 14-12 win. Australia, having already lost to the USA, had looked out of sorts and Fiji raced into a 14-0 lead with tries from Alowesi

Nakoci and Ana Maria Naimasi. Australia did hit back with scores from Faith Nathan and Charlotte Caslick but it was too late. It capped an outstanding day for Fiji.

Australia being dumped out also meant a new Olympic winner was guaranteed. Fiji lined up a semi-final date with New Zealand, who secured their place in the last four with a comfortable 36-0 defeat of the Russians, their second shutout against the same opponents in two consecutive matches. Portia Woodman scored two of the Black Ferns' six tries, while Michaela Blyde took her tally for the tournament to six.

Jasmine Joyce, meanwhile, scored a try in each half to help Great Britain into the medal semi-finals with a 21-12 win over the USA. Great Britain would face France in the semi-final after the French defeated China in their knockout match, a comfortable win in the end with a brace for Séraphine Okemba. France had already dealt a hammer blow to Canada's chances of progressing, showing no mercy in their final pool round and beating them 21-0.

On paper, New Zealand still looked clear favourites to reach and win the final. They had played Fiji 16 times in international sevens and won them all, including twice at the Oceania Sevens earlier that year. Reapi Ulunisau and Alowesi Nakoci had both been excellent though New Zealand's never-say-die attitude and brilliant captaincy from Sarah Hirini would surely see them through. Star winger Michaela Blyde had been nursing a hamstring injury, though an 80% fit Blyde was still better than most players on the planet. But Fiji had been superb over the two days, finding long-lost consistency, so a shock victory could not be ruled out.

Having only booked their ticket to Tokyo a month before, France's progression to the final four was an incredible achievement. Although the last major union to take up sevens – they only entered the qualification process for Rio at the last minute – they were massively supported by the continuity and clarity of vision that came from having the same coach for the past 11 years in David Courteix.

Great Britain too had achieved something special with a semi-final slot. For all their talent, losing their central funding in the months before the Olympics was a massive setback, but they had showed tenacity and togetherness in spades with Meg Jones and Jasmine Joyce among the best players at the event.

Both semi-finals were thrilling, with the only disappointment the fact that no fans were there to watch it live. New Zealand and Fiji could not be separated at full time, and it took an extra-time score to settle it. The match began with Gayle Broughton crossing the line in just the second minute to give New Zealand an expected lead early on, but Fiji were ferocious in defence and struck back a few minutes later through Vasiti Solikoviti.

Viniana Riwai's conversion edged Fiji in front, but Ruby Tui had the chance to put the Kiwis back in front on the stroke of half-time as she charged up the middle of the field from halfway, only for superb defence to force her to knock it on over the line.

Solikoviti then crossed for her second try a little more than a minute into the second half. It took an inspired effort from Portia Woodman to get New Zealand back into it and draw level. They scored again through Stacey Fluhler, but Tyla Nathan-Wong's conversion attempt hit the post and handed Fiji one last chance to win or level up the game. They did so through the raw pace of Reapi Ulunisau, who scored a spectacular try to send the game into extra time at 17-17.

Holding onto the ball for a full three minutes, New Zealand eventually broke through when Broughton beat three exhausted defenders to score her second try of the match and lock in a place in the final.

Speaking to me afterwards Sarah Hirini said she had not been surprised by how good the Fijians had been:

If you followed sevens diligently, you would know that they had the potential to play like that. We played them a month before the Games and we knew that they were really fit and that they still had a few weeks to go to keep working on that. We knew they would be the best Fiji team we'd ever played. It was obviously a game we were under pressure in.

Players went into different processes and situations in their minds and it became quite hard. At the end we had a couple of minutes before extra time when the coaches told us what way we'd be kicking off and so on but they didn't say anything much else other than what and when. They went into golden point mode and for us players we just needed to get the ball back and hold onto it and we'd score. We'd made errors in the game, myself included, but you have to completely forget about that and we did.

The best of the game

They would go on to face France, who were brilliant against a Great Britain team for whom Jasmine Joyce was once again outstanding. Two early tries to Anne-Cécile Ciofani and Séraphine Okemba put the French up 14-0 after just two and a half minutes, but Joyce got her side back into it with two well-taken tries as her pace was used to full effect.

But France were unrelenting, scoring either side of half-time as Ciofani and Coralie Bertrand both crossed for tries. Hannah Smith's try midway through the second half kept Great Britain just seven points adrift but France held on.

Having come through two incredibly tight games to reach the final, being tested by Great Britain and Fiji, this time New Zealand ensured there was no repeat of Rio. They were convincing in their quest to take home gold in the final, winning 26-12.

Sarah Hirini threw an early offload to Michaela Blyde to score and Gayle Broughton and Stacey Fluhler went over for a 19-5 half-time lead. Anne-Cécile Ciofani scored her seventh try of the tournament to draw France within seven points early in the second half, but Tyla Nathan-Wong went over to make sure of the gold medal.

Fiji took bronze, beating Great Britain to cap the end of an incredible journey for a team who had gone 16 weeks without seeing their families and who would have to quarantine for another two weeks when they got back thanks to ongoing Covid-19 restrictions. For several Fijian players, the Olympics had represented not just a first major tournament but the first time they'd ever stepped foot on an aeroplane and left the country. Head coach Saiasi Fuli told the media afterwards of the challenges in keeping the team together:

> Some of them, they tried to break camp and run home and we had to get them back and keep them at the camp and remind them that the journey will be quite a long one until we reach Tokyo.
>
> We identify them from athletics, some playing touch rugby in their village, and winning the bronze medal in the Tokyo Olympics is massive. They just learned rugby a year ago. They had no idea about [what rugby is]. So we had to do a massive job and 60–70% of our effort is just concentrating on core skills, how to catch, how to pass, tackle technique. That's before we implement tactical stuff.

The best of the game

Empty stands apart, women's rugby at the Olympics had been a story of personality, performance and triumph. From the magic of Ruby Tui in front of the mic to the wonderful instinct of Fiji on the field, the Olympics were a magnificent shot in the arm for women's rugby after its toughest of years.

There was New Zealand, raging favourites before the event with a brilliant leader in Sarah Hirini, who so sadly lost her mother earlier in the year, and on paper the best team the women's game has ever seen. But with that came the pressure. They had missed out five years ago and it haunted them. Their early wobble against Great Britain proved they were fallible, but in the end they were the top team and well deserving of their gold medal.

There was Great Britain, who played superbly in the circumstances and could leave with their heads held high, thinking perhaps of what might have been without the uncertainties of the past year. It seemed impossible that we would revert to a world where the team played just once every four years and that players like Welsh star Jasmine Joyce would go back to playing as an amateur in the lower echelons of Europe's sevens leagues.

There was Fiji, glorious Fiji, with perhaps the best backstory who became perhaps the story of sevens at the Olympics.

And there was France, who surprised many by reaching the Olympic Final just as they surprised many by getting to the World Cup Sevens Final. Perhaps we need to stop being surprised.

At the other end there was Canada, who finished a remarkable ninth. It was an incredibly poor return for such a talented and ambitious team but their build-up was marred by a row with their own union about allegations of bullying and harassment and the departure of their head coach. Their storyline was also punctuated by an embarrassing sideshow when men's coach Jamie Cudmore was sacked in the middle of the event for tweeting mocking and insulting messages about the team and the recent allegations. A fine mess.

There was Kenya too, with huge star Janet Okello, who brought joy to the field with their performances. They beat Japan and ran Canada close despite their lack of experience

at this level and left hoping for more exposure at sevens and
15s level.

And there was China who put in some fantastic
performances and reached an unlikely quarter-final.

The end of the competition hardly sparked wild celebrations
for those teams who had medals around their necks. There was
no alcohol allowed in the village and teams were still in close-
knit bubbles. New Zealand made do with pizza, chips and fancy
dress but would head home heroes, later named the best female
team of the entire Olympics.

Chapter Seventeen

The next grand stage

WHILE THE rescheduled 2021 Women's Rugby World Cup in New Zealand would eventually become a powerful celebration of women's rugby on the world stage, the build-up to the tournament revealed many of the cracks within the sport's infrastructure and systems.

In Wales, tensions that had simmered privately for years finally erupted into public view.

In September 2021, 123 former Welsh women's internationals released an open letter demanding urgent reform from the Welsh Rugby Union (WRU), accusing it of neglecting the women's game through the dismantling of development pathways, including the scrapping of the U20s and regional programmes.

The letter reflected growing frustration that top players were being encouraged to leave Wales to find competitive rugby elsewhere – a move widely interpreted as an excuse to avoid investing in a viable domestic league.

The signatories, which included influential figures such as Alecs Donovan, Gemma Hallett, Non Evans and Philippa Tuttiett, said they could no longer 'turn a blind eye to the inequality of provision', highlighting the contradiction between the union's public commitment to growing the game and its failure to support its own pathways.

They pointed to the team's poor results in the Six Nations as symptomatic of an environment on a downward spiral and warned that the WRU's 'inaction' had brought the programme to a long-feared crisis point.

Although the WRU acknowledged shortcomings and promised to restart some stalled initiatives, serious damage had been done.

The episode served as a sharp reminder of the struggle facing national unions: the challenge of meeting rising expectations (and justifiably so) from elite players and fans, while still operating within a semi-professional, mostly as yet commercially unprofitable, system.

The announcement later that year that 25 players would receive contracts marked a historic shift for Welsh rugby – but it was arguably progress born out of pressure, not vision and that too would bring its own challenges.

Ireland, too, found itself at the centre of controversy.

The IRFU's long-standing tensions with its women's programme were thrust into public view in 2021 following a now-infamous incident during the Women's Interprovincial Championship.

Images posted online showed players changing beside rubbish bins and graffiti-covered walls at Energia Park in Dublin. One Connacht player reported seeing rats near the temporary changing tents and when this was shared across social media, the embarrassment was keenly felt.

Although the IRFU apologised and launched an investigation, the debacle triggered a domino effect of scrutiny and internal upheaval in Ireland.

There had already been significant issues following Ireland's failed World Cup qualification campaign, with Adam Griggs stepping down as head coach and then former Wales international Amanda Bennett appointed to lead a review into what went wrong.

Hopes that this work might have rebuilt some stability were shorn when Ireland's director of women's rugby, Anthony Eddy, made public comments perceived to shift blame for failure for qualification squarely on to the players' shoulders, despite there obviously being huge challenges off the field around the programme too.

Many of the players were incensed by the finger pointing, with Ireland hooker Cliodhna Moloney taking to social media to liken his remarks to 'slurry spreading' and former international Jenny Murphy calling his stance 'spineless'.

What followed was a powerful escalation of crisis: a letter sent not to the IRFU, but to the Irish government, signed by 62 influential current and former players including Fiona Coghlan, Ciara Griffin, Lynne Cantwell and Sene Naoupu.

In stark terms, the letter, shared across Irish media and debated in the highest level of government, declared that players had lost 'all trust and confidence in the IRFU' and demanded external support to enact meaningful change.

The statement accused the union of 'substandard commitment', 'inequitable leadership' and 'a total lack of ambition' for what Irish women's rugby could achieve.

Somewhat amazingly, instead of taking the time to hear the players out, the IRFU responded defensively, rejecting the tone of the letter and expressing disappointment at its timing.

However, the backlash, combined with growing government and media scrutiny, couldn't be contained, forcing the union to backtrack and make several vital commitments.

Eventually under a new CEO, Kevin Potts, the IRFU accepted all 30 recommendations of the independent review, committed an additional €1 million to the women's programme (bringing the total budget to €4 million), and created a new head of women's performance and pathways.

Potts publicly apologised to the players for the organisation's long-standing failures, saying, 'If they felt they weren't being listened to, they are now.' Still, while structural reforms were set in motion, the emotional and cultural scars would take years to heal.

These events in Wales and Ireland were not isolated.

They were part of a broader shift within global women's rugby – where players, fed up with what they felt was poor focus, began to collectively demand better.

What became clear in the lead-up to the 2021 World Cup was that the fight for professionalism and equity in women's rugby was not only about contracts or facilities – it was about being heard and it was about visibility and many were no longer afraid to speak out.

Moloney, whose social media post had sparked a broader conversation and encouraged other players to speak out, arguably paid the heaviest price – being dropped from the Irish squad and not being selected for international play for several years. Elsewhere, momentum across the women's game continued to build.

After years of discussion and several thwarted attempts, a Women's British and Irish Lions tour finally began to seem possible, with the appointment of a 13-person feasibility group giving the project formal structure and direction.

At the same time, the RFU began the process of bidding to host the 2025 Women's Rugby World Cup, seeking to bring the tournament back to England for the first time since 2010.

With the prospect of a sold-out Twickenham for a World Cup final – far exceeding any previous crowd for a women's match – the bid proved successful, aided by significant government backing to improve infrastructure and drive participation through coaching, officiating and grassroots development.

Unlike previous tournaments, the 2025 event would be a multi-city and multi-region affair, with eight host cities selected across England.

On the pitch, England were preparing for a high-stakes series against New Zealand, who arrived for two Test matches before heading to France.

The Black Ferns had not played in over two years due to the pandemic, and the lack of competitive exposure made the series hard to preview.

England were clearly considered favourites going into the opener in Exeter, especially with a number of established Black Ferns like Portia Woodman and Kelly Brazier still reacclimating to 15s following the Olympics.

The match itself proved historic for multiple reasons: it marked the 100th officially recognised Black Ferns Test – but it also brought their heaviest defeat, as England ran in seven tries to secure a commanding and perhaps surprisingly large 43–12 victory.

A week later in Northampton, England were even more ruthless, winning 56–15.

The tour worsened for New Zealand as they went on to France and suffered further defeats – 38–13 in Pau and 29–7 in Castres.

Whether this was a case of historical underinvestment catching up or simply an inexperienced side struggling after two years off, the scale of the losses was something of a shock.

Alice Soper, a former player turned commentator, captured the urgency in New Zealand when she wrote that continuing 'on the same trajectory was not going to cut the mustard'.

England, she noted, had clearly moved ahead, and New Zealand would have to act swiftly to catch up in time for the World Cup.

Changes followed, with the appointment of Wayne Smith – a two-time men's World Cup winner – as a technical coach, a move that would later prove transformative, though at the time, it was unclear whether it would be enough despite Smith being joined by several other experienced coaches.

Around the world, more Test rugby was being played than ever.

Wales picked up a much-needed win over Japan, while Canada beat the USA 2–0 in a two-Test series.

Growth in the XVs game was also evident in emerging nations. Namibia played their first Test in eight years, losing to Zambia; Tunisia and Senegal both made their Test debuts; and Portugal returned to international action after a 27-year absence with a narrow 10–8 win over Belgium.

In England, an unusual twist led to a record-breaking moment. When a Covid outbreak forced the cancellation of a men's Barbarians match just 90 minutes before kick-off, the women's Barbarians fixture against South Africa was moved to the main billing slot. The game had been due to be a double header, but instead a crowd of 29,581 – then a record for a standalone women's Test – watched the Barbarians women run in 60 points in the only game of the day.

The game, broadcast in primetime on BBC1, handed women's rugby another high-profile national spotlight – albeit perhaps accidentally.

Sadly, the year ended on a sombre note with the death of US coaching legend Kathy Flores, whose lifelong advocacy for women's rugby had spanned generations and continents.

Her passing was followed by a fitting milestone when Emilie Bydwell was named head coach of the USA women's sevens team, becoming the first woman to lead a core World Series side.

Sevens returns

On the field, the World Sevens Series resumed in Dubai at the end of the year after 663 days, with Australia emerging victorious.

As 2022 began, the women's rugby calendar promised an intense and significant year, especially in sevens, where the

World Series, Commonwealth Games, and World Cup would all take place within a few months.

The postponed 2021 World Cup also loomed large, and before it, a revamped Six Nations – now in its own standalone window – was set to culminate in an England–France finale.

The World Cup year had arrived quickly, but nowhere was the urgency greater to get ready for it than in New Zealand, where the winless four-Test European tour had rung alarm bells. Fortunately, the launch of Super Rugby Aupiki – with four teams and long-overdue investment – signalled a step-change in domestic support and soon after, 30 national contracts were offered to Black Ferns players, giving them near full-time status.

Though England and France remained well ahead, the infrastructure was finally being put in place in New Zealand that meant surely their inconsistencies between World Cups might iron out.

Yet, there were still concerns about the World Cup itself.

There was doubt first that it would go ahead or be permitted to allow overseas fans in, and when Samoa and Hong Kong pulled out of qualifiers, there were further concerns about getting all the teams to the start line.

But in February, after multiple delays, the final qualification matches took place in Dubai.

Though originally slated as a four-team round-robin, only three teams made it to the pitch.

Colombia defeated Kazakhstan 18–10 in a shock result, especially given they played with 14 players for 65 minutes, but Scotland proved too strong in the final, booking their place at the World Cup with a dominant 59–3 win – giving them their first tournament appearance since 2010.

Coach Bryan Easson praised his side's composure and resilience through a drawn-out and uncertain qualification process.

Meanwhile, domestic competitions launched across Australia and New Zealand, with Super W attracting interest in particular for its inclusion of a Fijian team.

In Europe, the 2022 Six Nations came with full broadcast coverage for the first time, as BBC, RTÉ, and France Télévision committed to the tournament.

TikTok also joined as a title sponsor, marking a watershed moment in commercial investment and though England, as expected, dominated – winning all five matches, securing a fourth consecutive title and another Grand Slam, while conceding just 22 points – there were plenty of interesting storylines.

A record crowd of 15,000 turned out at Welford Road to see England beat Ireland, while the finale in Bayonne – sold out and thrilling – offered a fitting climax.

Yet England's supremacy was a reminder of the competitive gap still present.

The 2022 edition would be the last featuring fully amateur sides, with nations like Ireland moving towards contract models soon after.

In New Zealand, change continued at pace. In April, a damning independent review of the failed 2021 tour led to 26 recommendations for cultural and structural reform. Head coach Glenn Moore resigned, and Wayne Smith – initially involved in a background role – stepped forward to take on a front of house role.

He set out a bold public ambition, telling the team it would win the World Cup in front of 40,000 people at Eden Park later that year, and immediately began implementing technical changes.

In his own words, early training sessions convinced him of the team's potential and in his subsequent autobiography he wrote of his first experience leading the team's training.

You could immediately sense we were going to be okay. These girls are excited. They've got huge ability. They understand what we're doing. It's all very well to sell the style of the play; it's a little more difficult to develop the skills to be able to do it. You need dedicated learners.

In that very first session, we were teaching them to pass closer to the opposition. The players were used to passing a long way from the defenders, which allowed the opposition to slide off on to the next attacker.

We now wanted them square, passing without having to take the ball back in a swinging movement. No backward 'tick'. To pass off either foot, or even with your feet in the air, and to be close to the tackler.

We filmed the activities from end on, and I was amazed. The players were passing in waves going down the field and from behind I couldn't see the ball. They'd picked it up as quickly as that.

I started thinking, 'My throwaway line about winning at Eden Park in front of 40,000 people may become reality.'

As the Black Ferns entered the 2022 Pacific Four Series against Canada, USA and Australia, early improvements were on display.

They weren't perfect, but three wins from three gave them the title – and crucially some momentum.

In Europe, the sevens landscape saw a surprise rise from Poland, who won the European Sevens Championship in Krakow, losing only in the final to Ireland.

A decade earlier, Poland had been in the third tier of European sevens and their emergence was a striking symbol of how quickly progress could come.

On the global stage though, attention turned to the Commonwealth Games in Birmingham – one of the most high-profile editions in memory and the first major multi-sport event to award more medals to women than men, with 136 events for women compared to 134 for men.

Commonwealth glory beckons

The women's competition was an eight-team event with Australia, New Zealand and Canada qualifying via the World Sevens Series, while Fiji (Oceania), Scotland (Europe) and Sri Lanka (Asia) successfully came through the regional qualifiers.

Hosts England completed the line-up following news that from there on in a Great Britain team would be formed to compete on the World Series next year, making this event one of the few where they would in future get to represent their country.

Australia started as favourites after winning the recent World Series – a tag that was justified as the competition progressed.

There were early regulation victories for World Series teams against those from outside the series – Australia and England brushed aside South Africa and Sri Lanka – the latter playing outside Asia for the first time. Scotland performed creditably against Fiji, going into the break 14-5 down, but were unable to close the gap in the second half while New Zealand downed Canada.

England were then beaten by the Canadians in round two before Fiji shocked Australia with other results meaning that the host nation would have to beat New Zealand to make the last four. Unfortunately for them, the merciless Ferns dominated the first half, leading 21-0 before a Boatman try from the final play got England on the board. Three more New Zealand tries in the second period saw them safely through.

And so to the semi-finals, and it was a game for the ages between New Zealand and Australia.

First blood went to Australia through Maddison Levi, but the Ferns battled back and at the break were 12-5 ahead. The second half was even better, Australia pulling within two points with a second Levi try soon after the restart before they went ahead 17-12 with Levi scoring again. Cue nearly three minutes of incredible rugby as Australia hung on – despite Levi being shown a yellow in the final minute – to reach the final.

The second semi saw Fiji race to a 17-0 lead and eventually win out for a shot at a gold medal against the Aussies.

A nervy start in the final saw Australia grab the advantage, with Faith Nathan scoring two tries in the first three minutes and Madison Ashby add a third before the Fijiana had begun to settle.

As a result, Australia led 17-0 at half-time and when Maddison Levi added a fourth try in the first minute of the second half gold looked to be Australia's. But Fiji battled back and started to show the game that had taken them to the final. Laisani Miceisawana scored as the game entered the final minute, but Australia prevented any further score until the final play when Sesenieli Donu scored a consolation try for Fiji.

The gold ended an almost perfect year for the Australia side, who were surely going to go into the World Cup just a few weeks later as red-hot favourites.

Next up - a Sevens World Cup

Australia had referred to this event as an opportunity to win a 'Triple Crown' where they could become the first team to win the World Series, Commonwealth Games and World Cup in the same year – something New Zealand were not able to do in 2018 as they didn't manage to take out the World Series that year.

The World Cup in Cape Town therefore presented a historic opportunity.

With 16 teams taking part, the event was once again an important moment in the development of women's rugby worldwide, despite remaining somewhat in the shadows behind its better-known sisters – the Olympics, the World Series and the XVs World Cup.

Australia, as a reminder, won in 2009, and New Zealand in 2013 and again four years later in San Francisco where the happy accident of the collapse of a proposed two-centre World Cup forced the adoption of a pure knockout tournament, in the place of the usual pool and play-off phases.

This created a whole new feel to the event – different to both the Olympics and the World Series – where every match mattered, and left no room for the slow starts and second chances you get in a three-match, three-team pool. This was cut-throat rugby. Win or you are out. It was tough on the players, but exciting for spectators.

It was no surprise then that the same model had been adopted for the 2022 event.

All ten World Series teams qualified, their draw seeding based on Series points won between 2019 and 2022.

And as expected Australia lived up to their billing – beating New Zealand in a terrific final after a few days of excellent rugby and drama.

They only sealed their hard-earned win when New Zealander Tenika Willison missed a post-siren conversion attempt which would have levelled the scores at 24 apiece.

It was a tremendous final, with the two 2016 Olympic-winning warriors Caslick and 34-year-old Sharni Williams inspirational. Maddison Levi raced over for a hat-trick of tries on the right wing while speedster Faith Nathan went over for a tournament-leading eighth score.

Australia were the better team but the match showcased the familiar never-say-die spirit of New Zealand rugby as the Olympic champions fought back from 24-10 down with just over two minutes left.

Earlier, the Australians had beaten USA 17-7 in the semi-finals, with Caslick, who had also orchestrated the quarter-final

35-5 victory over England on Saturday, again instrumental in a much more testing affair, nabbing two tries before Alysia Lefau-Fakaosilea scored the clincher.

Co-captain Caslick was emphatic in her delight after the game:

'What we've achieved this year has been pretty awesome.

'We spoke about the '09 girls today and doing it for them. Hopefully, in three or four cycles, girls will be talking about us and what we achieved this year. The legacy of this Australian women's sevens is pretty fucking awesome.'

World Cup in focus

With the major sevens action of the year over, all eyes were now on the build-up to the World Cup in New Zealand with warm-up games and squad announcements on the horizon.

Italy sprang the biggest surprise of the lead-up with a 26-19 win over France, though France were experimenting with their starting team, while New Zealand, England and Canada looked strong in their warm-ups.

After all the delaying and the uncertainty the event was almost here and it had a familiar-looking format.

For the first four weeks of the event, the plan was for 12 teams to be playing in Auckland and Whangarei, aiming to qualify for the quarter-finals.

Both semi-finals and the final would be played at Eden Park.

The top two teams from the pool would qualify for the quarter-finals, plus the best two third-place teams from the three pools.

New Zealand, Australia, Scotland and Wales made up Pool A; Canada, the USA, Italy and Japan Pool B; and England, France, South Africa and Fiji Pool C.

This World Cup had two main lines of questioning going into it – could anyone stop England and could New Zealand complete a remarkable turnaround of form against the best teams and win at home?

England travelled on a then record run of 25 consecutive victories dating back to 2019, taking with them a dominant pack that had laid the foundations for their long winning streak. If there were any questions over them it was perhaps around the reliance on that power and whether in knockout rugby they would have the ability to flex – something that had not been required on their European travels thus far.

New Zealand opened proceedings against rivals Australia in what proved to be a thrilling and fitting opener.

Some 34,235 spectators attended the opening triple header in Auckland. How many were in their seats for this third fixture is impossible to say, but they were certainly stunned into silence as Bienne Terita (two) and Ivania Wong touched down to give the Wallaroos a shock 17-0 lead inside half an hour.

The Black Ferns hit back before half-time through Joanah Ngan-Woo and Portia Woodman, but Australia still led 17-12 at the break.

Awhina Tangen-Wainohu and Ruby Tui (twice) also crossed the whitewash after the break as the Black Ferns eventually confirmed a bonus-point victory at Eden Park as the hosts survived what would have been a huge upset.

The Wallaroos – who had never beaten the Black Ferns in 22 previous attempts – had perhaps never been closer to a breakthrough.

That New Zealand had found a way to win was perhaps the real story of the game, and that was a trait that would stand them in good stead later in the tournament.

England started with a trouncing of Fiji, who gave the Red Roses a tough opening half before falling away, while there were no other big surprises.

The closest game of the weekend came between Celtic rivals Wales and Scotland with Keira Bevan kicking a penalty five minutes after the full-time siren to give Wales a narrow victory in a nail-biting finale.

Megan Gaffney had scored the second of her two second-half tries in the 78th minute to draw Scotland level with Wales at 15-15 after they had trailed 15-5 at half-time.

But a Scotland error gave Bevan the last say in the match with a kick from close range and she nailed the penalty deep in extra time to spark a delirious celebration from her team-mates.

Perhaps the highlight of the opening weekend though was Italy and their win over the USA.

Italy so rarely play teams outside of the Six Nations that it was hard to call, and their first win was a brilliant result with Beatrice Rigoni and Veronica Madia outstanding as the half-back combination and Silvia Turani also excellent up front.

The pick of the games of round two was surely England against France with the two Six Nations heavyweights battling it out for top spot in their pool, and it didn't disappoint in a tight game edged by the tournament favourites 13-7.

After France lost star players Laure Sansus and Romane Menager to injury, England's Emily Scarratt scored the opening try in Whangarei.

Scarratt added a penalty either side of half-time before France scored through Gaelle Hermet when a stunning cross-field kick from Caroline Drouin was grabbed by Joanna Grisez, who sent Hermet over.

The finish was frantic but England held on, prompting head coach Simon Middleton to dismiss their tags as favourites after the game:

> I understand where the favourites tag comes from, but I think too many people are making us out to be too big a favourite.
>
> If that's a quarter-final or a knockout game, you are one bounce of the ball from being on the plane home.

That is what it's going to be like when you get to the biggest games. Hopefully it is a reality check for everybody who was probably making us more favourites than we are.

In the other pool games in round two, Scotland once again faced a heartbreaking and narrow loss, this time by two points to Australia; USA beat Japan, Canada downed Italy while the hosts hammered Wales 56-12. Fiji grabbed their first win, defeating South Africa.

No major shocks in the final pool round handed us a set of quarter-finals that looked like this: France v Italy; New Zealand v Wales; Canada v USA; and England v Australia.

None of the games were particularly close – a reminder that though the game was progressing, there were still far too few teams who compete with the top four or five sides, a challenge that may remain at the 2025 World Cup in England, this time with 16 teams competing.

The good news for this tournament was that both semi-finals were compelling.

Dow's solo try takes England into the final

There had been some critique of England's over-reliance on their driving line-out and power up front in the competition so far, but it was two brilliant tries out wide from star winger Abby Dow that secured the game 26 points to 19 against a gutsy Canada side.

Canada, always inferior in their resources than the nations they remained so close to in the rankings, were as fired up and physical as ever, playing a full part in what was the match of the World Cup so far.

England took the lead in the ninth minute when Marlie Packer, who had scored a hat-trick of tries in the quarter-final triumph over Australia, bagged another one after a strong line-out drive. Emily Scarratt converted and it was 7-0.

Six minutes later England scored their second try of the day and it was set up by full-back Helena Rowland.

Her purposeful run had the Canada defence on the back foot and she fed winger Abby Dow, who did the rest. It was unconverted, but after a quarter of an hour England were in control.

Canada needed something to spark life into their performance and it came in the 22nd minute when a good run and kick through by scrum-half Justine Pelletier was pounced upon by open-side flanker Karen Paquin.

Like Packer for England, she was a standout in Canada's quarter-final win over USA and she showed good pace to get to the ball first and score an unconverted try.

That breakthrough gave Canada confidence and they levelled things up at 12-12 five minutes before the break.

Just before half-time, England reset and gave themselves a 15-12 lead thanks to a penalty from Scarratt.

Scarratt kicked her second penalty of the match three minutes into the second half before England lost the influential Rowland to injury.

Canada then pressured as they looked for their third try, but England then turned defence into attack.

They turned the ball over on their own try-line and a brilliant open-field break by Claudia MacDonald set up her fellow winger Dow.

Dow had a lot to do, but she showed great pace and awareness to beat off the attentions of Canada winger Paige Farries to score a wonderful long-range try. Scarratt could not convert and it was 23-12.

Any thoughts that the try would knock the stuffing out of Canada were put to bed before the hour mark when they got right back down the other end and won a series of penalties.

After one penalty too many, England loose-head Vickii Cornborough was yellow-carded by referee Aimee Barrett-Theron.

Canada could not score against 14 players, but did so against 15 in the 67th minute.

It was replacement Tyson Beukeboom who went over for a try from close range and when De Goede converted from in front of the posts it was 23-19.

England were rattled, but they were handed a nerve-settler with a penalty from Scarratt in the 70th minute which put them 26-19 up.

The Red Roses managed the last ten minutes to make sure they reached a sixth successive Rugby World Cup Final but they did not look invincible and with New Zealand on the verge of their own amazing game against France, anything looked possible.

In the other semi-final, New Zealand edged to a 25-24 victory in a thrilling match having trailed 17-10 at half-time only for tries by Ruby Tui and Theresa Fitzpatrick to give the defending champions fresh hope.

A second try for the excellent Romane Ménager dragged France back into the contest, however, and the game hinged on a last-minute penalty miss from Caroline Drouin which let the Black Ferns off the hook.

It was heartbreaking for France who have still never reached a World Cup Final, but a reminder that New Zealand were never ever out.

It capped an excellent day's rugby watched, over the course of the two games, by about 23,000 spectators, handing the organisers the dream showdown.

England would have their long unbeaten record and winning mentality, while the Black Ferns would have an entire host nation roaring them on.

The final beckons

One of the most interesting storylines for New Zealand remained the role of Wayne Smith – a serial winner who was also in the camp working with, among others, the highly experienced Sir Graham Henry – both men heavily familiar with the pressure of World Cup finals.

New Zealand's dire 2021 showing meant that the team was playing almost without pressure – so low had expectations been going into it, while England had dilemmas of their own.

Having relied so heavily on their forward pack throughout the tournament, the close game against Canada was a reminder that champion sides often need greater flexibility than that.

There is a cliché in sport every time a major tournament comes round that promises that this will be 'the best yet'.

Of course that should always be the case – if each tournament is not better than the one before, something is going wrong somewhere – but this World Cup Final could lay claim to having been one of the best and most dramatic women's rugby games every witnessed.

Things started well for England with Ellie Kildunne, playing at full-back in place of the injured Helena Rowland, running in for the opening try after just three minutes

There was enough action in the first ten minutes for three finals and Amy Cokayne – who was called up to a Black Ferns camp as a teenager before choosing England – soon went over for her first of three tries in the Red Roses' trademark driving maul.

More drama came as a high tackle by Lydia Thompson on record World Cup try-scorer Portia Woodman resulted in a red card.

There could be no argument about Thompson's dismissal after she caught the unfortunate Woodman full in the face as New Zealand attacked down the left. It was a particularly sad exit for Woodman, one of the stars of the game and the tournament and a gutting way for the popular Thompson to leave her mark on the match.

New Zealand had relied on their unpredictable backline play in previous rounds but proved they could maul too as Georgia Ponsonby went over following a line-out immediately after.

Another England maul try – this time for Marlie Packer – prompted another Black Ferns response, with the Red Roses caught short as Leti-I'iga ran through plenty of open space to score her first try.

Again England turned to their pack, another try for Cokayne, as England's focus collided with New Zealand's chaos and Black Ferns prop Amy Rule closed out the half by peeling off the back of a maul to go over and make the score 26-19 in England's favour at half-time.

Things started to turn after the break. First Stacey Fluhler ran out of her own 22 and sent Scarratt the wrong way and the centre combined with Renee Holmes to go over before the full-back missed a conversion that would have tied the scores.

Suddenly England were struggling to contain New Zealand's backline and as the pressure mounted in their 22, Krystal Murray barged through Lucy Packer to put the Black Ferns ahead for the first time.

Such is England's faith in their driving maul, Zoe Harrison opted to kick for the corner instead of taking a penalty that would have tied the game again.

The Red Roses were rewarded as Cokayne completed her hat-trick before New Zealand joined England on 14 players because Kennedy Simon was shown a yellow card for a dangerous tackle on Abby Dow, who left the field for a head injury assessment.

Then came the Black Ferns' final and decisive strike. Theresa Fitzpatrick kicked ahead for Fluhler, who superbly offloaded the ball as she fell to the floor to send Leti-I'iga over to once more put New Zealand ahead.

Again, England had the chance to tie the scores with a penalty and again they kicked to the corner. This time, perhaps for the first time at this World Cup, their line-out let them down and New Zealand regained the ball to become champions for a sixth time, winning out 34-31.

For England to lose with a chance to win it through their famed line-out was a reminder of the cruelty of sport as they were left to watch New Zealand lift the trophy and rue their many opportunities.

France finished the tournament third after a fine win over Canada.

The 2021 Women's Rugby World Cup was a landmark tournament in every sense.

The final at Eden Park drew 42,579 spectators, the largest ever for a women's rugby match, contributing to a tournament total hallmarked by sold-out games.

Fans across New Zealand rallied behind the spectacle and the support for the Black Ferns grew massively.

With major milestones on the horizon in 2023, including World Rugby's long-awaited WXV competition, designed to level the playing field amongst the leading nations, the future looked exciting.

Another year of growth and change

Wales unfortunately began 2023 in crisis mode again, this time after a BBC documentary laid bare claims of sexism, bullying and sexual harassment at the WRU.

Amanda Blanc, now chief executive of the Aviva insurance company, also delivered a damning verdict on the union having sat as chair of the Welsh Professional Rugby Board, telling the union it had deep-rooted culture problems and describing its review in the women's game as verging on 'insulting to women'.

In her WRU leaving speech, Ms Blanc, on the 2021 *Forbes* most influential women in the world list, said she was questioned about whether she had 'sufficient business experience' to be the chairwoman of the WRU's professional board.

In her leaving speech, Ms Blanc recalled a 'truly offensive discussion' about reducing the sanctions for an elected WRU member after he had made misogynistic comments in public, including that 'men are the master race' and women should 'stick to the ironing'.

The resulting changes included a diversification of the Welsh board and the eventual hiring of the first ever female CEO of the union in Abi Tierney.

While the changes wouldn't have an immediate impact on the Welsh programme, eventually more resources and support arrived, with more women having a voice in decision-making, giving the women's game stronger support and advocacy.

The 2023 women's Six Nations was to make records for several reasons.

It was to be the first time every single team involved would feature players with full-time contracts – remarkable progress, given England went first just four year before at the start of 2019.

Their dominance, alongside France, had encouraged others to take the leap. Contracts are not, of course, the solution to all a team's ills, but they do make a huge difference to helping players to improve and recover, and will at least go some way towards levelling the playing field in the years ahead.

The tournament began with a final game for England's most capped player Sarah Hunter, who deserved her send-off in a fine win over Scotland.

Ireland reminded everyone that they had a mountain to climb, with their opening loss against Wales. They looked like a side sorely lacking game time having missed out on the World Cup, and though progress was being made off the field in Ireland, it would take some time to bed in.

It was already clear that the championship was heading for a finale between England and France in front of a record-breaking crowd at Twickenham

With 58,498 people turning up – a record by some margin – they were treated to a quite incredible match.

Off the field the RFU deserved great credit for the vision and the record, as the huge crowd were treated to a fantastic atmosphere and entertainment, which was thankfully matched by the play on it.

The cliché that rugby is a game of two halves could be invoked here with some gusto as England won the first half 33-0 but France the second 31-5.

France started well with some excellent carries and for the first seven minutes the game was played almost exclusively in England's 22.

But England hung on, thanks largely in part to two superb Hannah Botterman turnovers and when Helena Rowland made their first break of the game they scored – with Abby Dow finishing out wide. It was a sucker punch for what had been a dominant French performance so far and England built in confidence from it.

Marlie Packer was next to crash over, this time after a brilliant offload from Tatyana Heard as suddenly France looked incredibly fallible, struggling in the scrum.

England's power carrying was just too much for the French, with Tremouliere yellow-carded for a deliberate knock-on under pressure. Alex Matthews made the extra number count, driving over after another dominant scrum.

Zoe Aldcroft scored just before the break to make it 33-0 at half-time.

France were so much better after the restart with Gabrielle Vernier and Pauline Bourdon desperately trying to spark something in attack.

Bourdon's crisp and speedy passing resulted in a first try for Emilie Boulard and Gabby Vernier's brilliance was once again on show as she stepped Lucy Packer to race over for a second try and at 33-14 there was a glimmer of hope.

England went to their comfort zone, using their driving maul to help Lark Davies over the line and then France hit back again, this time through Charlotte Escudero, who dotted down from a driving line-out.

At 38-21 there were some question marks beginning to occur among the England fans, especially when Emiline Gros scored another and Vernier and Menager linked up to almost score what would have been the try of the game.

But England hung on – and hanging on they were at this point, to take the win.

A great game, on one of women's rugby's greatest days.

Attention could now at last turn to the launch of WXV with New Zealand and South Africa hosting the top two tiers of the new event – New Zealand welcoming the top six teams to WXV 1 across three match weekends in October and November while Cape Town would play host to the six-team second level WXV 2 with matches being played across October.

The advent of the competition saw immediate positives for many developing nations with all attempting to qualify into the various tiers, resulting in much-needed extra match time.

To WXV 1 first, and the competition in New Zealand saw the hosts welcome England, Australia, Canada, France and Wales to contest the top tier.

England went undefeated, defeating Australia 42-7, Canada 45-12, and then New Zealand 33-12 in the final showdown in Auckland.

New Zealand had also slipped to their first ever defeat to France at the event, losing 18-17 in a rematch of the 2022 World Cup semi-final. France, though, would go on to lose to both Canada and Australia in a reminder of their often-maddening inconsistencies.

England's captain, Marlie Packer, was named World Rugby Women's 15s Player of the Year during the finals' festivities.

Scotland topped their pool in South Africa, edging out Italy on point differential to win WXV 2 and end a good year, while in Dubai in WXV 3, which also doubled as a qualifier for the 2025 World Cup, Ireland secured the title after recovering from going 10-0 down in the first half against Spain to secure a narrow 15-13 victory.

Although the overall event was not perfect, for the first time the women's international game and consistent competitive platform gave a reliable annual structure across all tiers, offering crucial playing time.

The year ended with a new-look World Sevens Series – now called SVNS, with the women's competition now being given complete equal billing with the men – the same tournaments, same number of teams, same number of games.

The tournament would also build to a 'final' in Madrid in May where the competition should reach its climax, and where four team will be battling to stay in the series.

Promotion and relegation would be bigger than ever with the launch of a 12-team 'second tier' Challenger series, with three rounds producing four teams to challenge for places in next year's series, as well as providing a level of competition that would hopefully start to close the gap between teams in the series and those outside.

At the opening event in Dubai, Teagan Levi touched down either side of half-time as Australia ended New Zealand's 41-match winning streak to claim their fourth consecutive title at the location, going into the Olympic year in fine form.

Another year of growth

If 2024 was going to largely be about the Olympics, such was the pace of the growth of the game everywhere else that other massive storylines would also be generated.

At the turn of the year the British & Irish Lions announced initial details for the first-ever Lions Women's Tour in September 2027.

The 'Howden British & Irish Lions Women's Series' would take place in New Zealand with Lions team playing three Tests against the Black Ferns alongside pre-Test fixtures.

The commitment followed a feasibility study, sponsored by Royal London, which concluded that New Zealand would be the preferred Tour destination.

In addition – and perhaps crucially – were announcements about commercial sponsorship. Royal London was confirmed as 'Founding Partner of the Lions Women's Team' in a partnership that would also see investment in player development in the Home Unions through a special 'elite players' Pathways Funding grant'.

The insurers also said they would be investing in women's and girls' grassroots rugby across the UK and Ireland in the run-up to the tour.

But the announcement wasn't met with unanimous approval, with many questioning why the women's game was following a structure that might well make the game's imbalances even more imbalanced with the bulk of the Lions team likely to be English.

The thing to watch out for in the 2024 Six Nations was always likely to be the impact of contracts on teams like Ireland and Wales, and it was the game between these two in Cork in the early stages that produced one of the most commanding wins, with the Irish winning 36-5 after a tough couple of early results.

That Ireland would finish third spoke well of the positive changes happening there off the field including the arrival of Scott Bemand as head coach, while England were comfortable final-day winners in Bordeaux, in front of a big and hostile crowd, to take out the championship.

The tournament was also notable for the way in which star England full-back Ellie Kildunne at last was becoming one of the game's highest-profile stars, with her stunning displays and excellent insights and strong social media use, all combining to see her end the tournament as one of the most talked-about players.

On the other side of the world Canada beat the Black Ferns for the first time in their history to win the 2024 Pacific Four Series, with a 22-19 comeback victory over the reigning Pacific Four Series and Rugby World Cup champions.

In a match full of historical significance, Tyson Beukeboom officially reached 68 caps upon kick-off, becoming Canada's all-time women's caps leader.

'I still don't have words for it. It hasn't sunk in yet. We've hit so many milestones tonight,' said Beukeboom after the game.

'We knew we could do it. We just had to go out on the field and put the game down, and we did, and I think proud is probably the best word at the moment. It was so much fun to be out there tonight.'

With Australia taking out the first SVNs title, they would surely go to the summer's Olympics as red-hot favourites, with Paris about to throw up an incredible tournament.

Ferns Retain Olympic Gold in seismic sevens showcase

Over three sunlit days at Stade de France, more than 250,000 spectators witnessed New Zealand – not Australia – emerge as Olympic champions in what may go down as a transformative moment for the game.

Helped by ideal scheduling and clear, sunny skies, daily crowds swelled – 66,000 on Day 1, 68,000 on Day 2, and 69,000 for Finals Day – marking the third Olympic Sevens as a genuine blockbuster. And it delivered as such with upsets, comebacks, and a showcase of global depth making the event a perfect advert not just for the women's game but for rugby overall.

The drama began immediately. Great Britain downed higher-seeded Ireland, while Canada upset a sluggish Fiji –

who never recovered and bowed out quietly, a far cry from their Tokyo bronze. China, vastly improved from their previous Olympic outing, emerged as early fan favourites with a dominant win over Fiji and a spirited push against Canada securing them a quarter-final berth.

New Zealand breezed through Pool A, barely tested. In Pool B, Australia showed early dominance, though Ireland rattled them late while France and the USA coasted through Pool C, showing class and control.

The quarter-finals brought fireworks. New Zealand and Australia notched big wins, but the middle games were edge-of-the-seat affairs. USA edged Great Britain in a bruising battle, while Canada silenced a roaring French crowd with a superb win.

In the first semi-final, New Zealand were briefly rattled. USA's Alev Kelter bulldozed her way to an early lead and their defensive discipline held the Black Ferns at bay. But once Stacey Waaka opened New Zealand's account, the champions shifted gears. Michaela Blyde, all pace and poise, added two more scores – her eighth and ninth of the tournament – clinching an 11th straight win over USA.

Then came the shock of the tournament. Canada, scorching in the Paris heat, stunned favourites Australia for a second time in as many games.

Maddison Levi had put the 2016 champions up 12–0 with her 12th try of the competition, and Sariah Paki added another. But a breathtaking 75-metre solo try from Charity Williams before the break turned the tide. After half-time, Canada capitalised on Australian indiscipline. Asia Hogan-Rochester scrapped through a chaotic build-up to score, and Piper Logan outpaced Teagan Levi to seal a famous win.

Australia's heartbreak wasn't yet over and in the bronze medal match, USA claimed their first-ever Olympic sevens medal with a miracle try in the dying seconds.

With the clock in the red, Alex Sedrick sprinted the length of the pitch from her own posts to win it. Maddison Levi had earlier equalled Portia Woodman-Wickliffe's all-time Olympic try record, and looked to have secured bronze when her sister Teagan crossed late on, but USA's tenacity – and Sedrick's brilliance – proved decisive.

The gold medal match capped a monumental three days.

New Zealand co-captain Risi Pouri-Lane opened with a stunning solo effort, slicing through Canada's line to score under the posts. Ferocious Black Ferns defence pinned Canada deep until a high tackle from Woodman-Wickliffe earned her a yellow. Chloe Daniels capitalised, sprinting clear to equalise. Alysha Corrigan then intercepted a loose ball to send Canada into a shock half-time lead.

But New Zealand were composed. Michaela Blyde wrestled through three defenders after a lightning-quick Jorja Miller tap to restore the advantage. Then came the fairy-tale moment. Sarah Hirini – who had returned just 28 weeks after a serious knee injury – broke clear and offloaded to Stacey Waaka to seal the win, and the gold.

The tournament's legacy extended far beyond medals though.

Ilona Maher, already a fan favourite and advocate for body positivity, saw her influence sky-rocket. Her humour, empowering posts, and superb behind-the-scenes content from Paris exploded online.

Within a week of the Games, her Instagram following passed a million, eventually eclipsing Siya Kolisi and Antoine Dupont to become the most followed rugby player on the planet. Her reach – over eight million followers across platforms – became something of a cultural force.

Maher used that platform to highlight vital issues: the challenges faced by underpaid athletes, the importance of authenticity, and the potential of marketing players as global stars.

Her impact sparked serious investment too. Businesswoman and investor Michelle Kang pledged major backing to the USA women's programme after their bronze-medal heroics, but arguably, Maher's soaring profile may have proved even more influential – showing that rugby's future lies not just in team success but in unlocking the power of individual personalities.

With the USA set to host the men's and women's World Cups in 2031 and 2033, Maher is positioned to be a defining figure in rugby's American journey.

The year didn't end there.

The second edition of WXV added another layer of progress. England retained their crown with an unbeaten run, while Ireland shocked the world with a runner-up finish in the top tier, including a jaw-dropping 29–27 win over New Zealand, continuing their impressive progress.

Australia triumphed in WXV 2, and Spain lifted the WXV 3 title.

Sevens flourished. A record 787 international matches were played across 96 nations, including debuts for Saudi Arabia and Kiribati – underlining sevens' role in growing the game globally.

Meanwhile, 2024 also became the busiest year ever for women's XVs with 101 Tests, 13 non-Test internationals, and 45 participating nations. Andorra and Mexico made their Test debuts, while Jamaica, Norway, Romania, and Trinidad & Tobago returned to Test rugby after over a decade – perhaps the year's most uplifting development.

Notably, for the first time this century, England weren't among the most active Test nations in that year. That honour went to Fiji and Wales, who each played 11 Tests, reflecting how WXV and World Cup momentum has helped shift priorities across the landscape.

Now, all eyes turn to England in 2025.

A home World Cup, expanded to 16 teams and hosted across eight cities, looms large for a Red Roses team who warmed up with another Grand Slam in 2024.

But with women's rugby surging forward on all fronts – sevens, XVs, global reach, player stardom – the question now is not just whether England both as hosts and as a team are ready, or whether WXV has made a difference enough so that the gap between the best and rest decreases.

It's whether the sport is ready for what comes next.

Conclusion

'Being a supporter or participant in women's sports often feels like skiing uphill with a boulder tied to your back, listening to someone who took a ski lift to the top of the mountain with a feather in their hand mock you for not beating them.'

Lindsay Gibbs, *Power Plays*.

THIS BOOK tells the journey of a women's game over a period of 130 years, starting with Emily Valentine in 1887 and ending with women's rugby on the cusp of what will be the biggest and best-attended World Cup ever in England in 2025.

In between are the stories of remarkable volunteers who fought for the right for the game to be played, players who have entertained and taken the game to new heights and administrators and advocates and supporters who continue to accelerate it.

The pages tell a story of progress. It is one that we should celebrate, but they also recognise that there is further to go.

In every aspect of the game – from coaching to participation, commercialisation to governance, media coverage to athlete well-being and everything in between – the battles that started over a century ago may take a different form now, but they carry on.

Those involved in women's rugby have always had to fight to be treated with respect, but we remain some way off anything that looks like parity with progress outstanding on key areas like commercial investment, governance structures (where there are still far too few women in senior decision-making roles) and with the continuation of battles between players and their own unions for small asks like being listened to and taken seriously.

The lack of female representation at the top and in leadership positions especially matters to a sport in which women represent the fastest area of growth.

Attitudes too that women are not ready for a seat at the top table prevail. As recently as 2017, the then IRFU chief executive Philip Browne said that he was opposed to gender quotas on sports organisations suggesting that women did not have enough knowledge in the game to take up key positions.

Speaking to a government committee, Browne said:

> The suggestion by the government that it is considering the imposition of gender quotas on sports organisations is a concern for the simple reason that female rugby is still in its infancy, and it will be difficult to find suitably qualified female candidates with the accumulated rugby wisdom and skills set to fill such quotas without retreating to tokenism.

There has, as these pages have documented, been much progress in increasing investment into the game, and strong efforts are being made to generate commercial investment. Brands like Guinness, O2, Allianz, Royal London, Gallagher and Adidas are all big names involved in the game now with more to follow surely.

We stand too on the cusp of vital advancements in the field of competition: the ongoing Olympic cycle, a new global calendar for the game, increasing professionalisation, alongside advancements being made in domestic leagues like England's exciting PWR.

But all of these come with massive challenges and require careful and informed decision-making, particularly on how best to channel funding into a system that must avoid become unsustainable while at the same time meeting the rising expectations of players and fans for greater and greater resources.

What may hold our sport back most, though, is that there remains too often a lack of recognition that the women's game presents the single greatest opportunity for growth in rugby at every level, from participation to elite investment.

As former USA coach Pete Steinberg is fond of saying, too many running the game see women's rugby as a 'cost and not an investment' and fail to see the long-term growth opportunity.

I think about the quote that opened this chapter a lot.

Gibbs wrote it in response to a fiasco in college women's basketball in the USA where images went viral of the weights rooms allocated to the women's and men's teams at the NCAA finals tournament.

The difference in the quality of facilities was so stark it was almost laughable. Gibbs, in her brilliant newsletter which tackles sexism in sport, set out just how tired she was of the constant battle for women's sports to be respected or, at the very least, not embarrassed.

It's hard not to feel the same when you advocate or champion for women's rugby to be seen, valued and respected. But, as Gibbs rationalised, we must choose to be optimistic.

There are more advocates and campaigners putting pressure on people to support the game than ever before. Alice Soper in New Zealand is determinedly calling out inequities while also doggedly working to build an active and supportive community for players at all levels while the launch of several organisations, including one I am involved in with Jenny Mitton called Women of Union, seeks to provide more support.

Media coverage is rapidly improving too, as is female representation in it. We have brilliant broadcasters like Sara Orchard at the BBC, writers like Sarah Mockford and Fiona Thomas at *The Telegraph*, and writers and broadcasters like Rikki Swannell, all of whom are experts on the women's game – and male allies like Nick Heath, Stephen Jones, Paul Morgan and many more.

There are now so many dedicated women's rugby podcasts that it is hard to name them all while ex-players like Ireland's Fiona Coghlan, New Zealand's Melodie Robinson and Wales' Philippa Tuttiett have emerged as excellent commentators and pundits in recent years.

We have amazing ambassadors on and off the field, many of whom you've read about on these pages. I am determined to continue to play whatever role I can in making sure they are well known and commended for what they have done for our brilliant sport.

When this book was first completed in 2021, it ended with the women's game taking centre stage in Tokyo – a moment of both celebration and reflection.

But in the years since, women's rugby has accelerated so rapidly that an update was not just timely, but essential.

Rugby's greatest opportunity for growth lies in women and girls – in participants, fans and commercial markets that remain under-developed and this realisation seems to have progressed rapidly in the past few years.

So no, the boulder has not disappeared – but the slope is a little less steep; the number of skiers is growing and more of them are now asking why the ski lift only ever seems to go in one direction.

There is no going back.

Acknowledgements

IT'S IMPOSSIBLE to list all the people I interviewed over the years for this book by name, especially as some spoke to me in an off-the-record capacity, but I do want all of those who gave up their time so willingly to know how incredibly appreciative I am that they shared their thoughts, insights and memories with me.

To all the people quoted throughout the various pages of the book, thank you so much for your time and your thoughtful contributions as well as your patience with subsequent follow-ups. Thanks too for everything you have done and continue to do for women's rugby.

Thank you to Scott Reeves who first approached me about writing a book about women's rugby over a decade ago and who has stuck with me valiantly! I appreciate your time, massive patience, and energy. We got there in the end!

To all at Pitch for coming on board and taking the project on with great support and insight and for helping to finally make this happen – thank you so much!

Thank you to Stephen Jones, one of the original media champions of women's rugby (and still the only journalist to cover every Women's Rugby World Cup), for the lovely foreword and for the constant words of encouragement, interest and support for me and the game itself.

To John Birch, who really is the epitome of the very best kind of male ally in women's sport. Your amazing dedication, hard work and passion for the game has been a constant source of help and delight to me and I am certain that without you, Scrumqueens.com would struggle to have had the impact it has. Thank you for reading this book numerous times and giving very helpful pointers along the way. Long may you love the game!

To all those who supported the development of this book by taking the time to read it along the way and offer me thoughts and pointers, especially Sarah Mockford, Sara Orchard, Melodie Robinson, Alice Soper, Maggie Alphonsi, and Sue Anstiss – it was hugely appreciated!

Thank you so much to those who helped to provide such great images for the book including Dom Rumbles, Karen Bond and Charlotte Harwood at World Rugby, the team at Inpho in Ireland and Anne Parsons and Kerri Heffernan. To my brilliant mum and dad for instilling a love of books in me. No matter what we did or didn't have growing up there were always books and, alongside that, great encouragement to read them.

Finally, and most importantly, to my wonderful wife Sarah for all your support, motivation and patience and your help in designing the cover! Scrumqueens.com would not have existed without the support of your agency Make it Clear, and I am eternally grateful for all the work you have put in to building and maintaining the website, as well as your long-standing good nature about all the hours I dedicate to writing about the game. Thank you too for your amazing dedication to women's rugby through years of volunteering at Teddington. People like you are what make our game so great. Me and our own two little queens at home are very lucky to have you.

My own journey in the women's game from a teenager learning the ropes in Midleton, through to playing at Highfield, UCC, Wasps and Teddington, has included meeting some incredible people who work very hard to support and run the game. All of them have played a part in me sitting down – eventually – to write this book.

There are remarkably few people paid to work in women's rugby and so to all the dedicated coaches, administrators, players, supporters, writers and advocates out there who do it all because they love it – thank you and keep going!

There's so much more to come.

Bibliography

Chapter 1

Fenwick, Kirby, The stories we tell matter: the history of women's sport must not be overlooked (www.theguardian.com/sport/2019/mar/08/the-stories-we-tell-matter-the-history-of-womens-sport-must-not-be-overlooked)

Birch, John, *The Remarkable Emily Valentine* (www.scrumqueens.com/blogs/anonymous/remarkable-emily-valentine, 2010)

Curtin, Jennifer, *Before the 'Black Ferns': Tracing the Beginnings of Women's Rugby in New Zealand, The International Journal of the History of Sport* (33:17, 2071-2085, DOI: 10.1080/09523367.2017.1329201, 2016)

Palenski, Rob, *Rugby: A New Zealand History* (Auckland: Auckland University Press, 2015)

Trevor, Captain Philip, *Rugby Union Football* (London: Chapman & Hall, 1903)

Furse, Lydia J, *Cardiff v Newport, the Ladies Story* (www.worldrugbymuseum.com/from-the-vaults/clubs/cardiff-v-newport-the-ladies-story, 2018)

Prescott, Gwyn, *The earliest photograph of a women's team?* (https://cardiffrugbymuseum.org/articles/earliest-photograph-women%E2%80%99s-team 2019)

Curtin, Jennifer, *Why are we still ignoring women's rugby?* (www.newsroom.co.nz/lockerroom/why-are-we-still-ignoring-womens-rugby, 2018)

Ferguson, Andrew, *How a courageous duo helped women's rugby league kick off in 1921* (www.nrl.com/news/2018/12/23/how-a-courageous-duo-helped-womens-rugby-league-kick-off-in-1921/, 2018)

Leigh, Mary H, and Thérèse M. Bonin, *The Pioneering Role of Madame Alice Milliat and the FSFI in Establishing International Trade and Field Competition for Women.* (*Journal of Sport History*, vol. 4, no. 1, University of Illinois Press, 1977)

Furse, Lydia J, *'Barrette: Le Rugby Feminin in 1920s France'* (The International Journal of the History of Sport, DOI: 10.1080/09523367.2019.1634555)

Chapter 2

Gomez, Carole, *Le rugby à la conquête du monde – Histoire et géopolitique de l'ovalie* (Armand Colin, 2019)

USWRF History Project, *A brief history of the first women's collegiate championships* (www.uswrf.org/post/a-brief-history-of-the-first-womens-collegiate-championships, 2020)

World Rugby content, *The story behind the first ever women's international,* (https://www.women.rugby/news/570629, 2020)

USWRF History Project,, *Million Dollar* Babies (https://www.uswrf.org/post/million-dollar-babies, 2020)

Wertheim, Jon, L, *Unusual tolerance for pain, Candi Orsini cheerfully takes her lumps in the flicks and on the rugby field.* (Sports Illustrated, August edition, 1996)

Chapter 3

Harvey Helen, *Women's rugby – from hand-me-down jerseys to professional contracts*: (www.stuff.co.nz/sport/112488887/womens-rugby-from-handmedown-jerseys-to-professional-contracts, 2019)

World Rugby content, *The Class of '91: Between the Lines* (https://www.youtube.com/watch?v=4BeDBO0iObs, 2020)

World Rugby content, *Jervey: WRWC 1991 was an experience of a lifetime* (https://www.rugbyworldcup.com/2021/news/238440, 2017)

Birch, John, *Remembering WRWC '91: The Soviet Union* (https://www.scrumqueens.com/features/remembering-wrwc-91-soviet-union, 2016)

Walsh, Daire, *I was aware we weren't accepted: The journey of Ireland's first-ever women's rugby captain* (https://www.the42.ie/trailblazers-jill-henderson-ireland-rugby-5407372-Apr2021/, 2021)

House of Rugby content: *The real story of England's heroic 1994 World Cup winning team* (https://www.youtube.com/watch?v=cy6Jx_SYwQw, 2020)

Chapter 5

Bathgate, Stuart, Pioneers celebrate 25th anniversary of first Scotland women's international (https://www.theoffsideline.com/pioneers-celebrate-25th-anniversary-first-scotland-womens-international/)

Signes, Emile, Sevens in Olympics, a PreHistory of Women's Sevens (http:// princetonrugby.com/wp-content/uploads/2016/02/Sevens-in-Olympics_-a-Prehistory-of-Women27s-Sevens.pdf)

Chapter 6

Stuart, Lewis, Scotland crowned European champions, The Times, 2001

Kervin. Alison, England's world falls apart in final challenge, , 2002

Richardson, Charles, *The inside story of the 2001 British and Irish 'Lionesses' – and how a proposed tour was brutally blocked (The Telegraph,* www.telegraph.co.uk/rugby-union/2021/07/02/inside-story-2001-british-irish-lionesses-proposed-tour-brutally/, 2021)

ESPN content: *Wallaroos hit by cut in funding* (http://en.espn.co.uk/scrum/rugby/story/43584.html, 2002)

Parker, Charlie, *Female rugby players warn of widespread sexism at dinners* (The Times, *https://www.thetimes.co.uk/article/female-rugby-players-warn-of-widespread-sexism-at-dinners-9mttvswrc, 2019)*

Bowes, Ali and Culvin, Alex, The Professionalisation of Women's Sport: Issues and Debates (Emerald Publishing Limited, 2021)

Chapter 7

Hallett, Gemma, *How the WRU failed its women (https://medium.com/@gem_68313/how-the-wru-failed-its-women-c8e1132f8be, 2020)*

Chapter 8

Spencer, Catherine, *Mud, Maul, Mascara: When fighting for a dream can make and break you* (Unbound, 2020)

Chapter 10

Giteau, Kirsty, *Women's game needs backing (www.scrumqueens.com/news/giteau-womens-game-needs-backing, 2010)*

Donnelly, Ali, *Landmark nine game deal penned between world's top two* (www.scrumqueens.com/news/landmark-nine-game-deal-penned-between-worlds-top-two, 2011)

Doyle, Gary, *The team that came from nowhere to win a Grand Slam and slay the All Blacks* (www.the42.ie/ireland-womens-rugby-team-5169404-Aug2020/, 2020)

Chapter 11

Birch, John, *Sensation on the Rovato mud* (www.scrumqueens.com/news/sensation-rovato-mud, 2013)

Cummiskey, Gavin, Twist of fate led Claire Molloy to a rugby career with Ireland (www.irishtimes.com/sport/rugby/international/twist-of-fate-led-claire-molloy-to-a-rugby-career-with-ireland-1.2959857, 2017)

Chapter 12

Rugby Coach Weekly Podcast: The Final: The Remarkable and Untold Story of the 2014 RWC (part four) www.rugbycoachweekly.net/rugby-coaching/podcasts/the-final-the-remarkable-and-untold-story-of-the-2014-rwc-part-four/

Chapter 13

Cummiskey, Gavin, *Ireland lose their way in the dark at Ashbourne RFC* (www.irishtimes.com/sport/rugby/international/ireland-lose-their-way-in-the-dark-at-ashbourne-rfc-1.2103589, 2015)

Rowan, K and O'Reilly, P, *Six Nations, Two Stories* (O'Brien Press Ltd, 2015)

Pommier, Benjamin, *Tournoi européen : l'équipe de France féminine joue sa qualification pour Rio, ce week-end* (www.lepopulaire.fr/limousin/sports/actualite/rugby/2015/06/18/tournoi-europeen-lequipe-de-france-feminine-joue-sa-qualification-pour-rio-ce-week-end_11486797.html, 2015)

Donnelly, A, *Walsh calls for more integration for women's game* (https://www.scrumqueens.com/news/walsh-calls-more-integration-womens-game, 2016)

Chapter 14

Rowan, K, *USA coach Pete Steinberg: World Cup format is 'slap in the face' for the women's game* (www.telegraph.co.uk/rugby-union/2017/08/16/usa-coach-pete-steinberg-world-cup-format-slap-face-womens-game/ , 2017)

Cummiskey, G, *Ruth O'Reilly: 'The guys in the blazers need to decide if this is something they are serious about,* https://www.irishtimes.com/sport/rugby/international/ruth-o-reilly-the-guys-in-the-blazers-need-to-decide-if-this-is-something-they-are-serious-about-1.3198674, 2017)

BIBLIOGRAPHY

Chapter 15

Donnelly, A, *Black Ferns awarded first-ever contracts* https://www.
rugbyworld.com/countries/new-zealand-countries/black-ferns-awarded-
first-ever-contracts-91999, 2018)

Slot O, *Will it take a strike to resolve this? Women's rugby contract crisis
(https://www.thetimes.co.uk/article/will-it-take-a-strike-to-resolve-this-
womens-rugby-contract-crisis-fm28rbz6s, 2018)*

Myers, R, *England's Red Roses smash Scotland* (www.thetimes.co.uk/
article/a155f1a0-4839-11e9-ab90-7b64c665210d, 2018)

Stevenson, S, (*twitter.com/sumostevenson/
status/1145533098362150912, 2018)*

Chapter 16

Orchard S, *Rugby and brain injuries: World Cup winner Kat
Merchant has lower cognitive capacity (*www.bbc.co.uk/sport/rugby-
union/55306949, 2020

Thomas F, *Nic Evans exclusive interview: 'I'm too scared to find out if I
have dementia (www.telegraph.co.uk/rugby-union/2020/12/10/nic-evans-
exclusive-interview-scared-find-have-dementia/, 2020)*

Sky Sports content, *Ireland women kit launch a poor effort* www.
skysports.com/watch/video/12059737/ireland-womens-kit-launch-a-
poor-effort,2020

Donnelly, A, *Alphonsi on rugby, race and what needs to change.* (www.
scrumqueens.com/news/alphonsi-race-rugby-what-needs-change, 2020)

Back the Girls Podcast, *Episode 4: The legend, Tails. (www.open.spotify.
com/episode/1kv4F8KSgNJonfr88aapz0, 2021)*

Kuznetsov, D, *We sat in the grass during the day, afraid to move, so that
the militants would not notice. Rugby player of the Russian national team
from the Dagestan village will perform at the Olympics* (https://www.
sport-express.ru/olympics/tokyo2020/rugby/reviews/olimpiada-v-tokio-
bayzat-hamidova-istoriya-regbistki-sbornoy-rossii-iz-dagestanskogo-
sela-1809944/, 2021*)*

BBC content. *We are at the Olympics, be happy!* (https://twitter.com/
bbcsport/status/1421244212792549376, 2021)

Dart, T, *Fluid Fiji defeat Team GB in Olympic rugby sevens bronze medal
match,* www.theguardian.com/sport/2021/jul/31/fluid-fiji-defeat-team-
gb-in-olympic-rugby-sevens-bronze-medal-match, 2021)

About the author

Ali Donnelly is one of women's rugby's most authoritative and knowledgeable voices. She ran the influential and award winning Scrumqueens.com from 2009-2025, covering the breadth of the international women's game, and has written extensively about the game, including for publications including the *Irish Examiner, Guardian, Times* and *Rugby World.* She is also the co-founder of Women of Union, which is dedicated to supporting and championing women working in rugby. She has worked in senior communications roles for a range of high-profile organisations, including Sport England, the UK Prime Minister's Office, and the BBC.